REPRESENTING ISLAM

FRAMING THE GLOBAL

Edited by Hilary Kahn and Deborah Piston-Hatlen

REPRESENTING ISLAM

Hip-Hop of the September 11 Generation

—⁂—

KAMALUDEEN MOHAMED NASIR

INDIANA UNIVERSITY PRESS

This book is a publication of

Indiana University Press
Office of Scholarly Publishing
Herman B Wells Library 350
1320 East 10th Street
Bloomington, Indiana 47405 USA

iupress.org

Manufactured in the United States of America

Library of Congress Cataloging-in-Publication Data

Names: Kamaludeen Mohamed Nasir, author.
Title: Representing Islam : hip-hop of the September 11 generation / Kamaludeen Mohamed Nasir.
Description: Bloomington : Indiana University Press, 2020. | Series: Framing the global | Includes bibliographical references and index.
Identifiers: LCCN 2020005984 (print) | LCCN 2020005985 (ebook) | ISBN 9780253053039 (hardback) | ISBN 9780253053046 (paperback) | ISBN 9780253053053 (ebook)
Subjects: LCSH: Rap (Music)—Religious aspects—Islam. | Hip-hop—Religious aspects—Islam. | Rap (Music)—Social aspects.
Classification: LCC ML3921.8.R36 K36 2020 (print) | LCC ML3921.8.R36 (ebook) | DDC 782.421649088/297—dc23
LC record available at https://lccn.loc.gov/2020005984
LC ebook record available at https://lccn.loc.gov/2020005985

1 2 3 4 5   25 24 23 22 21 20

To my wife, Kalsum, and our three children, Luqman Hakim,
Sumayyah, and Hajar

CONTENTS

PREFACE

IT IS MY INTENTION, IN this book, to capture the diversity of hip-hoppers who purport to be affiliated to Islam—from the Five Percenters to the Nation of Islam (NOI), to the hip-hop hijabis, to those who locate themselves within the *nasheed* genre, to artists who are inspired by the religion and its religionists. All of them, in their own expressions, have laid claim to representing Islam in their craft either through fronting Muslim causes or reading Islam in a new light. Today, these cultural icons, more so than religious leaders, are bringing the discourses of Islam into the public domain and in unapologetic terms.

This book was a long time in the making. I started thinking seriously about the subject matter during the start of my PhD in 2008, but it is only after writing five other books that I am returning to what has been a soundtrack of my youth. Hip-hop has always captivated me at many levels—the beats, the powerful lyrics, the artists, and, of course, the lives they project. Growing up in a working-class Malay background, my friends and I always dwelled on music and sports as ways out of our rut. Throughout my youth, I had contemplated being a soccer player despite doing well in school and had even spent time going for trials at the biggest club in the city. The short story is that I am now an academic.

For many Malays who go down the musical route, hip-hop often becomes their genre of choice. But it was only in my varsity days that I got my first taste of Islam-inspired hip-hop. In my freshman year at the National University of Singapore in 2000, a student activist introduced me to a Los Angeles–based group called Soldiers of Allah. The student, who was active in *da'wah* movements on and off campus, downloaded the group's tracks from the now defunct free file-sharing website Napster.

It was almost a full decade later, in the middle of my PhD, that I first gave a presentation at Western Sydney University called "Discovering 'Nasheed' in Hip-Hop: A Study of Muslim Youth." Western Sydney's vibrant hip-hop scene has been the subject of much scholarly and media attention. Living in the suburbs of Bankstown for a couple years was indeed inspiring and sowed further interest in me to develop this project, and I continued to return periodically to seek inspiration. Much has happened since my first hip-hop talk at my alma mater. The scene has evolved at lightning speed, and my understanding of it has been much enriched through my conversations with various scholars at critical junctures of the conceptualization of this book.

While I was a visiting scholar at NYU's Hagop Kervokian Center and CUNY's Graduate Center, and in my subsequent visits to New York City, I had the opportunity to seek out various hip-hop scholars and sociologists of religion who enriched my understanding of the hip-hop scene. The time Bakari Kitwana and I walked the streets of Harlem from the Schomburg and finally settled down at a Dunkin' Donuts, talking about the state of hip-hop studies, is one of my fondest memories. The few days I spent at the Schomburg, in an event celebrating hip-hop pedagogy, left a lasting impression on me. There, I had the good fortune of listening to hip-hop-scholars Jeff Chang and Chris Emdin and watching Jasiri X give a powerful performance. The session, which showcased hip-hop's potent influence on inner-city kids and how music can be creatively harnessed to do good, is something I still share with scholars and policy makers in my home country.

The people of the Committee for the Study of Religion at the CUNY Graduate Center, led by Bryan Turner, provided many insights when I spoke there. Sujatha Fernandes, whose wonderful work I greatly benefitted from, pointed me in the right directions. Hip-hop and religion scholar Monica Miller invited me to share my research at Lehigh University, where I also met an astute fellow hip-hop academic, Christopher Driscoll. Michael Gilsenan, for whom I was a research assistant in my postgraduate days, was always generous with his time. He advised me on the project over the years whenever we got to meet in New York and in Singapore.

I have to give huge props to the Fulbright program for sponsoring my stint at UCLA that allowed me to experience up close what hip-hop on the West Coast is like. As part of Black Awareness Month, Fulbright delegates had the opportunity to engage with community and youth representatives. There were invigorating discussions about the cultural significance of Martin Luther King, Harriett Tubman, and hip-hop figures like Kanye, Jay-Z, and Lupe. UCLA's Cheryl Keyes and H. Samy Alim, renowned hip-hop scholars in their own right, shared with me fresh perspectives and sources that made me consider different dimensions of the project that I would have otherwise quite foolishly neglect.

Ann Kerr, UCLA's Fulbright coordinator, engaged me and my son in conversations about hip-hop and basketball. Ann's son, of course, is Steve Kerr, head coach of the Golden State Warriors and Chicago Bulls legend. It is no coincidence that the Fulbright stint includes a day where scholars across California are brought together to take in a game atmosphere. In a lot of ways, an NBA game is the biggest advertisement for hip-hop and shows off its glitzy side. Although I had realized this relationship for a while through my correspondences with hip-hop fans and watching games on television, nothing compares to being able to soak in the fanfare at LA's Staples Center.

I am grateful to John Voll and Khaled Abou Fadl for their encouragement and for extolling the importance of studying Islam's relationship with popular culture. Sherman Jackson made me question the value of doing this work and why I had set on this journey in the first place. These reminders were what I needed in those exact times. In Singapore, Khairudin Aljunied and Sam Han shared their inputs during lunches and coffee breaks no matter how juvenile my ideas. At Indiana University Press, I would like to thank Jennika Baines, Stephanie Smith, Allison Chaplin, and Elaine Smith for ensuring a smooth publication process. Especially to Elaine, thanks for your wonderful work and for persevering with my manuscript through a difficult time.

Toward the end of this project, I had the opportunity to discuss different facets of the book with participants in two public lectures at the Royal Melbourne Institute of Technology and Western Sydney University and in two workshops at Georgetown University and the University of Freiburg called "Reorienting Islam in Southeast Asia" and "Rocking Islam: Music and the Making of New Muslim Identities" respectively. Half of the papers presented at the conference on Islam and music at Freiburg were on hip-hop and covered countries such as Germany, Morocco, Egypt, Indonesia, and the United States, cementing not just the scholarly interest in hip-hop but also demonstrating the global influence of the genre across the continents.

It is inevitable, given the number of years I have worked on this, that parts of this book have been published in various academic platforms, appearing as articles in the *Journal of Sociology* and the *Journal of Religious and Political Practice* and as chapters in the *Handbook of Hyper-Real Religions* and *Globalized Muslim Youth in the Asia Pacific*. I would like to thank Sage, Routledge, Brill, and Palgrave for use of these materials, which I reworked for the purposes of this book.

My wife, Kalsum, was with me every step of the way in the making of this book. She painstakingly read through drafts of the manuscript and has always been at once my harshest critic and my biggest fan. Finally, this book is dedicated to my son, Luqman Hakim, and daughters, Sumayyah and Hajar. They often reminisce longingly of the semesters we spent as a family when I was visiting NYU and UCLA, working on this book. Here's to more adventures ahead!

Kamaludeen Mohamed Nasir
Singapore, April 29, 2020

REPRESENTING ISLAM

INTRODUCTION

Anthem of a Generation

The New World Order was born on September eleventh.

—Immortal Technique, "The Cause of Death"

GLOBAL EVENTS AND THE RISE of religiosity in the Muslim world have placed young Muslims under the scrutiny of politicians, academics, and the media. The leading roles of Muslim youth in the Arab Spring, the ensuing concerns about Muslim migration to the West coupled with episodes such as the release of the anti-Islamic short film *Innocence of Muslims*, and the various retaliations against the *Charlie Hebdo* caricatures of Prophet Muhammad have sparked a worldwide backlash against young Muslims in particular. They find themselves increasingly depicted as armed and dangerous. In many academic writings and news headlines, young Muslims are perceived as carriers and purveyors of Islamic fundamentalism. This is, in itself, a new development in the study of Muslims globally, in part inspired by Samuel Huntington's 1996 book *The Clash of Civilizations and the Remaking of World Order*, where he asserts that Islamic fundamentalism was born out of the failure of Muslim nations to provide economic and political development for their people.

Since the terrorist attacks in New York City on September 11, 2001, Huntington's thesis has been revitalized and extended to include the stigmatization of an emergent generation of young Muslims. Young people already present a challenge to modern societies and are often seen as threats who need to be reined in and socialized to the norms of adult mannerisms and worldviews. As a result, young people find themselves subjected to multiple authorities, be it parental authority, school regulations, religious dogmas, or state sanctions.

1

In the present climate, where the migration and demography of Muslim communities globally are generally characterized by a large proportion of young people, the threat of sociopolitical instability caused by a Muslim youth boom has given much weight to the clash of civilizations thesis. The implications of this on young Muslims are far-reaching.

Moral panic and fear of young Muslims have come to define an entire generation. Contrary to their parents, who lived in an era that was not characterized by a war on terror, this unique generation has not known anything other than intense securitization, be it in Muslim- or non-Muslim-majority countries. In the minds of many young Muslims, the war on terror signifies an all-out attack on their Islamic identity. Most young Muslims are neither passive nor violent, but the hyperscrutiny imposed on their religious communities has put their faith and piety in question.

This book is about young Muslims who have embraced and appropriated hip-hop music as their anthem in response to surging Islamophobia following September 11. Many were still in their teens and twenties in 2001. Since then, they have come into the public sphere in response to vociferous calls for Muslims to embrace their religion in a more moderate manner and to be more flexible in their adherence to the articles of faith. Some young Muslims emerged from this asserting, reaffirming, and fortifying their Islamic religious identity while others have creatively engaged in a rereading of their faith. Hence, many young Muslims have had to come to terms with their piety regardless of whether or not they claim to be devout. For those who consider themselves religious, September 11 has presented them with the ultimate challenge of defending their religion and religious practices, such as fasting during the month of Ramadan, performing daily prayers, or observing the hijab.

The way the September 11 generation navigates their own Islamic identity with the tenets of Islam that are broadly observed by the world's near two billion Muslims of various regional and denominational differences is a fragile balance. Some feel this negotiation of identity and faith calls for a distinction to be made between Muslim hip-hop, simply hip-hop that is produced by self-identified Muslims, and Islamic hop-hop, music that attempts to reconcile the genre with the values of the religion to emphasize theological clarity. I find these rhetorical distinctions unnecessary. Many Muslim hip-hoppers engage, to varying degrees, in an examination of their religious identity when crafting their music. Further, practitioners and scholars hold diverse opinions according to differing principles about what qualifies as Islamic music, so who ultimately defines the genre is an intrinsically contentious process. Last, many Muslim musicians are also engaged in fighting Islamophobia both locally and abroad and pursue causes that are essentially Islamic in nature, such as speaking truth in the face of tyranny and fighting for fairness and humanity, even though the delivery may upset Islamic sensitivities. These musicians are thus constantly traversing and practicing the seamless distinction between Muslim and Islamic hip-hoppers, and the use of terminology in this book embodies this fluid negotiation.

Nonetheless, many even among those who accede to not "practicing" their religion find themselves in positions of having to reexamine their identity amid enhanced scrutiny. Popular youth culture often becomes the common arena whereby these acts of piety, in all their diversity, are performed. Hip-hop is currently the most visible and popular of them all.

On the eve of September 11, *Time* magazine ran an article entitled "Hip-Hop Is the Most Important Youth Culture on the Planet."[1] Hip-hop's unstoppable rise in popularity culminated in 2018 with American hip-hop artist Kendrick Lamar winning the Pulitzer Prize for music for his album *"DAMN."* This achievement, which was the first Pulitzer Prize awarded to a nonjazz or nonclassical musician, immortalized the genre's place in music's hall of fame. Notwithstanding that, also in 2018, China banned hip-hop songs from its airwaves. Whether hip-hop is embraced for its exceptional musical quality or repudiated as a threat, what is certain is its potency and deep resonance with young Muslims all over the world. This sentiment is captured by the French hip-hop artist Médine in his iconic track "Arabospiritual." The song documents his personal journey following the twin towers attacks and the boycott of his previous album, which he simply called *11 Septembre.*

Moi j'ai le mal du siècle	I have the evil of the century
Depuis qu'à Manhattan les tours jumelles ne décorent plus le ciel	Since the Manhattan twin towers no longer decorate the sky
Sans vouloir romancer mon parcours officiel	Without wanting to romanticize my official career
J'ai déposé ma plume au profit d'un retour spirituel	I put down my pen in favor of a spiritual return
Individuelle retraite au sein des mosquées de quartier	Individual retreat in neighborhood mosques
Aucune scène, aucun concert viendra me perturber	No scene, no concert will disturb me
Un aller simple pour le voyage intérieur	One way for the domestic journey
Afin de réparer les cœurs que la vie matérielle détériore	In order to repair the hearts that material life deteriorates
Une éponge à la place de la mémoire	A sponge instead of memory

Moi j'ai le cerveau perméable à toutes formes de savoir	I have a brain permeable to all forms of knowledge
Ne souris pas j'ai des sourates sous les soupapes	Do not smile I have suras under the valves
Et j'aspire à devenir un Livre Saint sur pattes	And I aspire to become a Holy Book on legs
Lorsque enfin l'envie de rapper me dépasse	When finally the desire to rap exceeds me
Moi en 2004 ma destinée me déclasse	Me in 2004 my destiny downgrades me
Premier album : c'est l'autopsie d'une catastrophe	First album: it is the autopsy of a catastrophe
"Eleven September" seulement présent dans quelques stores …	"Eleven september" only present in some stores …
Je suis un Muslim qui fait de la black musique	I am a Muslim who plays black music
Pourtant je n'ai rien de black je suis tout pâle j'ai même du sang toubab	Yet I have nothing black I am very pale I even have toubab blood

This book is a critical study of the culture and consciousness of hip-hop among a particular generation of Muslims referred to as the September 11 generation. The very notion of a generation is central to my study. Karl Mannheim (1952) proposes that when members of a generation galvanize themselves by the experience of historical events from similar vantage points and are exposed to similar traumatic experiences, they can influence society by challenging conventional norms and offering new cultural visions. Moreover, Edmunds and Turner (2005) argue that generations identify themselves in terms of historical and cultural traumas, which are produced by a diversity of social processes by members of national, social, or global groups. They contend that generations act strategically to bring about change. When generations utilize their economic, political, and educational circumstances to innovate in the cultural, intellectual, and political spheres, they shift from being a passive age cohort to a self-conscious one.

Muslim hip-hop by the September 11 generation is unique in a number of aspects. First, their religious identity has resulted in the securitization of an entire cohort of people. This is carried out to an extent that results in a conflation of their religious identity with diverse ethnic and national identities. Second, in appropriating the genre, young Muslims have engaged in a selective Islamization of hip-hop culture. This ranges from the fusing of Islamic iconographies in their music to engaging in a particular form of bodily discipline. Third, youth activism and promotion of hip-hop as a craft come at a time of unprecedented social media penetration. This allows hip-hop to flourish in many urban cities and thrive across the various governmental spectrums—from liberal to authoritarian regimes.

Hence, this is a study of a unique cohort of Muslims living in the post–September 11 age; for these youth, hip-hop culture provides an important framework of social identity and offers the space to form ethnic, generational, and transnational solidarities. The emergence of young Muslims as the new blacks drives them to appropriate hip-hop, albeit with some tensions, to gain legitimacy in mainstream society. Glocalized forms of hip-hop emerge as a reflection of socioeconomic status that is intimately linked to locality. Diasporic young Muslims in urban settings, for example, are subjected to official doctrines of multiculturalism in their host countries. As the next chapter will demonstrate, between the formation of a global Muslim youth hip-hop culture and manifestations of its glocalized forms, the notion of social justice remains central to Muslim hip-hop practitioners. This theme within Muslim hip-hop is likely to thrive given the social status, both real and perceived, of many Muslim minorities.

Hip-hop originally referred to African American urban youth culture born in poor neighborhoods of the South Bronx of New York. It manifests itself in the form of rapping, graffiti, a particular way of dress, a linguistic style, and other cultural identifiers. Bakari Kitwana, a close observer of the hip-hop scene in the United States, defines the hip-hop generation as "young African-Americans born between 1965 and 1984 who came of age in the eighties and nineties and . . . share a specific set of values and attitudes" (2002, 4). Kitwana's formulation of the hip-hop generation coincides with the concept of Generation X. Likewise, the hip-hop generation that Kitwana describes emerged out of several driving forces—"the visibility of black youth in popular culture, globalisation, the persistent nature of segregation, public policy surrounding the criminal justice system, media representations of black youth, and the general quality of life within the hip-hop community" (2002, 4). Since then, quite a number of scholars have studied hip-hop culture from a generational perspective (Fernandes 2011; Clay 2012).

In *Close to the Edge: In Search of the Hip Hop Global Generation*, Fernandes highlights the potential of critical hip-hop among the younger generation and describes how, for example, Khaled Sabsabi, a.k.a. Peacefender, an award-winning Sydney-based visual artist and one of Australia's pioneers in bringing hip-hop workshops to the community, worked to eradicate the objectification of women during the Sydney event she attended. This form of hip-hop, at times termed "conscious hip-hop" or "reality hip-hop," has, since the inception of the genre, been used as a platform for activism by minoritized groups. In an interview in 2005, Khaled put it powerfully: "Living in South West Sydney is about being confronted with universal issues about migration, displacement and the language of exiles—of diasporic communities searching for their sense of place and most importantly purpose" (Fernandes 2011, 189). While these studies are illuminating and have been instrumental to my own, I believe the identification of young Muslims as the September 11 generation has been inevitable and instructive to both their production of and relationship with hip-hop.

One of the key areas of struggle for most Muslim youth is the media's negative portrayal and misreporting of issues and events relating to Islam and Muslims. Scholars have documented widespread negative depictions of young Muslims across media outlets. There have been a number of post–September 11 books that build on Edward Said's formative work, *Covering Islam: How the Media and the Experts Determine How We See the Rest of the World*, which focuses on the misrepresentation of young Muslims in mainstream media (Said 1997; Poole and Richardson 2006; Gardner, Karakaolus, and Luchtenberg 2008; Petley and Richardson 2011; Pennington and Kahn 2018). These scholars have been critical of the moral panic constructed by the media through the demonizing of young Muslim subjects. They have also documented the impact of such reporting on Muslims who feel that the media has curtailed their freedom of expression and silenced their voices. Young Muslims commonly believe that being Muslim alone might subject them to the suspicion of criminality regardless of their behavior. Others have observed how the media routinely characterizes crimes committed by Muslims as "Muslim crimes" while never mentioning the religion of non-Muslim criminals. Not surprisingly, young Muslims believe they are being singled out for being Muslim. In my previous book, *Globalized Muslim Youth in the Asia Pacific* (Kamaludeen 2016b), I reference studies of youth respondents experiencing significant adversity in school, including various forms of harassment, bullying, and stigmatization coming from peers and figures of authority. These works are unequivocal in their view that the media generates anti-Islam sentiments that often result in discrimination, physical abuse, and retaliation against Muslim communities.

A striking observation is that "color," or more accurately, phenotypical features, are a key component of media and public discourses. As a result of the problematic emphasis on biological traits when constructing the Muslim other, many non-Muslims who share the "Muslim look," such as South Asian Hindus and Sikhs or Arab Christians, are subject to anti-Muslim discrimination and violence. Being perceived as a Muslim has real, and at times fatal, consequences.

In 2013, the Sikh Coalition reported that more than seven hundred attacks or bias-related incidents against Sikhs, including the 2012 fatal shooting of six people at a Sikh temple outside Milwaukee, Wisconsin, had occurred since September 11. In the fall of 2013, a Sikh professor from Columbia University was severely injured while walking near Central Park. He was surrounded by a group of approximately twenty men, who punched and kicked him while shouting "terrorist" and "get Osama."[2] A few months earlier, a woman shoved an Indian Hindu man to his death off a train platform in Queens. When confronted by police officers, she bragged: "I pushed a Muslim off the train tracks because I hate Hindus and Muslims—ever since 2001 when they put down the twin towers, I've been beating them up."[3] Another horrific anti-Muslim attack occurred in New York City three years later. In August 2016, a South Asian imam (religious teacher) and his assistant were shot and killed execution style in broad daylight.[4]

A personal anecdote with respect to color occurred on the very first day I arrived in Australia, a white-dominated country. I was walking on the streets of Sydney with my cousin in the summer of 2008. Despite both of us having a mixed Malay-Ceylonese parentage, a Caucasian man passing by yelled in a threatening tone, "Fuck off, niggers!" I realized then that dark-skinned Muslims, or rather those who look Muslim, suffer from a double jeopardy. On the one hand, they are victims of increasingly pervasive Islamophobic attacks, and on the other, they are associated with the negative stereotypes surrounding blackness—aggressive, sexually promiscuous, and ultimately dangerous.

The September 11 and hip-hop generations have been further shaped by the digital age and the social media wave (Han and Kamaludeen 2016). The increasing high usage of smartphones among young people makes this demographic the most significant users of social media, which is characterized by profile-specific demands for information on the one hand and user-generated content on the other. The simple act of liking a post, following a page, or subscribing to a news feed allows one to fashion his or her social sphere in the vast digital space. The collaborative filtering mechanism of these platforms recommends pages or links based on the user's recent activities, and the underlying algorithms bring more personalized content onto the viewer's information streams, filtering out what he or she is more likely to reject. While social media seems "liberating" for its users, it is at the same time limiting views to such an extreme degree that incomplete and/or inaccurate information are rampant—an ironic development for this information age. While beyond the scope of this monograph, it suffices to note how social media platforms such as Facebook (2004), YouTube (2005), Twitter (2006), and Instagram (2010), among others, are increasingly producing exclusive thought communities on a global scale. Today's youth are forming virtual communities and networks that serve their preferences and identities—the hallmark of this generation.

Studies of Muslim youth and also of hip-hop are poorly served when it comes to comparative studies of popular culture across national boundaries and countries of origin. We are still waiting for a single volume that compares and contrasts young Muslims from different ethnic origins across cities. What we have are books that take a state- or ethnic-centric approach to the study of hip-hop culture. In this sense, Hisham Aidi's *Rebel Music: Race, Empire, and the New Muslim Youth Culture* (2014) is a breakthrough. It shares the title of an MTV series that examines how young people from all over the world appropriate music to engineer a brighter future for themselves and their communities, at times to their own detriment. In the same vein, Aidi's book shows the multiple ways young Muslims are experimenting with music to create social change. Aidi's timely contribution not only has hip-hop as a subject but also discusses rock, blues, and jazz among other musical genres. By focusing exclusively on hip-hop culture, I aim to extend his arguments on the appropriation of this art form by African Americans to Muslim immigrants and other native populations alike. This is done through a sustained engagement with various axes of analyses and through the lens of concepts such as human rights, authenticity, and the body.

This volume also builds on Sohail Daulatzai's *Black Star, Crescent Moon* (2012), which examines how black culture interacts with the Muslim world through popular culture such as literature, music, and cinema. Daulatzai's work is the only academic book I know that seriously examines a Southeast Asian country as one of the focal points in the development of black culture. He does this by tracing the engagement of Malcolm X and other black activists, and he highlights the 1955 Bandung Conference, where the former Indonesian president Sukarno famously called for a new Asia and a new Africa in his opening address. Daulatzai's book shows how the call for solidarity feeds the Nation of Islam (NOI)'s reorienting of blackness as Asiatic in origin and Malcolm X's linking of the experiences of African Americans as similar to that of colonization in the third world. The thread of Islam then becomes an unbreakable cord that African Americans can trace all the way to Africa and Asia. Nonetheless, by drawing on the September 11 generation as an analytical tool, I expand Daulatzai's conceptualization of what he has called the "Muslim International" as the intertwining experiences of black Islam and the Muslim third world. While limiting the scope to hip-hop, I broaden the empirical field to include not just other Southeast Asian countries, which are not seen as third world today, but also hip-hop coming out from the first world, either through their indigenous populations, like in Singapore and Turkey, or through migrant populations born and bred in countries like Sweden and France.

This book is divided into six chapters. It starts by exploring my own experiences with hip-hop culture in my home country and then tracing the entrenched roots of Islam within hip-hop culture. As with jazz music, the relationship of hip-hop within African American social movements such as the Nation of Islam in the early years was not all that straightforward or easy. To foreground the global appeal of Muslim hip-hop, which is heavily influenced by the United States, the chapter discusses the various strains of black Islam and the changing complexion of Islam in the country. Yet it has to be acknowledged that, in very significant ways, Muslim hip-hop has successfully decentered its African American roots. For a truly global study of Muslims, this chapter also calls for a provincializing of Islam from its usual Middle Eastern bias or even from the current Eurocentric trend of overly focusing on immigrants in Western countries. This allows the monograph both the conceptual and the empirical space to examine the practice of Muslim hip-hop in places such as Southeast and Central Asia, for example, areas that are not usually associated with the genre.

The next chapter deals with Muslim hip-hop's struggle for authenticity. I explore how a predominantly African American art form has gained a foothold in the Muslim world and how authenticity is negotiated both through conversations with African American Muslim hip-hoppers and a significant degree of homological imagination on the part of young Muslims (Kamaludeen 2012). Does practicing hip-hop make an individual less Islamic? As we will see throughout the pages of this book, Muslim hip-hop practitioners regularly defend their religiosity on Internet forums and in published interviews. On the surface, hip-hoppers struggle to reconcile their craft with the authenticity of their Islamic piety. Hence, summoning images of courage from personalities in Islamic history in their music, for example, confers upon young people a symbolic status and an "authenticity" derived from a connection with a glorified Islamic past. Second, contestations over authenticity also exist in the form of hip-hop that is produced and consumed. Muslim hip-hoppers are also engaged in conversations with other hip-hop practitioners over the authenticity of their craft. As hip-hop jargons travel across national boundaries and religious lines, the terms often lose their original meanings. Instead, new meanings are imbued, consciously or unconsciously, either to make them more in sync with theology or more generic to fit consumer tastes. Although hip-hop specialists like Anthony Kwame Harrison (2009) contend that racial authenticity and hip-hop authenticity are increasingly decoupled, there is evidence of center-periphery relationships within the hip-hop *ummah* as young Muslims often talk about looking to their Western counterparts for inspiration and, at times, validation.

The following chapter examines the global human rights activism of young Muslims through their participation in hip-hop culture. The increased awareness of Muslim identity in the post–September 11 era inadvertently influences and permeates the consumption of popular youth culture. This chapter contends that the hip-hop *ummah* attempts to draw from the struggles of the African American experience to articulate the human rights concerns facing their communities. The right to appropriate hip-hop as a means to express their predicaments also brings its young practitioners into conflict with moral entrepreneurs who act as gatekeepers to the religion. However, the human rights activism of young Muslims is bridging the seemingly irreconcilable gap between hip-hop and piety, serving not only as important frameworks of social identity but also providing the space to forge generational and transnational solidarities.

Next, the book explores the effect of hip-hop on the Muslim body. The chapter explores how the body is used as a site of contestation not only in multicultural and secular environments but also in highly controlled religious environments like Afghanistan. One area of contention pertains to performativity and the management of the female body. It is not an exaggeration to say that the world is obsessed with the Muslim female body. More often than not, amid all the attention and passionate back and forth about female oppression and empowerment in Islam, one critical group is not represented at all—Muslim women themselves. Through an exegesis of the hijab issue and the overall place of Muslim women in the hip-hop industry, this chapter discusses the debates over who has the right to speak for Muslim women. This issue of the compatibility of values, of whether Islam is in sync with hip-hop culture, is also evident if we examine the performativity of hip-hop culture among contemporary young Muslims. In this regard, hip-hop can be seen as a response to the disciplining of the body that governs Islamic music. Nonetheless, we also witness explicit attempts by hip-hop practitioners to Islamize hip-hop performance. Additionally, the controversy surrounding the involvement of Muslim women in hip-hop and the existence of eminent and emerging female artists such as Miss Undastood, Poetic Pilgrimage, and Mona Haydar provides the backdrop to discuss issues of gender and hip-hop music, terrains that have been well traversed by hip-hop scholars including Tracey Sharpley-Whiting (2007) and Michael P. Jeffries (2011).

The following chapter examines how popular Muslim youth culture in various global cities mirrors the different paths taken by their respective nations since government policies to manage youth and Muslim communities shape the possible variations of Muslim youth culture. Muslim youth form the backbone of Muslim-majority countries, but for many other countries around the world, the condition of Muslim youth indicates the degree of success of their espoused multiculturalism and minority policies. The increasing securitization by nation-states and the focus of the general public on their Muslim minority populations have led to tough questions over what it means to be Muslim. Although not without exceptions, the micromanagement of Muslim youth tends to result in youth culture taking on more assimilative attributes, as opposed to a laissez-faire management, which leads to a more competitive environment. In the latter, there is greater experimentation of "Islamic" expression that contributes to the larger identity market. A study of young Muslims and hip-hop benefits from information gleaned from recent works published on Muslims and rock music. Mark LeVine's (2008) *Heavy Metal Islam* and Salman Ahmad's (2010) *Rock and Roll Jihad*, for example, document the economic and social risks rock musicians are subjected to by choosing to practice their craft. Government management of hip-hop artists builds on its previous engagements with rock culture, which came into prominence at least a couple of decades before hip-hop. However, even in authoritarian countries, the state's reaction to hip-hop is visibly changing. This shift in governmentality is made more apparent when hip-hop is compared to how nations relate to Muslim rock music (LeVine 2008; Wallach, Berger, and Greene 2011).

The final and concluding chapter critically examines the hip-hop axiom of *keeping it real* within the context of the September 11 generation. The ability to keep it real is complicated by a distinct characteristic of millennial religiosity, which is defined by an individualization of religion and a reconfiguration of religious edicts to suit modern dilemmas. This is exemplified by the extensive borrowing and sampling of black music of the NOI and Five Percenter strains by Sunni Muslim groups, which has led to a clash of theologies and a hyperreal reading of Islam and its terminologies. At the same time, Muslim hip-hop practitioners regularly make adaptations to their craft based on their individual or collective affinities. Their social and political status, language, and geographical locations, among other factors, offer them a rich reserve of symbols and identifiers from which they can adopt and appropriate. In the process of reimagining their identities and how they would like to be perceived, young Muslims are ultimately engaging in a reconstruction of tradition and thus challenging preconceived notions of the "real."

To borrow a hip-hop terminology, the methodology that I use in this book can be called *sampling*. I utilize the words of individual artists and groups to create a soundtrack of a generation. By both locating the words of these artists within a specific contextual background and in their own social milieu, and also examining them through conceptual tools like human rights and authenticity to see how these discourses contribute to grander narratives that resonate outside the confines of their locality, I unveil how the music may reveal dominant trends among contemporary Muslim hip-hoppers to frame a particular issue in a specific way. I do this by oscillating between what C. Wright Mills in *The Sociological Imagination* calls *personal troubles* and *abstracted empiricism*. For purposes of data collection, I use two main sources. I make use of freely available interviews of hip-hoppers conducted by newspaper journalists, magazine editors, academicians, and online websites. They provide a rich resource for understanding the raison d'être and context motivating artists, why they see their existence as crucial, and how they rationalize their actions. Then I will look at the lyrics and music videos of their songs.

These rhymes provide powerful insights into the reality of their social conditions and what issues they feel strongly about. The lyrics and videos highlight both the conscious and at times unintentional choice of words and images that artists appropriate, evoking positive or adverse reactions among their consumers. As with a soundtrack comprising artists of diverse backgrounds, the sounds and narratives of the artists are multifarious and layered but collectively capture the different aspects of life as part of the September 11 generation. In truth, in many instances, artists resist the dominant sociopolitical norms that seek to hijack their identity and paint them with a single brushstroke.

These strategies of Muslim youth resistance can be gleaned through a study of youth consumption of hip-hop through the new media. This book explores the vibrant "underground" hip-hop culture of the digital sphere. This is an especially crucial platform in illiberal countries where criticisms of state-society interactions and interethnic relations are taboo. For hip-hop practitioners within these localities, the new media becomes an avenue for them to do hip-hop and continue the conversations when traditional outlets have been shut. There is also increasing evidence of an education of hip-hop culture among urban minority Muslim youth through social media sites such as YouTube and MySpace. These virtual spaces thus provide rich data for the book to gain an entry into the everyday lives of young Muslim hip-hoppers.

Literature and media often portray young people as empty vessels susceptible and vulnerable to shifting fashion trends and the latest commodities found in the market. Large companies have geared their marketing campaigns to specifically target youth and tap their spending power. However, not only do young Muslims make rational choices in their consumption, but these choices are also influenced by global affairs as they partake in solidarity movements with young people from other parts of the world. On the one hand, these large movements showing solidarity with groups of Muslims who are victims of oppression elsewhere in the world can be understood as another aspect of globalization. On the other, they can be viewed as a form of polarization at a global level.

Hence, this book looks at the complexities of *representing* Islam. To place these complexities within the matrices of power, the correct questions should follow. Who can represent Islam? How is Islam represented? Can musicians represent Islam? Can women or, for that matter, female musicians be the face of the Abrahamic faith? In this age that many scholars of religion have characterized as defined by a crisis of religious authority—an era that has seen the rise of digital religion, for example—the answers to these questions are no longer local or direct. In their quests to find answers, and to reconcile their craft with personal piety, musicians who attempt to resolve these questions engage in representing Islam in fresh, modern ways. Some do this by going back to the classical texts to show the diversity of Islamic positions on the issues at hand while others insist on a contextualization of religion to suit the social conditions of today. The battle is ultimately, to use a popular jargon in the hip-hop lexicon, over the right to *represent*.

NOTES

1. Tony Karon, "Hip-Hop Is the Most Important Youth Culture on the Planet," *Time*, September 22, 2000, http://content.time.com/time/arts/article /0,8599,55624,00.html.

2. Julie Cannold, "Possible Hate Crime: Sikh Professor Says He Was Beaten by Men Yelling, 'Get Osama,'" CNN, September 24, 2013, https://www.cnn .com/2013/09/23/justice/new-york-sikh-possible-hate-crime/index.html.

3. Marc Santora, "Woman Is Charged with Murder as a Hate Crime in a Fatal Subway Push," *New York Times*, December 29, 2012, https://www.nytimes .com/2012/12/30/nyregion/woman-is-held-in-death-of-man-pushed-onto -subway-tracks-in-queens.html.

4. Eli Rosenberg and Nate Schweber, "Imam and His Assistant Killed in a Shooting Near a Mosque in Queens," *New York Times*, August 13, 2016, https:// www.nytimes.com/2016/08/13/nyregion/queens-mosque-shooting.html.

ONE

—∿—

SONGS RATHER THAN SCREAMS

SURROUNDED BY THE WEALTH OF one of the most expensive cities in the world, hip-hop thrives in Singapore's economically depressed Muslim communities. Once a rite of passage for young working-class Muslims, over the past two decades, hip-hop has acquired a much wider fan base. According to Triple Noize, a popular hip-hop group in the early 2000s, 80 percent of their supporters are from the Malay Muslim community, and a significant number are middle-aged. While Triple Noize anticipated youth support, enthusiasm from middle-aged fans surprised the group: "Also, got one time kiter ader [when we] perform kat [at] somewhere in Geylang then most of the makcik2 [middle-aged Malay women] there got excited lah! They are soo supporting & that minute we know that they are acherly [*sic*] genuine supporter" (Triple Noize interview in anakmelayu.com, quoted in Kamaludeen 2016b).

Triple Noize's rise in widespread popularity coincided with that of *Singapore Idol*, a youth singing competition for ages sixteen to twenty-eight. A spin-off from its British counterpart, *Pop Idol*, the competition resulted in a few surprises. Although Malay Muslims represent only 15 percent of the Singaporean population (slightly more than half a million people), all three *Singapore Idol* winners hailed from the minority Muslim community—Taufik Batisah (2004 winner, with 62 percent of the votes), Hady Mirza (2006 winner, with 70 percent of the votes), and Sezairi Sezali (2009 winner, percent win withheld). The show was canceled after these three consecutive wins by local Malay Muslim males. In 2007, a similar singing competition called *Live the Dream* was held in Singapore for competitors aged twenty-five to sixty-five. As in *Singapore Idol*, the outcome of the show was also entirely dependent on viewer voting through SMS (Short Message Service). Affendi and By Definition, the winners of the solo and group categories respectively, were, once again, Malay Muslim males.

Despite their musical achievements, Malays are the most financially challenged community among the official ethnic groups in Singapore. The income per capita of Malay families lags far behind those of the majority Chinese and minority Indian and Eurasian communities. Malays also experience disproportionately higher rates of incarceration, substance abuse, gang-related crimes, divorce, and poor health compared to other ethnic groups. The discourse of the "Malay Problem" has been a prominent mainstay of Singapore politics since the country's independence in 1965 and has been dominated and sustained by scholars and the power elite (Kamaludeen 2007; Rahim 1998) and internalized by the target population. This has manifested in self-loathing and the development of a siege mentality among many in the community. In a similar vein to what is occurring in the United States among the African American populace, the sporting and entertainment industries—particularly the music scene—have presented fertile and dynamic arenas for young Malays to explore their identities and creativity. Singing and talent competitions have offered sanitized, populist platforms for the minority Muslim community to proclaim viable national ambassadors from within its own community.

This success of Muslim youth has not gone unnoticed by the state, which often exploits them to showcase the success of meritocracy and multiracialism in Singapore. As Prime Minister Lee Hsien Loong stated on December 5, 2004, "Taufik and Sylvester—a year ago no one knew them but they had talent and grit. They won Singaporeans' hearts and won contest, they were finalists. Taufik's mother is a cleaner and was not able to attend many performances as she worked long hours, but from that background and his ability and talent, Singaporeans recognised it and you can organise your friends to vote for your favourites. But in the end, the right man won . . . so Singapore must be a land of opportunity for all of us."[1]

Almost all spheres of social life in Singapore are governed by the state's policy of multiracialism. For example, public housing, in which most Singaporeans find themselves living, is apportioned according to a racial quota. Political representation, at least at the grassroots level, also incorporates racial quotas with each sizable constituency having to field at least a member of a racial minority. There are, of course, still major inequalities. Since independence in 1965, all three prime ministers, the country's most powerful political office, have been Chinese men, two of whom are from the same family. The state's preoccupation with race and the CMIO (Chinese, Malay, Indian, Others) model explicitly affects migration patterns in Singapore to the detriment of minority groups because of the government's insistence on maintaining a quota of each racial group (Kamaludeen and Turner 2014). The effect of this model is to preserve racial dominance by the Chinese majority, which constitute about 75 percent of the population of the city-state. Ultra-low birth rates among Singaporean Chinese have resulted in liberal migration policies to attract the Chinese diaspora from Malaysia, China, Indonesia, and the greater region. Conscription, more specifically the requirement that all able-bodied males serve in the defense forces over the course of their adult life, is also heavily influenced by race. Malay Muslims, find themselves disproportionately assigned to domestic vocations such as policing and firefighting as opposed to more prestigious positions in the navy, air force, commandos, and heavy artillery where Malay Muslims are substantially underrepresented. It is important to the state, however, that the appearance of multiracialism is upheld. Hence, the *Singapore Idol* competition provides a valuable platform to portray the success of multiracialism as an official state ideology.

The first *Singapore Idol* headed a local hip-hop group of his own called Bonafide. Despite impediments in the local music industry that curtail the reproduction of these hip-hop talents, such as strong censorship laws and the lack of a viable market to ensure the survivability of indigenous artists, various initiatives have emerged within the community itself. The love affair between Singaporean Muslims and hip-hop predates the *Idol* competitions, and the affiliation can be traced back as far as the Malay Muslim rap duo Construction Sight, who emerged triumphant in the Asian singing competition *Asia Bagus* in 1991. Notwithstanding, it is undeniable that this affinity has increased exponentially since the turn of the new millennium.

By virtue of the Internet, global networks have formed within the Muslim hip-hop community. Reputed for its vibrant hip-hop culture (Maxwell 2003; Fernandes 2011), Western Sydney's diverse Muslim population offers insight into the depth of challenges young Muslims face, as well as how they manifest in popular culture. Fernandes's book *Close to the Edge* traces the hip-hop movement in the streets of Chicago, Havana, and Western Sydney. She charted her journeys throughout the diverse hip-hop scene of suburban Sydney with her sidekick, Waiata, a young woman of Aboriginal descent, discovering a plethora of ways that hip-hop has been consumed and appropriated by Sydney residents. She documents her frustration with how a section of the youth are "consuming and imitating unrealistic images of African Americans," emphasizing misogynistic, hypersexualized bravado that is coupled with gratuitous violence. She recalls how hip-hop artist Mohammed performed in a Sydney event wearing "a chain with a cross studded with fake diamonds," rhyming to shooting and stabbing with belly dancers "grinding their hips together with his" (Fernandes 2011, 126–27). The glorification of misplaced "black attributes," such as the objectification of women, for example, has led, paradoxically, to the dissociation and divergence from both the black other and the Arab self—the very gap that hip-hop practitioners want to close.

"BLACK ISLAM" AND HIP-HOP

Hip-hop was born in an age of segregation and institutionalized racism and served as a social critique against police violence and the inequality experienced by African Americans in every aspect of their lives, from employment and education to public accommodations and mass incarceration. It is essential that this book trace the nascence and evolution of Muslim hip-hop in light of the influential civil rights movement of the 1950s and 1960s. Although most of the earliest hip-hop artists like DJ Kool Herc and Grandmaster Flash were not Muslims, the presence of Islam and longtime leader of the Nation of Islam Elijah Muhammad were palpable at that time. Afrika Bambaataa, one of the founding fathers of hip-hop, acknowledges that he was "heavily influenced by the beliefs of Elijah Muhammad and the teachings he gave Malcolm X and Muhammad Ali and others." Afrika Bambaataa remarks that "everything [Elijah Muhammad] said about dealing with life, nationalities, religion and self" resonated with him.[2]

Shortly after its inception, hip-hop was publicly adopted by the NOI and the Five Percenters movements. The NOI, started in the 1930s, and its splinter group, the Five Percenters, which was conceived in 1964, emerged out of the struggle for civil rights, a movement that sought to address African Americans' "innermost concerns" and to provide "a survival kit" against economic marginality and political discrimination. These groups were instrumental in organizing protest movements in the country.

> In the case of black culture, protest [is] inspir[ed by] the people's innermost concerns. Needless to say a protest culture such as we have in the major urban black centres is also in important psychological respects a survival kit. It also suffers from too shamelessly [*sic*] a preoccupation with certainty and the need for the elimination of ambiguity. It would be a serious cultural tragedy if this protest culture should lose touch with traditional African cultural forms. It should continue to enrich itself from this source in its specific idiom. On the other hand, some strands of the current urban black culture are absorbed from the black experience, notably in the United States and post-colonial Africa. (Manganyi 1982)

As Cornell West (2001, 142) evinces in his book *Race Matters*, "The basic aim of black Muslim theology—with its distinct black supremacist account of the origins of white people—was to counter white supremacy." Although black Muslims can be Sunni, Shiite, and Ahmadi, here West alludes to the NOI and Five Percenter strains when he writes about black Muslim theology. Hip-hop became a deliberate strategy, especially among these groups, to disseminate messages of black empowerment amid the racist attitudes of the time. Louis Farrakhan, long-term member and leader of the NOI, recognized the influence of hip-hop early on and to this day has sought to harness its power on a global magnitude: "You don't wanna come here sit 'n' listen to Farrakhan for two hours, that's a little bit too much. But turn on the box and the [Public Enemy] are getting to you with the Word, and whities sayin' 'Oh, my God, we gotta stop this!' But it's too late now, baby! When you got it—it's over, when the youth got it—it's over . . . the white world is coming to an end."[3]

Farrakhan, a professional musician in his own right, rose to fame in the 1950s as a vocalist, calypso singer, dancer, and violinist. Although he was asked to give up music in order to commit himself fully to Islam, in the last few decades, Farrakhan has become a father figure in the hip-hop community by defending artists who have come under fire for their lyrical content. This development seemed unlikely in the beginning given NOI's position on popular music, which was initially ambivalent at best. Edward Curtis IV argues in his book *Black Muslim Religion in the Nation of Islam, 1960–1975* that Elijah Muhammad never had total jurisdiction on the subject given the tremendous influence of music in the everyday lives of African Americans. This resulted in disagreement among the group's leadership over the "the appropriate role of music in community entertainment" (2006, 173). What is clear is that music did not have much of a place in the movement's infancy.

In the late 1960s, for example, Elijah Muhammad was harshly critical of jazz and its musicians. A 1969 issue of the NOI's publication, *Muhammad Speaks*, came with the pronouncement that "the Honorable Elijah Muhammad teaches us not to listen to Jazz music." Those who invite dancers and musicians are deemed "indeed very weak believers in Islam. . . . The idea that people who call themselves Muslims would present such an affair to invite others to hear disgraceful music is a discredit to their belief" and "such a weak follower is trying to hold on to the ways of this filthy American society." Although music still played in the bazaar and at the mosque, up to the early 1970s, there was an official NOI media blackout on Muslim artists and their music (Curtis 2006, 172–73).

The change in NOI's attitude toward popular music did not begin with Farrakhan's support of hip-hop artists but earlier, with Wallace Warith Deen

Muhammad's ascension as leader of the NOI after the demise of his father, Elijah Muhammad. Farrakhan's influence on the music world was only made possible by the monumental shift of the NOI's stance toward popular music in the mid-1970s during Warith's reign. Martha Frances Lee, author of *The Nation of Islam: An American Millenarian Movement*, notes that Warith instituted a number of doctrinal reforms to prevent the group from becoming too insular and to encourage its growth and engagement with society at large. In the mid-1970s, *Muhammad Speaks* also reoriented itself toward this new disposition and began viewing the popular music industry more favorably. In June 1975, Stevie Wonder, who had previously dedicated his seven Grammy Awards in honor of Elijah Muhammad, was featured in the paper. Later that year, in an unprecedented event, Kool and the Gang performed at the Muhammad family residence in Chicago (Lee 1996, 65).

It is undeniable, however, that as a seasoned musician, Farrakhan has naturally brought NOI's patronage of hip-hop music to the next level. He has provided support and individual counsel to numerous rappers and has arbitrated some of the most high-profile disputes in the industry. In 2009, hip-hop superstar Calvin Broadus, a.k.a. Snoop Dogg, gave a stirring speech at the annual NOI's Saviours' Day Convention. Calling himself the leader of the hip-hop community, Snoop Dogg highlighted Farrakhan's contributions both as a mentor and a peacemaker in the industry and maintained that he will always look to the minister for guidance. Also participating in the event were big-name rappers such as T.I. and Doug E. Fresh.

As Farrakhan had envisioned, the Muslim hip-hop *ummah* (Islamic community) from across the continents has taken to rap groups such as Public Enemy like a fish to water. Public Enemy, perhaps the most influential hip-hop group of all time, is a New York–based act founded in 1986 and renowned for their sharp social commentaries on the realities facing the black community. They were one of the earliest hip-hop groups to attain international fame, and their iconic track "Fight the Power," which is still quoted and played in many contemporary films and dramas, is generally regarded as one of the most powerful songs of its genre. The group's lyrics repeatedly pay tribute to the NOI. William Eric Perkins (1992, 41–42), author of *Droppin' Science: Critical Essays on Rap Music and Hip Hop Culture*, is of the view that just a year after the group's formation, Public Enemy became the spokesperson for black consciousness in the mold of Malcolm X, Elijah Muhammad, and Louis Farrakhan. In fact, Perkins argues that the group is not merely influenced by the NOI but is its biggest champion by a considerable degree.

By using their rhymes to criticize political elites in the United States, Public Enemy inspired Youssef and his comrades to do the same in Algeria. Youssef and other teenage members of the Algerian rap outfit Intik, who sought asylum in France during the military repression in the late 1980s, credited the American hip-hop group with bringing out the rage in them. As Youssef eloquently expressed, "Some people took the route of resisting by fighting with weapons, but us, we're against violence, so our resistance was using our song, our lyrics; the language of words, not of weapons" (Drissel 2009, 132). A global icon in Islamic music, Maher Zain, puts it another way: "I believe that if you want to speak to the world, you make a song. . . . People would rather to listen to songs than screams."[4] This potent and creative use of words, what I have called poetic jihad, would be a source of both struggle and empowerment within the hip-hop *ummah*.

The practice of hip-hop, as evident in the lexicon of Muslim black hip-hoppers in the United States, illuminates the fluidity and variegated nature of Islamic representations in the urban United States. The struggle to define Muslim hip-hop is most poignantly marked by the friction among Sunni Muslims, the NOI, and the Five Percenters. To be sure, the majority of allusions to Islam in American hip-hop spawn from adherents of the Five Percenters (known more often among its members as the Nation of Gods and Earths), which Clarence 13X formed in the thick of the civil rights movement as a breakaway group of the NOI. Present-day members include influential figures in the American hip-hop scene, such as the Wu Tang Clan, Busta Rhymes, and Rakim. The Five Percenters reject the NOI's notion of Farad Muhammad as "Allah." On the contrary, they believe that the black man himself is God, that ALLAH is actually an abbreviation for Arm Leg Leg Arm Head, and that Islam stands for I Self Lord And Master.

The group refers to women as Earth and believes that the female body must be covered, as three-quarters of Earth is covered with water. Therefore, Five Percenter women cover their hair and wear clothes that conceal their figure. Michael Muhammad Knight, in his book *Why I Am a Five Percenter* (2007), addresses the apparent power imbalance in the God/Earth nexus and the sexism in the group's ideology with considerable depth. In the chapter he aptly called "Battlefield Earth," Knight observed that allusions to a divine feminine, thus positioning women on par with the black man's standing as God, are met with the harshest of criticisms. Acknowledging that, at times, he did come across Five Percenters who accord "full theological equality" to women, the popular belief that pervades the movement is that women should play a secondary role. Common metaphors include that of men as the Sun and women as Earth in the solar system and Five Percenter's media idealizing men as the "intellectual, economic and cultural head of his family" while emphasizing the reproductive role of women. Knight argues that not much thought was put into the roles played by women until much later, after the founder's death, which might account for the disproportionate ratio of men to women in the movement. However, he contends that theologies constructed around the figure of a strong man are not exclusive to the group, that individuals have the "right to name himself or herself, whatever name is chosen," and that not all Five Percenter women want to be God and instead find fulfillment in their roles as Earth.

The name Five Percenters is derived from the teaching that 85 percent of people on Earth are oblivious to and will not arrive at the Truth. Of those who do know the Truth, 10 percent will use their knowledge to their own benefit by exploiting the ignorance of those who are unaware. Hence, only the remaining 5 percent are conscious of the true nature of the black man as God or Allah (Nuruddin 2006). In a sense, the Five Percenters have reinterpreted Sufi ideals, especially the concept of *tawheed*, or the oneness of God, which is at the root of Sufism's metaphysical and pantheistic interpretations. Sufis believe that humans are the images of God, and, being an extension of God, they are to some extent divine. The spiritual journey has led Sufi sheikhs and masters to claim a human form of God status, a station where God sees through the lens of his chosen ones and these chosen Sufi masters see with the eyes of God. This is the final stage of *fana'* (annihilation), a state of selflessness where the ego has been subdued and God is allowed to take control. Five Percenters have taken this to the next level by claiming that men can be and are Gods themselves. Referring to black men as Gods places the Five Percenters in direct contradiction with the first pillar of Islam, which is the belief in the oneness of God. Thus Sunni Muslims consider the Five Percenters' theology blasphemous (just as they might do for the NOI) while the Five Percenters place Sunni Muslims in the 10 percent category.

In this book, unless relevant to the context and themes I am describing, I will not be making a hard distinction between *Muslim hip-hop*, hip-hop as practiced by self-declared Muslim artists of various orientations, and *Islamic hip-hop*, hip-hop that strictly adheres to the precepts of Islam. Abdul Khabeer (2007) has mapped out the Islamic hip-hop project quite vividly, albeit in the US context. Islamic hip-hop might object to the use of certain musical instruments, avoid the use of vulgarities, impose a strict body regimen during on-stage performance, and broach matters that are closely knit with religious doctrine. According to Zaher of Deen Squad: "Everything we do, God is always in the equation. . . . We ask God to bless everything that we do. . . . What's going on in the world right now is so bad, what we are doing now is the cure."[5]

It cannot be denied that among a significant segment of those who try to marry hip-hop with Islam, such as Poetic Pilgrimage, Deen Squad, Native Deen, the Brothahood, and many other outfits and their fans, issues such as uttering profanities as part of performance, for example, are important considerations, and I allude to these practices throughout.

In this book, however, I also seek to include hip-hop, produced by those affiliated with Islam, that might not traditionally fit into the category of Islamic hip-hop. In my research, I have discovered that a broad range of Muslims take great pride in contributing to the discourse on hip-hop and Islam. They play active roles in promoting, defending, and representing the religion. Hence, to limit the discussions to a particular subsection would not do justice to the whole spectrum of individuals participating in the conversations. My claim that I do not make a hard distinction between the terms *Islamic hip-hop* and *Muslim hip-hop* is evident in the fact that I only mention the former a handful of times in the book in favor of the latter, which I find more inclusive. I have gone to great lengths to include hip-hoppers of diverse Islamic orientations, putting forth their own attempts at representing Islam and leaving interpretations to their own varied perspectives and experiences. Whether the avoidance of vulgar language and tattooing is more authentically Islamic than the struggle for social justice is not something that I argue in this book. I do not provide a hierarchy of who is more Islamic; instead, I aim to present social reality in its many complexities. This manuscript is not an exercise in theology, and I prefer to leave that to the readers' discretion. In fact, some Muslim artists, like Ice Cube, do not proclaim to be aligned to any particular group at all. Ice Cube, who is touted as one of the most talented lyricists of his generation and a successful Hollywood actor, defines himself as a "natural Muslim, 'cause it's just me and God. You know, going to the mosque, the ritual and the tradition, it's just not in me to do. So, I don't do it."[6]

Debates about the nature of Islam are still ongoing as scholars come to terms with the growing potency of popular culture and as disparate communities interact with one another. Muslims belong to larger, more structured communities, and it is clear that, from very early on, the practices and piety of various schools of Islam are intricately woven and have influenced and borrowed from one another. This is a point made by Zareena Grewal in her book *Islam Is a Foreign Country: American Muslims and the Global Crisis of Authority* (2014), where she argues that there is a tendency among academicians and the press to frame Islam in terms of false binaries, such as that of native Islam and immigrant Islam, black Islam and Arab/South Asian Islam, American Islam and foreign Islam, when there is actually symbiosis among them. These dichotomies are often convenient ways to classify people into good Muslims and bad Muslims. In truth, even before the civil rights movement, diverse migrant Muslim communities were already heavily involved in domestic politics and social issues, and many of these communities had adherents to their orientation of Islam from the "native" black population.

While it is well documented that black Muslims like the NOI have been active in the sociopolitical scene since the 1930s, it is less known that Islam has had a very long history in the United States. Approximately 20 percent of slaves brought to the United States in the 1700s were Muslims. A few hundred Muslims were even documented to have fought in the American Civil War in the 1860s. Muslim immigration from Europe started slowly after the end of the war. By the early twentieth century, Bosnian, Polish, Albanian, Indian, Syrian, and Arab mosques had sprouted up all over the country, serving their respective communities while also engaging the society at large. The Ahmadiyyahs, an Islamic sect from South Asia, focused on proselytizing to African Americans and migrant communities and were active in championing issues of racial segregation and institutionalized racism. Richard Brent Turner, in *Islam in the African American Experience*, argues that it was the Ahmadis who gave African American Muslims their first taste of multiracial solidarity and that they were probably the most influential Islamic group in the United States until the 1950s. The American Ahmadiyyah mufti was made president of a conglomerate of diverse Muslim groups in the 1920s, and the Ahmadiyyahs were seen as strong allies of the civil rights movement (Turner 2003, 130–31).

Besides the anthropological and sociological evidence for the importance of self-identification as a form of meaning making, it is essential to note that the ideologies of groups like the NOI are not static but have, in fact, evolved over time to be more in line with mainstream Islam. Like Sunni Muslims, the NOI believes in the five pillars of Islam, which are composed of the oneness of God (*tawheed*), the five daily prayers (*salah*), fasting in the month of Ramadan, compulsory charity (*zakah*), and pilgrimage for those who are able (*hajj*). It is pertinent to look at the NOI's changing stance on fasting as an example of its transformation. Although the NOI initially appointed December as the month to fast, in 1988 Farrakhan announced, during his travel to the United Arab Emirates, that Ramadan would be observed with the rest of the Muslim *ummah* on the ninth month of the Islamic calendar. In his speech "Ramadan: Fasting Strengthens Discipline," published in *The Final Call*, the NOI's newsletter, Farrakhan stated that since members of the community had matured in their understanding of the faith, they should now try to adhere to the Qur'an as precisely as possible. In *Roc the Mic Right*, H. Samy Alim claims that Farrakhan also reinterpreted the group's notorious dictum of the white man as "devils" and abstracted it to refer to the struggle with "the devil within," which, if left unchecked, will lead to harmful thoughts, deeds, and desires. This deracialized metaphorical interpretation of "devil" brings the NOI's teachings, which have been highly influential in the hip-hop nation, much more in line "with other modalities of Islam than one might think." Indeed, most Muslims, including members of the NOI, would agree that at the heart of Islam is "self-improvement, the *jihad bil nafs* [the struggle against oneself], [which is] the basis for community development, *jihad fi sabil Allah* [the struggle in the way of Allah]" (2006b, 37–38).

Many hip-hop outfits, like the Wu Tang Clan and the Roots, are a blend of mixed "Islamic" members. Since the 1980s, there has been an influential group of former Five Percenter and NOI hip-hoppers who have publicly embraced Sunni Islam, including Ghostface Killa and Raekwon from Wu Tang Clan. Moreover, the NOI itself shifted closer to Sunni Islam when Warith Deen Mohammed, the son of Elijah Muhammad, assumed the helm.

Much has been written about the effect of waves of migration on black Islam in the United States. In 1965, the United States passed immigration reforms that repealed the prior national origins quota, which had favored Europeans. As a result, immigrants from Asia and the Middle East came in droves. Mass immigration in Los Angeles, like many cities across the United States, led to the mushrooming of mini enclaves of immigrants, who quickly established Little Bangladesh, Koreatown, Chinatown, and Persian Square. In fact, due to the half a million or so Iranians residing in southern California alone, Los Angeles has been nicknamed Tehrangeles. This demographic shift played a significant role in the exposure of African American Muslims to the diversity of thought within Islam as practiced globally.

Although the post-1965 surge of migration was a significant factor in reshaping Islam in the United States, it was the epochal moment of Warith's assumption to leadership that led to the largest mass conversion to Sunni Islam in the United States. His ascent to power could not have been more dramatic. On February 25, 1975, just moments after his father passed away, Warith emerged from the NOI's South Side Chicago mosque with a Qur'an in his hand, proclaiming, "We have to take this down from the shelf. We say we are Muslims. What my father taught that is in this book, we will keep. What is not in this book, we have to give up." He swiftly renamed the NOI as the World Community of al-Islam in the West, which later came to be known as the American Muslim Mission and then the American Society of Muslims. In 1981, Louis Farrakhan and a few thousand members broke away from Warith's group to revive the Nation of Islam. The pair made a public reconciliation in 2000, declaring their unity (Esposito 2008). However, as discussed prior, the "Warith Deen effect" had a permanent impact on NOI's ideology by bringing it into the center of Islamic thought.

Sulayman S. Nyang, professor of African Studies at Howard University, credited Warith Deen with re-Islamizing and re-Americanizing the movement: "Here's a man who inherited an organization that most scholars of Islam would describe as heretical before [Mohammed took over]. That mythology has been replaced by sound theology rooted in Islamic orthodoxy. The people had to make a 180-degree turn" (Turner 2003, xxii). While Elijah Muhammad had blasted America for its mistreatment of African Americans and preached against patriotism, even persuading then twenty-eight-year-old Warith to take up a jail sentence for not enrolling in the military when he could have gotten off with community service, Warith adopted a markedly different direction. Yvonne Haddad, a scholar of American Islam, claims that although Warith "knows there is much about America that is racist . . . he's working with it to change it. He is extremely important in making Muslims look at themselves as Americans and emphasizing their American identity."[7] Since the mid-1970s, black Islam has acknowledged its former marginality and repositioned itself as less confrontational. These shifts have afforded Muslim hip-hop a national space, a more cosmopolitan outlook, and ultimately a global audience.

Even though this was true before, by the 1980s, it was clear that black Islam could no longer be equated exclusively with the NOI and the Five Percenters. For example, many black artists now are not only avowedly Sunni, but they are also Salafi or Sufi. One famous case of such a reorientation is the black Dar ul-Islam movement (Curtis 1994). Prior to Warith Deen's ascension and interventions, Dar ul-Islam was the biggest native Sunni group, with thirty-one affiliated mosques in the mid-1970s. Under the changes instituted by Deen, the movement markedly changed direction and became avowedly Sufi in the early 1980s, inevitably leading to fragmentation in the group.

Although the Five Percenters consider themselves representatives of Islam, they might not necessarily see themselves as Muslims due to obvious theological clashes with mainstream Islam. For instance, the Five Percenters have rejected the very definition of a Muslim that literally means "someone who submits." The group does not accept the five pillars of Islam, instead valuing their freedom from strict rules, structure, and hierarchy. According to Yusuf Nuruddin, these contestations with Islam are long-standing and seen clearly in public high schools, with the Five Percenters calling Sunni Muslims "Soon to be Muslims" who teach "that the True and Living God is a Spook"

(Nuruddin 1994, 129). Likewise, Sunni Muslims have been known to criticize the Five Percenters for engaging in heresy or committing *shirik* (associating partners with God). Author Daniel Genis, who learned about the Five Percenters while spending ten years in prison, puts it this way, "If the Nation of Islam is actual Islam's eccentric nephew, then the Nation of Gods and Earths, as the 5 Percenters are called, is that nephew's unhinged offspring."[8] The Five Percenters' quest for official recognition continues to this day. It was not until 2003 that the thousands of incarcerated Five Percenters were given the right to practice their religious beliefs in prisons. Before that, they were brushed aside as a criminal gang.

These differences aside, it cannot be denied that much of the Five Percenters' inspiration—as manifested in its vocabulary and iconography—is derived from mainstream Islam. In addition, Five Percenter artists have made a lasting impact on the hip-hop *ummah*, or what H. Samy Alim has called the transglobal hip-hop *umma* (2005), as seen in the lyrics and music that have influenced contemporary Muslim hip-hoppers the world over. I will discuss the Sunni co-optation of the NOI and Five Percenters' expressions, style, and terminologies, consciously or otherwise, as young Muslims attempt to empower themselves by harnessing and tapping into the raw emotions of anguish and anger. Hence, it is empirically and conceptually important to include all self-described adherents of "Islam" in this study.

PROVINCIALIZING ISLAM, PROVINCIALIZING HIP-HOP

To a significant extent, hip-hop as practiced by its young Muslim activists has provincialized its center. Dipesh Chakrabarty (2000) has called for a provincializing of Europe in order to bring the subalterns (subjects) back into the discourse and the writing of history. Chakrabarty advocates provincializing Europe to decenter the discourse emanating from Europe and to treat it as just one of many other discourses. The provincializing Europe project stems from the understanding that the recording of "Eastern" history has been constructed by westerners through their encounters, real or imagined, with the "West." The terms *East* and *West* are thus hyperreal terms referring to certain figments of the imagination whose geographical referents remain somewhat indeterminate.

In order to fully appreciate the complexities of Muslim hip-hop culture and the global conversations within the hip-hop *ummah*, in this book I call for both a provincializing of Islam from its conventional Middle Eastern center and a provincializing of hip-hop from its American center. Chakrabarty's thesis, which is firmly supported by historians and sociologists, asks the critical question of how we can reconcile ourselves with the legacy of a traditional center of influence in the age of globalization. Young Muslim hip-hoppers also grapple with this question. When comparing the experiences of young Muslims living in highly authoritarian countries where religion is heavily regulated with their counterparts in countries with much more liberal religious views, one obtains a novel angle from which Muslims can be studied. Examining the convergence and divergence of the lived experiences among similar social groups of Muslim youth allows one to deconstruct the myths that reduce social pathologies to particularistic ethnic problems. A comparative framework also highlights the positive and negative features of both models of governance and explains the differences between the specific patterns of behavior that emerge, debunking the notion that a given outcome may be expected in all countries of a similar type. In challenging the assumption of center-periphery relationships as espoused by world system theorists, it is vital to provincialize the Middle East in the study of Islam and Muslims around the world. Locating the dilemmas of Muslim youth within a transnational perspective illuminates the complexities of globalization, the nation-state, religion, and youth culture in all their nuances.

MUSLIMS AS THE NEW BLACKS: PROVINCIALIZING HIP-HOP FROM ITS AFRICAN AMERICAN ROOTS

Despite hip-hop's contentious origins, Boyd (2002) postulates that hip-hop will allow the rest of the United States to assimilate with African American culture. Today, hip-hop's reputation is synonymous with African American culture, but this was not how it started. Many scholars have pointed to hip-hop's diverse and cosmopolitan beginnings not just in terms of racial mix (Flores 2000; Rivera 2003) but also music. Since the early days, deejays such as Afrika Bambaataa, DJ Kool Herc, and Afrika Islam have incorporated beats from soul, rock, jazz, reggae, calypso, and even Bugs Bunny soundtracks to appeal to their audiences (Schur 2009).

Boyd's assertion of the assimilative powers of hip-hop at the national level may even be modest given its global impact. Many individual observers, social activists, and academics have commented that "Muslims have then, ironically, become the new 'black' with all the association of cultural alienation, deprivation and danger that come with this position" (Alexander 2000, 15). Trevor Phillips, former chairman of the United Kingdom Commission for Racial Equality, remarked that "Muslims are the new Blacks."[9] Indeed, Muslims in the United

Kingdom have replaced black West Indian minorities as the most victimized group in terms of hate crimes and racial abuse. Phillips's observation is supported by the fact that comparisons between Muslims and blacks have become commonplace in the European mainstream press, new media, and academic circles. Many allude to the intense securitization young Muslims have had to endure post–September 11. In addition, minority Muslims themselves have adopted hip-hop attributes to a point that comparisons are often made to African Americans. In 2003, Simon Wong, the manager of Jams the Club, remarked that "Malays are the blacks of Singapore. They're more artsy, talented and have a better sense of rhythm than other ethnic groups here."[10]

From the perspective of Muslim youth, assimilation with black culture takes root even beyond the US context and is greater than the aesthetic appreciation of hip-hop culture as a musical form. The predicament and social realities of African Americans resonate deeply with them. This resonance, combined with voracious consumption of hip-hop culture by young Muslims, gives rise to a form of homological imagination that is driven, in part, by how hip-hop is commonly appropriated by urban minority youth to advance human rights (Kamaludeen 2015). According to Mahmoud from DAM:

> I used to hear African Americans talk about poverty and I would look around me and see the type of place where we were living was the same as what they were rapping about. I would hear them rap about drugs; here in Lod we have more drugs dealt than anywhere else in the Middle East. They would rap about friends gunned down and we have many friends who were killed. Tamer has friends who were murdered; I have friends that were murdered. They used to rap about the way black folks were divided against one another; this was music I believed I was living. A lot of people ask me, "why don't you like Arabic music?" "It's not that I don't like Arabic music but I wasn't feeling Arabic music. Arabic music talks about love, about flowers in a beautiful world and my life didn't reflect that. The stuff I was feeling was hip-hop." (Nashashibi 2011, 157)

In *Studying Popular Music*, Richard Middleton stresses that homologies are "structural 'resonances' . . . between the different elements making up a socio-cultural whole" (1990, 9). *Homology* in the Bourdieuan sense refers to "the source of the functioning of the consecration of the social order" that conceals the power relationships just as it serves to manifest itself under the pretense of neutrality (Bourdieu 1988, 204). Following Bourdieu, I maintain that in imagining a singular and shared habitus, young transnational Muslim hip-hoppers "are united in a relationship of homology, that is, of diversity within homogeneity characteristic of their social conditions of production" whereby "each

individual system of dispositions is a structural variant of the others, expressing the singularity of its position within the class and trajectory" (Bourdieu
1990, 60). As subsequent chapters will show, Muslim hip-hoppers continue to
draw from the African American struggle for civil rights in the United States,
including the language, icons, and history. As Bourdieu perceptively identifies,
"presuppositions, a doxa, and the homology between the producers' position
and their clients' is the precondition for this complicity, which is all the more required when fundamental values are involved" (Bourdieu 1984, 240). Although
the relationship is no longer that of producer/client, conflated identities persist
as young Muslims of the September 11 generation continue to put their stamp
on hip-hop culture. It can be said that an individual hip-hop artist at any societal level is engaged with a relation of homology that is tied to a set of activities
or commodities that are themselves characterized relationally.

The combination of hip-hop and the African American experience has given
urban minority youth new cultural expressions and a sense of troubled history
to claim solidarity with and also extract ideals of resistance (Aidi 2014). Hip-
hop and rap are increasingly Islamized and appropriated by Muslim youth in
many parts of the world. Hip-hop's social commentary and confrontational
style are lending a voice to Muslim youth to battle public misconceptions of
Islam. This is juxtaposed against attempts by moral entrepreneurs to manage
young people through music. More significantly, this book argues that, for the
most part, studies of youth culture among minority groups neglect their connectivity with the larger mainstream culture—in this case, through hip-hop.
Hence, a more balanced study of the exclusion of minority youth needs to take
into account the complex and sometimes paradoxical ways mainstream culture
penetrates and interacts with the lived experiences of minority youth.

In the case of hip-hop culture, this homological imagination is played out
through two structures: (1) the hierarchy of hip-hop culture that can be traced
from its specific African American roots to its diasporic manifestations and
(2) the mental structures of its Muslim youth practitioners. Although it is important to note that the adoption of hip-hop culture among globalized Muslim
youth exhibits a significant degree of homological imagination, it is not exer-
cised in toto. This is most evident through examining the evolution of hip-hop
idioms and jargons.

Taking into consideration the mass consumption of hip-hop culture among
predominantly Muslim youth globally, the Islamic hip-hop lexicon seeks to
reinstate the original meanings that have been "distorted" by African American Muslim theological beliefs and reproduce symbols that now have a "realer
than real" feel to them. This is predominantly accomplished by mainstreaming

hip-hop jargons to adopt a more "authentic" connotation to satisfy Sunni Muslim requirements or even making them ambiguous to refer to a plurality of religions. The result has been the appropriation and transposition of various hip-hop idioms to employ more global and conventional interpretations. Muslim hip-hoppers routinely consume and co-opt NOI and Five Percenter hip-hop, despite its origin in a subversive movement within the domain of Islamic theology, and transform it into a more consumerist and palatable medium to voice their discontent.

The hip-hop generation is not limited to African American youth consuming a particular form of street music. Contemporary hip-hop music is used by diverse social groups who find themselves at the margins of society. In the context of this study, hip-hop lends a voice to Muslim youth who utilize hip-hop activism as a vehicle either to assimilate into mainstream society or, on the other hand, to create an alternative identity of the other. In the post–September 11 era of increased Islamophobia, hip-hop has also been used to battle public misconceptions of Islam as well as to articulate everyday injustices experienced by Muslims locally or globally.

THE HIP-HOP *UMMAH* AND THE STUDY OF GLOBALIZATION

The notion of a hip-hop *ummah* has been around for decades. In 1995, members of A Tribe Called Quest—composed of Q-Tip, a.k.a. Kamaal Ibn John Fareed, and Ali Shaheed—teamed up with the late Jay Dilla to form the hip-hop production collective known as the Ummah. The collective got its name from its founding members, who are pious Muslims. And, despite a name that signifies global Muslim solidarity, the production team was heavily involved in the mainstream music industry, having collaborated on the albums of heavyweights such as Whitney Houston, Busta Rhymes, and Janet Jackson. In 2012, the hip-hop magazine *The Source* ranked Q-Tip as the twentieth top lyricist of all time. In an interview in 2009, Q-Tip reflected on the formation of The Ummah and its paradoxical nature:

> Yeah just to kind of keep it like . . . I don't want to get too glossed on it. It was the same thing for The Ummah. That's why I came up with The Ummah, because I felt it was the brotherhood. That word (Ummah) means brotherhood. But the problem with The Ummah and even now with me with Tribe. . . . With Ummah, just because I was the face, people would automatically assume sometimes, like with that "Sometimes" remix, that I produced it or that I did the beat when it was Dilla. So, people would get

confused sometimes over that and think that just because I'm the face of it, if it says The Ummah it means that I did it or credited it as such. And that wasn't the case. So, he (Dilla) wanted to make sure that he got known for what he did.[11]

In an industry that places a premium on charisma and individual personality, it becomes challenging to speak of an *ummah* within the hip-hop community. As Q-Tip illuminates, the ideal often does not manifest in reality. Hip-hop consumers often view creative works attributed to the community as the work of the leader of the pack, which can cause tension within the collective. As Q-Tip stated, "I think everyone should just be allowed to believe what they want to believe, as long as they don't transgress against the next person. . . . It doesn't make a difference what you are. I read the Quran and it appealed to me. At the time, I was agnostic and it really breathed spiritually back into me. For me it's really a cushion, it's cool. I'm cool with it."[12] More significantly, Q-Tip embodies the diversity and level of tolerance inherent in the hip-hop *ummah*. While there are many calls for the oneness of the *ummah* amid assumptions of the existence of a homogenous and monolithic collective, especially in the contemporary landscape of political Islam, the hip-hop *ummah* defies this.

One of the most powerful unifying concerns of this generation of Muslim hip-hop practitioners is the consciousness of living in an age where they and their friends, families, and whole communities are increasingly securitized (Maira 2016; Masquelier and Soares 2016). Recognizing the Muslim hip-hop *ummah* as part of the September 11 generation presents a more critical perspective of its status and identity that goes beyond a nation-state narrative, allowing us to see connectivity on a global platform. A crucial observation in this regard pertains to how, despite the African American hip-hop scene holding much clout over the genre, the nodes of cultural influence in Muslim hip-hop are increasingly dispersed. The constant and necessary engagement with global processes in attempting to unpack Muslim hip-hop gives it the potential to make important contributions to the study of globalization through seeking to understand how Muslim youth have responded to these processes in the context of and in spite of their specific localities. Thus far, studies of young Muslims have generally not adequately captured their responses to the challenges of globalization or their capacity for agency. Many studies claim that young Muslims are out of place in their communities. They also are deemed to be alienated from a generational perspective when pitched against their elders and from an intercultural aspect, as they are unassimilated in larger mainstream society.

My study departs from the cultural alienation thesis that pervades scholarly works and popular media—a thesis that assumes that those who embrace a subculture do so exclusively as a result of feeling marginalized. The cultural alienation thesis is often used as a discursive strategy to preserve the sanctity of the dominant culture, be it national, ethnic, or subcultural, from the contamination of Muslim youth. On the contrary, the appropriation of hip-hop, as with popular youth culture in general, acts as a mediating element in the ability of Muslim youth to gain acceptance in mainstream society. This is achieved, albeit with some tensions.

Even as we speak of the September 11 generation and making sense of the "hip-hop *ummah*," it is important to note that they cannot be conceived homogenously. As Bennett (2000) advocates, the process of globalization will not impose homogeneity. Rather, it will emphasize and foster the "local," which he defines not as a physical space but as a set of discourses. Social actors assume the meaning and significance of their practices not solely by virtue of their engagement with dominant social structures such as the state but by their embeddedness in local politics and social or cultural relations. Discursive practices, however, are also intimately associated with the production and consumption of popular music. Musical texts that originate elsewhere, such as Five Percenter lyrics, for instance, are routinely read and understood by people living outside the United States whose sensibilities are formed by the culture of the locality in which they reside. It must be noted that local sensibilities are themselves heavily influenced by exposure to musical texts that originate elsewhere. Either way, hip-hop as practiced by young Muslims takes on multifarious, glocalized forms that illuminate their local conditions. The following are some examples.

Minority Muslim youth hip-hoppers commonly use terms made popular by African American hip-hoppers, such as *outlaws* and *outsiders,* to refer to their perceived estranged social position vis-à-vis the larger mainstream society, drawing from what Imani Perry (2004) has called hip-hop's "outlaw culture." From my observations in Western Sydney, an area with a significant presence of Muslim migrants, young Muslims have long been stigmatized as unrefined and are reputed to be laden with social problems. The accents of people who reside in these communities are derogatorily labeled *woggie* or *westie* and hold less cultural capital in a predominantly white Christian nation. An amalgamated form of language emerges out of these power relationships. As a diametric response to conventional decorum, "Lebspeak" (Cameron 2003) is born among second-generation Lebanese youth by fusing hip-hop expressions into their everyday speech. These conversations between hip-hop and local culture lead to the formation of glocalized jargons like "'fully sick bro,' 'awesome, Habib' (a form of 'mate'), Yallah (let's go), other than the more colourful swearing ('mo-fo', for example)" (Butcher 2008, 374). The language of hip-hop among young Muslims is inexorably interwoven with local flavors and draws inspiration from antagonisms similar to those found in domestic conflicts. In Germany, diasporic Turkish youth in Berlin (Soysal 2004) found their voices in a limiting discursive space through the landscape of hip-hop that governs their stories through a ghetto narrative and hip-hop lexicon. The "angry street talk" of Turkish youth in Berlin resonates with other groups, such as London's Fun-Da-Mental, the United States' N.W.A., and Paris' NTM. The use of these terminologies tends to be a double-edged sword. On the one hand, the perceived shared social conditions with the African American experience are precisely the appeal for Muslim youth, but, on the other hand, the discursive constraints within the hip-hop vocabulary necessitate that young Muslims adopt an "us versus them" attitude.

These dynamics of glocalization can also be observed in Singapore, which is home to an interesting mix of black street language, Ebonics, and Singlish, a colloquial form of localized English that manifests in everyday speech among adherents of hip-hop (Mattar 2003). Young hip-hoppers suspend their local identity and adopt a global identity through the deployment of Ebonics and the juxtaposition of the East Coast–West Coast antagonism onto the local landscape. A vibrant "underground" hip-hop culture, as exists in many urban cities, especially thrives in illiberal environments and enjoys a substantial following among young Muslims.

Besides serving as a powerful medium for these battles, the Internet allows youth to traverse national and ethnic boundaries. The growing role of cyberspace in the everyday lives of young people, who theoretically have the freedom of space and place on the Internet, has upended the efficacy of state regulation of conventional media such as television. Ironically, it is exactly this fear of unknown places and spaces that has been driving states toward regulating the Internet. Gary Bunt asserts that a primary role of the Internet is to continue the dialogue where traditional sources stop. In the context of global cities, "the application of the Internet is having an overarching transformational effect on how Muslims practice Islam, how forms of Islam are represented in the wider world, and how Muslim societies perceive themselves and their peers" (Bunt 2009, 3). In these urban cosmopolitan cities, young Muslims play a crucial role in advancing the rights of their diasporic communities through hip-hop. For youth living in Muslim-majority countries, however, their assertion of citizenship through the Internet takes a different slant. Hip-hop activism on the

Internet played an important role in the Arab Spring, transforming the newest sensations in cyberspace into revolutionary heroes.

Two important works have emerged recently on the significance of piety in the context of hip-hop culture. Monica Miller's *Religion and Hip-Hop* (2013) rightly argues that scholarship on hip-hop tends to have preconceived ideas of religion that are then rigidly juxtaposed unto the empirical landscape. Reading hip-hop culture solely through the lens of theology misses much of the social processes that influence the everyday lives of youth on the streets. This perpetual struggle between hip-hoppers and moral entrepreneurs is also set against the backdrop of the stereotyping of hip-hop culture and black youth as deviant. Ebony Utley's *Rap and Religion* (2012) documents how religion is appropriated by hip-hoppers as a tool of empowerment and legitimation. From the most gangsta of hip-hoppers to the mildest of *nasheed* singers who fuse hip-hop into their music, God is an important feature evoked from time to time. These observations are pertinent to the social realities of young Muslim hip-hoppers of the September 11 generation and are themes I develop in this book.

A *Forbes* article titled "3 Areas of Society Hip-Hop Culture Will Dominate by 2020" predicts the imminent rise and dominance of hip-hop in politics, education, and corporate culture.[13] More and more world leaders are making references to the genre and affiliating themselves with hip-hop artists; universities have started teaching courses on hip-hop culture, with artists having a regular podium in the institutes of higher learning; and, albeit very slowly, the complexion of the corporate hierarchy is showing fledgling signs of greater diversity. Noteworthy is the article's failure to acknowledge religion as a domain that has been influenced by hip-hop. What will become even clearer in the following pages is that the link among African Americans, Islam, and hip-hop has come full circle.

Initially, black Islam of the NOI and Five Percenter strains was seen to appropriate elements of mainstream Islam as a means of empowerment. Hip-hop became the instrument through which much of these found expression. As a result of the global popularity of the genre among young Muslims and the migration of Muslims to the United States, hip-hop and black Islam evolved to encompass some of these collisions and conversations. Moreover, globalized young Muslims have appropriated hip-hop culture beyond the spatial and conceptual imaginations of the genre's founding fathers, harnessing the power of hip-hop to fight battles such as Islamophobia, state oppression, and patriarchy. All these social processes inform hip-hop culture in the United States today. Hip-hop is now more than just a sound. It is a vehicle of identity formation, a pulpit for proselytizing, an arena to have fun, and a weapon for social activism.

NOTES

1. "PM Lee Outlines Vision for Singapore and PAP," *Channel News Asia*, December 5, 2004.

2. Graham Reid, "Afrika Bambaataa Interviewed (1988): The Shape of Things Hip-Hop and Political to Come?," Elsewhere, October 18, 2010, https://www .elsewhere.co.nz/absoluteelsewhere/3603/afrika-bambaataa-interviewed-1988 -the-shape-of-things-hip-hop-and-political-to-come/.

3. Louis Farrakhan, "The Origin of the White Race: The Making of the Devil," speech delivered at Mosque Maryam, Chicago, March 23, 1989.

4. Lisa Siregar, "A Portrait of the Artist as a Young Muslim," *Jakarta Globe*, May 2, 2011, http://www.thejakartaglobe.com/archive/a-portrait-of-the -artist-as-a-young-muslim/.

5. Rua'a Alameri, "Islamic Hip-Hop Duo Deen Squad Empower Hijabi Women with New Single 'Cover Girl,'" *Al Arabiya*, March 8, 2017, http://english .alarabiya.net/en/features/2017/03/08/Islamic-hip-hop-duo-Deen-Squad -empower-hijabi-women-with-new-single-Cover-Girl-.html.

6. "Chillin' with Cube" (Film), *Guardian*, February 25, 2000, https://www .theguardian.com/film/2000/feb/25/icecube; see also Marlow Stern, "Ice Cube on Donald 'Easy D' Trump: 'Everybody Is Getting What They Deserve,'" Daily Beast, February 10, 2017, https://www.thedailybeast.com/ice-cube-on-donald -easy-d-trump-everybody-is-getting-what-they-deserve.

7. Don Terry, "W. Deen Mohammed: A Leap of Faith," *Chicago Tribune*, October 20, 2002, https://www.chicagotribune.com/news/chi-021020 -mohammedprofile-story.html.

8. Daniel Genis, "Word Is Bond: An Ex-Con Explains the 5 Percenters," Daily Beast, April 12, 2014, https://www.thedailybeast.com/word-is-bond-an -ex-con-explains-the-5-percenters.

9. Haider Zaman, "Essence of Accountability," *DAWN*, July 23, 2004, https:// www.dawn.com/news/1066243.

10. "Eh Yo, Trip!" *Straits Times*, September 7, 2003, http://newspapers.nl.sg /Digitised/Article/straitstimes20030907-1.2.32.3.aspx.

11. "Exclusive: Q-TIP Interview," MOOVMNT, April 19, 2009, http://www .moovmnt.com/2009/04/19/exclusive-q-tip-interview/#.V47uBfl97IU.

12. Hattie Collins, "The Tipping Point," *Guardian*, November 15, 2008, https:// www.theguardian.com/music/2008/nov/15/q-tip-urban-music-hattie-collins.

13. Ogden Payne, "3 Areas of Society Hip-Hop Culture Will Dominate by 2020," *Forbes*, May 24, 2018, https://www.forbes.com/sites/ogdenpayne /2018/05/24/3-areas-of-society-hip-hop-culture-will-dominate-by-2020 /#3259f5aba149.

TWO

—ɷ—

SOMETHING THAT IS OURS . . . AND STILL AUTHENTICALLY ISLAM

EMPIRE, AN AWARD-WINNING MUSICAL DRAMA that aired in the United States in 2015, examined the issue of authenticity in the hip-hop industry. Shortly after the series began, the *Atlantic* ran an article asking the question, "Is *Empire's* Depiction of the Hip-Hop World Authentic?"[1] The *Atlantic* reviewers noted that although the show addresses issues of social class—for example, when Lucious and Cookie, the husband-wife founders of the Empire label, regularly berate their privileged sons, Andre, Hakeem, and Jamal, for not having "lived the authentic street life"—the series' portrayal of the hip-hop industry as being stuck in gang wars, drive-by shootings, and assassinations was anachronistic.

In the show, the pressure for the heirs of Empire to flaunt their authenticity is exacted by the anxious parents, who, besides having to manage the business, worry about their company's street credibility and its ability to produce music that is socially relevant. These issues are portrayed as not mutually exclusive in the cutthroat industry and hence are a constant Achilles' heel of the multi-million-dollar company. Season four introduces a politically conscious Muslim rapper named Preacher Azal who is also a tattoo artist. Preacher Azal's role is to question the authenticity of Empire's music, which he believes is driven primarily by money and status. Preacher Azal criticizes Jamal for his position as a star entertainer born into hip-hop royalty. In the track "Good Foot," in which he collaborates with Jamal, Preacher Azal raps, "I guess heart was a lost star. . . . I ain't in the business of making you top five, I'm just in the business to keepin' the hope alive."

The series also attempted to capture, from very early on, the embeddedness of Islam in the hip-hop industry. Its fourth episode depicts Lucious and

Cookie trying to steal Titan, a superstar rapper with NOI roots, from a rival recording company. Since Titan, "the most authentic artist since Tupac," is incarcerated for his involvement in a shooting, Cookie cannot contact him directly and therefore decides instead to approach Titan's mother. Knowing that Titan and his family are devout members of the NOI, Cookie wears a hijab in an overt show of respect when she meets Titan's mother in her home. Lucious later meets with Titan in prison, tempting him to sign with Empire for an extravagant sum of money sufficient to help rebuild Titan's community. These interweaving themes of Islam, criminalization, incarceration, and personal atonement are recognizable in the lyrics of Tupac Shakur and other hip-hop artists.

Hip-hop series, like *Empire*, are becoming some of the favorite television shows of young Muslims worldwide. Previously, *The Cosby Show* was one of the first television series showcasing a successful African American family to have achieved international success. With its portrayal of an African American family made up of a father who was a doctor, a mother who was a lawyer, and children who were doing well academically, the show shattered stereotypes in its time. The show was uplifting and empowering for many African Americans and provided a much-needed respite from the harsh realities of their lives, including popular culture's abysmal portrayal of African American life only in ghettos and projects. However, *Empire*'s version of a successful African American family is a radical departure from *The Cosby Show*, as *Empire*'s depiction of the hip-hop industry is overshadowed by the strong presence of outdated violent behaviors.

While the inclusion of some elements of gangsta hip-hop and criminality may be necessary for a historically authentic narrative, it is the show's enduring themes of family, solidarity within the community, and finding agency through music that are more likely responsible for its global resonance among fans. Just as *Empire* grapples with issues of authenticity, so do most Muslim hip-hoppers, who struggle to reconcile their craft with their Islamic piety. With hip-hop's notorious associations, does practicing hip-hop make someone less Islamic? If so, how do Muslim hip-hop practitioners transcend this as individuals and as a collective? It seems that one strategy is to summon images of courage from personalities in Islamic history. This confers upon the youth a symbolic status and an "authenticity" derived from a connection with a glorified Islamic past. At another yet equally fundamental level, mainstream Muslim hip-hop also serves as a challenge to the authenticity of hip-hop's "Muslim roots" derived from the NOI and Five Percenters. Besides this ideological departure, Muslim hip-hoppers also struggle to be authentic to hip-hop's other cultural repertoires: fashion, jargons, and street demeanor. They therefore adopt various transformative strategies, successfully or not, to create a space for themselves within the Muslim *ummah*.

REACHING THE ROOTS OF HIP-HOP AUTHENTICITY

The rich history of Islam in America is well documented in hip-hop. There are many hip-hop songs that make references to Islam and Muslim/non-Muslim relations.

> Oh you a Muslim now, no more dope game
> Heard you might be comin' home, just got bail
> Wanna go to the Mosque, don't wanna chase tail
> I seems I lost my little homie he's a changed man
> Hit the pen and now no sinnin' is the game plan
> (Tupac Shakur, "I Ain't Mad At Cha")

Tupac's song "I Ain't Mad at Cha" discusses the conversion of one of his close friends to Islam. From Afrika Bambaataa to Tupac to Jay Z, Islam is often represented quite prominently in both lyrics and, at times, music videos, the latter, for example, through Muslim fashion, gestures of prostration, and raising both hands in supplication.

Although African American hip-hop has been filled with Muslim symbolism since its inception, Muslim hip-hoppers struggle to come to terms with their own authenticity. Nuruddin (2006) asserts that there are strong "science fiction motifs" in the ideology of the hip-hop of the NOI and the Five Percenters. The overarching myth revolves around the work of a menacing and somewhat crazy black scientist called Yakub who existed six thousand years ago in a time when the Original People, who were black, lived singularly on planet earth "like gods in a technologically advanced utopia" (Nuruddin 2006, 147). Nuruddin presents, as evidence, a work called *An Original Man: The Life and Times of Elijah Muhammad*, written by Claude Clegg, that describes the NOI leader's life from 1934 until his death in 1975. In this work, Clegg (1997, 49) states:

> Yakub had a super intellect and thirst for knowledge. He began school
> at age four and displayed a penchant for scientific inquiry. Known as the
> "bigheaded scientist" on account of his unusually large cranium which
> symbolized his vanity as well as his mental powers, he earned degrees
> from all of the colleges and universities in the land by the age of eighteen.
> Though one of the preeminent scholars of the Nation of Islam, his greatest
> achievement took place outside of school when he was just six years old.
> While toying with two pieces of steel, he learned the secret of magnetism,

that opposites attract. The larger lesson for Yakub was that if he could create a race of people completely different from the Original People, that race could attract and dominate the Black Nation through tricknology—tricks, lies and deception. The essence of the black man, which consisted of a black and brown germ, was the key to creating such a race. If he could simply graft or separate these germs until none of the original black genetic code was left, he would be able to create a species of man, called "mankind," who would rule the earth forever.

According to the myth, Yakub and his sixty thousand followers were banished to an island called Pelan due to the havoc they wreaked in the capital, Mecca. In Pelan, Yakub constructed laboratories for genetic engineering and engaged in an elaborate eugenics project where he created a master race that was "physically weak, spiritually and morally depraved, yet intellectually cunning" that he could control to be the undisputed leader on earth (Nuruddin 2006, 148). The NOI's theology mentions that the history of the Original Man happened in twenty-five-thousand-year sequences, with Yakub being the latest cycle. In fact, in an earlier cycle, a scientist, in his failed attempt to detonate planet earth, had flung a large chunk of earth into space, and this became the moon (Nuruddin 2006). The theology of the NOI also refers to the Mother Plane, known to the world as an unidentified flying object (UFO). Louis Farrakhan describes the Mother Plane in great detail in the following speech:

> The Honorable Elijah Muhammad told us of a giant Mother Plane that is made like the universe, spheres within spheres. White people call them UFOs. Ezekiel, in the Old Testament, saw a wheel that looked like a cloud by day, but a pillar of fire by night. The Honorable Elijah Muhammad said that that wheel was built on the island of Nippon, which is now called Japan, by some of the original scientists. It took 15 billion dollars in gold at that time to build it. It is made of the toughest steel. America does not yet know the composition of the steel used to make an instrument like it. It is a circular plane, and the Bible says that it never makes turns. Because of its circular nature it can stop and travel in all directions at speeds of thousands of miles per hour. He said there are 1,500 small wheels in this Mother Wheel, which is a half mile by-a-half-mile. This Mother Wheel is like a small human built planet. Each one of these small planes carry three bombs. . . . That Mother Wheel is a dreadful looking thing. White folks are making movies now to make these planes look like fiction, but it is based on something real. The Honorable Elijah Muhammad said that the Mother Plane is so powerful, that with sound reverberating in the atmosphere, just with a sound, she can crumble buildings.[2]

Although Muslims from the Sunni and Shiite traditions would write off the NOI and the Five Percenters' theology as heresy, their hip-hop jargons have appropriated many terminologies from the Islamic tradition. For the Five Percenters, Harlem is *Mekkah*, Brooklyn is *Medina*, Queens is *the Desert*, and the Bronx is *Pelan* while New Jersey is *New Jerusalem*. The beliefs of the Five Percenter hip-hoppers are often codified in their lyrics. For example, the phrase *whassup G* refers to another black male adherent and not *gangsta*, as is often believed. In addition, popular hip-hop slang such as *represent* and *break it down* can also be traced to the influence of the Five Percenter hip-hoppers. So too can the expressions *word* and *peace*. The popular hip-hop expression *peace* originates from the Moorish Science Temple, the Muslim precursor to the group (Fauset 2001, 42). *Word* is an exclamation of the Five Percenters affirming the truth in the statement of another God (Nuruddin 1994, 127).

The influence of the Five Percenters transcends the art of rapping, inspiring other pillars of hip-hop culture such as break dancing. The informal circle, where b-boys and b-girls perform their moves in rotation, is the cypher, a Five Percenter innovation. The cypher (or cipher) represents any circle or cycles where lessons are being taught. It has become the authentic and sacred space to perform break dancing (Schloss 2009). Cyphers also depict the hip-hop oral culture of battling and rhyming in small-sized speech communities. James Peterson contends that "the ritual of rhyming as practiced by emcees and wannabe emcees incorporated discreet inclinations and impressions regarding the cipher from within the rubric of Islam" (2014, 85). Muhammad Michael Knight's book *The Five Percenters: Islam, Hip-Hop and the Gods of New York* (2007) and Felicia Miyakawa's *Five Percenter Rap: God Hop's Music, Message, and Black Muslim Mission* (2005) meticulously detail the ideology of the group and their deep influence on hip-hop culture.

Inheriting a culture that is already rich with symbolism and iconography alluding to Islam, Muslim hip-hop practitioners find themselves having to creatively navigate a minefield of jargons:

Hip-hop's changed, ain't a black thing anymore G
Young kids in Baghdad showing 2 on 3
Holla West Coast?! Naah, West Bank for life
Upside Down, holla for my Moros aight
Spit rhymes in Arabic on the same level like Jada
You wouldn't know if you should head bang or belly dance playa
I'm that type of sand nigga type of Johnny Conchran yaw dig
World wide like H. C. Andersen, I won't quit

Don't depend on the rap game, I depend on my brain
Ya stereotype me; I knock you out like Prince Naseem.
(Outlandish, "El Moro")

This song, by Danish Muslim hip-hop group Outlandish, demonstrates how the genre has mutated and how it is appropriated beyond its Five Percenter origins. Linguistically, this is done via the inversion of the term G. While maintaining the symbol as a popular hip-hop jargon, its usage here is closer to the *gangsta* insinuations. The term *gangsta* is also commonly used in popular culture as a show of black empowerment and hypermasculinity, a term of endearment for people in the "fam" or who are part of the "crew," not unlike the blaxploitation movies of the 1970s, when hip-hop was coming into its own. Used in this way, the word has been stripped of its theological origin, which was intended to refer to the Five Percenter notion of God. In Outlandish's "El Moro," Outlandish ceases to refer to the African American struggle on the streets and has instead produced a rallying cry to galvanize a young Muslim generation that feels under siege globally. The esoteric messages and insider language of the NOI and the Five Percenters that are codified within hip-hop jargons are often beyond the comprehension of its consumers. Nonetheless, by and large, hip-hop language has become normalized and is reproduced among the global hip-hop *ummah* to represent symbols that are detached from their intended meaning. Not coincidentally, the first Javanese rap song to break into the scene in Indonesia was by a group called G-Tribe.

While it seems that Muslim hip-hop today has done violence to its "authentic hip-hop roots," historically, a schism within the African American Muslim hip-hop community had already occurred over objections to the NOI or Five Percenter theology. African American Muslim hip-hop has long embraced the oratorical style of Malcolm X, an eminent civil rights leader and Islamic activist. Shortly after joining the NOI, Malcolm X rapidly became one of its most influential leaders, starting Temple Number 11 in Boston, expanding Temple Number 12 in Philadelphia, and heading Temple Number 7 (generally considered the epicenter of the movement) in Harlem. His assassination in 1965, shrouded in conspiracies and just a year after his conversion to the more mainstream Sunni tradition, cemented his place not only in black history but in global popular culture. Malcolm X has since become a central figure in Muslim hip-hop, with many hip-hop songs invoking his name and speeches. Richard Brent Turner, scholar of black Islam in America, reveres Malcolm X for his clout and contribution to hip-hop culture, crediting him with the conversion of African American youth to mainstream Islam.

Malcolm X's impact on Islam has extended far beyond the United States. For many indigenous Australians, the gateway to Islam happened through the discovery of the life journey of Malcolm X. Peta Stephenson, in her book *Islam Dreaming: Indigenous Muslims in Australia* (2010, 244), documented conversions to Islam and "the prominence of a single recent historical model—Malcom X—in their decision to convert." Many indigenous people identify themselves as angry and relate to the African American struggle for equality. Champion Aboriginal boxer Anthony Mundine embraced Islam after reading the autobiography of Malcom X, a crucial document in Aboriginal conversions. Sonny Bill Williams, who is of Samoan descent and was a cult figure in Australian rugby before becoming the first Muslim to play for the New Zealand All Blacks, considered Malcolm X and Muhammad Ali as two important men who shaped his life. It is not difficult, then, to fathom that Muslim hip-hop, which is bursting with references to Malcolm X, would find a ready audience among these communities. Popular American hip-hop stars such as Snoop Dogg and Ice Cube, who are both close to the NOI, have reached out to Australia's Aboriginal populations in their interviews and performances to support the community and highlight cultural convergences. In 2008, Snoop Dogg visited Redfern, an area in inner-city Sydney known for its concentration of indigenous people (Warren and Evitt 2012).

However, owing to the complexity of his personal background, replicating Malcolm X in global Muslim hip-hop usually comes at the expense of ignoring the structural conditions that make up his habitus. These include but are not limited to Malcolm X's own unique life story and to him being a part of generations of African Americans having to reconcile their history of slavery while staring at institutionalized discrimination in the US. The symbolic status of figures such as Malcolm X can also be viewed as a product of secular consumerism; he is romanticized as a symbol of the rebellion, as a Che Guevara of the Muslim world. Even so, seen in this way, hip-hop artists are perpetually applying what C. Wright Mills calls the "sociological imagination," the attempt to connect history and biography. The realization that there are aspects of Malcolm's struggles that speaks to the lives of Muslims globally fuels hip-hop activism and makes it even more potent.

While the NOI and the Five Percenters have arguably been the most prominent movements related to hip-hop, Sunni Islam also serves as a source of musical and cultural inspiration in the hip-hop community. Sunni Muslims look toward followers of "al-Islam" (in hip-hop parlance) such as Q-Tip (Fareed Kamal), Lupe Fiasco, and Mos Def. Today, they are among the most highly acclaimed hip-hop artists and are lauded as representatives of hip-hop's school of Afrohumanism and positivity. However, even as the global Muslim hip-hop movement has managed to reconcile its practice with the "authentic Muslim roots" of African American hip-hop, the latter endures a tenuous relationship with Islam at a fundamental level. In the following two sections, I discuss the two main prongs its practitioners undertake to engage with this debate.

DA'WAH BEATS (IN) HIP-HOP

The most important and basic question concerns the permissibility of music in Islam. The religious fatwa on the status of music in Islam is diverse and ranges from a total prohibition of music to allowing musical instruments as long as the song complies with Islamic precepts, such as the prohibition against uttering profanities.[3] Rantakallio's (2013) study of Muslim hip-hop identities on the website Muslimhiphop.com records the quandary facing Muslims who produce and consume Islamic hip-hop while having to rethink their identities on various fronts. Deen Squad expressed their frustration in their track "Deen over Dunya," a Tupac remix that featured Quadir Lateef: "It's a shame a lot of people are against us cos we can dakwah and our duty is to spread love . . . cos we reach out to the youth way better than them." Some of the dilemmas facing Muslim hip-hop artists are encapsulated in the online comments on Muslim youth forums, which are reproduced here:

> I know this is a controversial request, but 3 brothers and myself are Islamic Rappers, we've gotten alot of critisism over the years and we've heard it all . . . but im gonna ask anyway, coz i believe that what we do is from our heart, our intention is good and we genuwinly wanna help the youth, they are more likely to listen to Lyrics that educate them in a "cool" way rather than some old bloke giving a 2 hour lecture . . . anyway, my request is . . . we are looking for a Muslim DJ in Victoria to produce some beats for our flows . . . we are to perform at a huge Islamic function soon, and we need some customized beats ASAP! if anyone who is reading this knows of any PROFESSIONAL Muslim DJ's who are qualified to produce some krayzie beats please leave a reply. (lyrikaloo1, posted March 1, 2005; Kamaludeen 2016b, 78)

> im seriously fed up of this haram police saying music is haram and blah blah. firstly are you perfect?? no none of us are we are all human. and also some of you are acting as if making a music video is the worst thing a muslim can do. as muslims we should be worrying about the bigger things out there such as isis or the "muslims" committing murdering people but no we should worry more about those making music videos rather than the muslims who are giving Islam a bad name. also we all know some stuff are debatable such as music theres not a clear teaching on the ruling of music. and most importantly when watching this video i dont recall their being any swearing

or bad lyrics. all of his music videos are spreading good messages there not your typical music vide with swearing so from that point of view no harm done. secondly in this day and age this may be one of the few ways we can try to engage young kids in islam. and also why are you even on youtube heck why are you even on this video?? but seriously in the end i think we have more important things to worry about rather than on some muslim making a music video (taz874, posted November 2015).[4]

Commenters lyrika1001 and taz874 express the intricacies and tensions of the consumption of hip-hop among Muslim youth. When commenting on the original video of "Muslim Queen" by Deen Squad, which has since been taken off YouTube, taz874 succinctly described the multifaceted debates between consumers of hip-hop music and their detractors. Muslim youth seek to have their generational voice heard in interpreting what is considered "halal music." Hip-hop practitioners, in particular, have taken on two broad intersecting pathways to be authentic to their Islamic beliefs: (1) by infusing hip-hop into *nasheed* and (2) by Islamizing hip-hop itself.

The form of music most agreeable to many Islamic scholars is *nasheed*. As an Islamic-oriented musical piece, it is traditionally sung acapella and performed with basic percussion. However, even within the *nasheed* genre, the permissibility of the female voice has been a contentious issue. The new generation of *nasheed* singers have nonetheless included women and incorporated various instruments to advance their craft, provoking debate within the Muslim community. It is understandable, then, that one of the deliberations within the Muslim hip-hop *ummah* is between the terms *Muslim hip-hop* and *Islamic hip-hop*. To put it simply, the term *Islamic hip-hop* is used by Muslim hip-hoppers to reconcile themselves with Islamic religious requirements in music.

Attempts at bringing hip-hop culture closer to one's religiosity, express it in the public sphere, and harness its potential as a missionary tool are not exclusive to Muslims. There have been a host of books, including *Holy Hip Hop in the City of Angels* and *The Street Is My Pulpit*, that document, from Los Angeles to Nairobi, the transnational reach of what has interchangeably been called Christian hip-hop, holy hip-hop, and gospel hip-hop (Zanfagna 2017; Ntarangwi 2016). Zanfagna (2017, 2) contends that while Islam "has historically been the most prominent religious ingredient in hip-hop's diverse stock," Christian hip-hop slowly emerged onto the map of holy hip-hop in the mid-1980s.

However, the phenomenon of "Islamic hip-hop" is fairly recent, aided by the mass migration of Muslims to the West in the mid-1960s and later as a direct result of the religious revival that affected the Muslim world in the 1980s. Western hip-hop groups that are often associated with the genre, such as the

UK's Mecca2Medina and the United States' Native Deen, did not become active until the mid-1990s and post–September 11. The main elements of Islamic hip-hop are that it may restrict the types of musical instruments used, excludes expletives (like hip-hop's Christian version), and frequently draws upon issues of doctrinal import. On the other hand, practitioners of Muslim hop-hop, which refers to Muslims doing hip-hop, may be more liberal in their craft. Either way, many hip-hop activists go out of their way to Islamize their music and performance, driven by the belief that hip-hop can be compatible with one's Islamic convictions as it is merely a vehicle for self-expression.

In addition to incorporating musical instruments and allowing women to participate, *nasheed* has evolved to include other elements of popular music. An ethnomusicologist of Indonesia, Anne Rasmussen, notes that "the recent appropriation of the sound and look of American 'boy bands' for the *nasheed* movement . . . signals the substitution of Western aesthetics at the expense of both Arab and traditional musical styles" (2010, 168). Contemporary *nasheed* is malleable. New research on music in Muslim Southeast Asia points to the centrality of the *nasheed* genre with the emergence of *nasheed*-themed movies such as *Syukur 21* (Gratitude in the twenty-first century) and *Stanza Cinta* (Love stanza), as well as *nasheed* boy bands. These have strong followings, especially among the educated and middle classes (Daniels 2013; Sarkissian 2005; Barendregt 2006, 2011). Many scholars of *nasheed* have traced the nascence and growing popularity of the movement to a form of "campus Islam." In the 1970s, Islamic activism among impassioned university students gave rise to Islamic revivalism. Islamic renewal in Muslim communities continues into the millennium, especially among educated and middle-class youth. It is no wonder that creative, youthful *da'wah* and reformist movements have grown out of this development. According to Rasmussen (2010), one such Indonesian group is Snada, whose name is derived from the words *senandung* (a tune or song that is hummed or sung softly) and *da'wah*. The group's members are all students from the University of Indonesia who met in a prayer room on campus in 1994. By 2004, the group had released ten albums.

These developments provide fertile ground for fusing hip-hop into *nasheed*. Collaborations with the more mainstream and traditional *nasheed* singers have allowed Muslim hip-hoppers to project a more authentic Islamic identity. KRU, an acronym for Kumpulan Rap Utama (Leading rap group) and Malay for "crew," is arguably the most successful rap group in Malaysia. The group formed in 1992, and the three brothers have been credited with revolutionizing the Malaysian music scene with their blend of hip-hop and pop. Forging alliances across the industry and bringing others into the fold of their unique sounds, they also own a thriving entertainment company, KRU Studios, that in the new millennium has produced *nasheed* songs for groups like Rabbani.

Musical collaborations and performative fusions, however, come with challenges. While rap and *nasheed* collaborations are popular, a minor controversy broke out when one of the most famous Malaysian rap groups, Too Phat, teamed up with popular *nasheed* vocalist Yasin for the song "Alhamdulillah" (Praises to Allah). The song claimed not just nationwide but regional success. In 2003, they invited Singaporean hip-hop outfit Ahli Fiqir to perform with them in the Anugerah Bintang Popular BH. Despite the contents of the song, the group presented a commercialized Western appearance. Most of the rappers were dressed in casual T-shirts and jeans while Malique from Too Phat wore an Adidas sweater and DJ Cza donned an NBA jersey with *New Jersey* emblazoned on the front. Joe Flizzow, one half of hip-hop duo Too Phat, came under criticism for his "authentic" hip-hop performance of the song. While his counterpart, Malique, and all the other singers remained seated, Joe, wearing dark glasses, a wristband of pan-African colors, and a silvery chain, swaggered up to the front of the stage amid his rap. He started his rap with the verse "Make me a soldier in the path of Allah," and some fans were offended by what was deemed a lack of respect to the song and to Allah. This incident is symptomatic of how certain rituals of hip-hop authenticity are considered problematic in the context of an Islamic tradition. For example, wearing chains, the symbolic act of chaining, and showing off one's social status are key hip-hop signifiers. Yet, these are considered inappropriate even though they do not transgress the specific Islamic injunction for Muslim men not to adorn themselves with gold jewelry.

Blending *nasheed* and hip-hop presents even greater difficulties for female rappers. The collaborations are almost always between male *nasheed* singers and hip-hop performers. In the aforementioned gig by Too Phat, Yassin, and Ahli Fiqir, the female member of Ahli Fiqir was excluded from the performance. The reasons women rappers are not included are complex and cannot simply be put down to a strict interpretation of religion. Female involvement in hip-hop is also entangled with issues of cultural tradition and the nature of the state. The intricacies of the participation of Muslim female hip-hoppers will be discussed in chapter 4 of this book.

Despite occasional fiascos, hip-hop and *nasheed* collaborations have become a mainstay of Muslim popular culture. National television and radio programs have started to air *nasheed* and hip-hop performances side by side, and the differences between the two have increasingly blurred. Australian hip-hop group the Brothahood released a video recorded in Abu Dhabi of their impromptu acapella rendition of "Assalatuwassalam" with Malaysian *nasheed* group Raihan. Raihan, listed from 2008 to 2016 on "The Muslim 500," an annual publication ranking the five hundred most influential Muslims in the world, also collaborated with Mecca2Medina on the track "Do You Know Him?" In both songs, members of the group Raihan sang praises to Allah and the prophet while members of the Brothahood beatboxed and Mecca2Medina rapped:

All the way from Malaysia to the UK, USA, and Africa
All in Islam
All over the world
We have to unite because of Allah and him
Who? Rasulullah

On occasion, *nasheed* groups sometimes "cross over" to hip-hop. For instance, the Indonesian group the Night Pray, which was formed in 2010, now fully embraces the hip-hop genre. This has led to calls for a redefinition of the two genres, and predictions of the dissolution of distinctions between the two have arisen. According to Joe Lee:

What makes a nasyid act these days, well . . . nasyid? Like jazz that has transformed itself into so many different sub-genres, nasyid has undergone so many changes to the extent that many are wondering what exactly its identity is. Should religious songs be only sung in the contemporary pop and folksy styles that many of the earlier nasyid groups have restricted themselves to, or should they move over to more adventurous and experimental terrain such as pop and hip-hop? Many singers have already cast away the all-too-familiar religious garb and headgear for the more casual wardrobe. Along with that goes the vocal style, the more religious references in the lyrics, the musical stylings. . . . The consequences at the moment are that many nasyid crossovers succeed only in making a lame attempt at pop. A shame though, after pioneer nasyid groups such as Raihan, Rabbani and Nowseeheart have defined what mainstream nasyid is all about. But the reality is that things are changing for *nasyid* and if the trend continues, the genre may soon just mean all songs with humane and moral messages.[5]

Greater fusion of hip-hop and *nasheed* groups and sentiments such as those cited prior have prompted some *nasheed* practitioners to reexert the "authenticity" of their genre. The Night Pray, on their official Facebook page, describes hip-hop music in general as chaotic, often affiliated with a club or party atmosphere. The group claims that their music is a religiously inspired *senandung* and a strand rooted in "hiphoplogy." The trio characterizes their *nasheed* music as consisting of five components. They aspire for their songs to contain meaning that supports *da'wah*, have a nice tune and arrangement, and provide content that is lyrical and poetic. They desire to produce music that can be enjoyed by every strata of the *ummah*. Finally, they aspire to ensure that their music does not contain any political motivations, does not promote the special interests of any particular group, does not highlight differences within the community, and does not engage in hip-hop lingo that would be seen as "trash talking." In short, they seek to refrain from using any language that would negatively affect the unity of the *ummah*.[6]

In a similar fashion, many hip-hop artists and listeners evoke the concept of *niyyat*, or intention, in producing or consuming music. Although they do not go to the extent of arguing that the ends justify the means, the "good" of music is often emphasized (Shannahan and Hussain 2011). For example, the good intention of harnessing the potential of music to advance social causes does not make cursing on stage acceptable, but there is widespread recognition of the beneficial aspects of music and of honing one's craft. This modality is not intrinsic to hip-hop and has been adopted by Muslim singers of other genres. Rhoma Irama, a popular Muslim-Indonesian musician, record producer, and composer of many songs that have been much studied in academic circles, went further in arguing that music is a crucial tool in doing *da'wah*. Tapping on his experience of more than three decades in the music industry, he mapped out a guideline that "*da'wah* music" has to satisfy (2011, 188):

1. the structure of the songs has to be beautiful and interesting;
2. the lyrics have to be strong, make sense, and present a good argument to touch people's hearts;
3. the melody, lyrics, and rhythm have to be harmonious; and
4. the singer and composer have to make the lyrics relate to every-day life in order to give people good examples to follow.

The purpose of the song, its relevance to its consumers as well as issues of aesthetics, forms the backbone of *da'wah* music. For the September 11 generation, however, several factors have elevated the expectations of *da'wah* music to a new level. Despite careful qualifiers about their craft and how they have positioned their work with respect to their faith, the involvement of Muslim youth in hip-hop customarily presents a challenge to religious gatekeepers who view aspects of hip-hop as contrary to Islamic values. Hip-hop predominantly signifies a form of Western moral degradation and a state of normlessness. For example, in Singapore and Sydney, many Muslims are resistant to welcoming hip-hop into their communities. Ibrahim Mohamed Ali, former chairman of Al-Falah Mosque, located at the heart of Orchard Road in Singapore, a retail and entertainment hub that is also a popular youth hangout, recounted how two mosques tried to hold hip-hop events at the National Youth Park and were then criticized for going against the norms of the Muslim community. "It's a very sensitive balance,"[7] he said. Mainstreamed contemporary Muslim hip-hop also has to respond to the shifting dynamics of *da'wah* in the new age.

The potential of *da'wah* is increasingly apparent to religious elites. Louis Farrakhan is somewhat of a pioneer in tapping into the influence wielded by hip-hop's megastars. Other Muslim outfits have started to follow his lead. Sufi groups are known to embrace hip-hop groups, knowing full well the implications of being linked to a controversial group. Joseph Hill (2016), in studying the Senegalese Fayḍa Tijāniyya Sufi movement, explored a number of ways that rappers and religious elites have sought to reconcile hip-hop's presence in the community. He noted that the sentiments of the local populace have changed drastically from restrained endorsement to lavish praise since the years following September 11. Even the founder's youngest son is known as Baay Mbay "Emcee" Niasse for once harboring dreams of becoming a hip-hop artist before becoming a religious elite in the community. The movement has a strong diasporic community and even counts non-Senegalese hip-hoppers in the UK such as Muhammad Yahya from Native Sun and his wife, Sukina Douglas of Poetic Pilgrimage, as their representatives. By 2014, almost all in the locality regardless of age, gender, or educational status had good things to say about the rappers' involvement. Hill contended that the successful immersion of hip-hop artists and their craft into the religious group, to the extent that it is deemed an act of piety, is done through four ways—appealing to the greater good, evoking the authority of divine inspiration, going back to theological discourse, and embodying the characteristics of what is traditionally regarded as a "good Muslim," such as being steeped in religious knowledge and manifesting exalted virtues.

Despite headway in gaining the religious elites' acceptance of hip-hop, activists like lyrikao01 have decidedly referred to their craft as a form of preaching and conveying in a "cool" manner. Abdul Khabeer (2016), in her book *Muslim Cool: Race, Religion, and Hip Hop in the United States*, points to the development of a new form of identity politics where Americans find fresh ways of being Muslim through negotiating their ideas, fashion, activism, and engagement with the state through the lenses of blackness and hip-hop culture. This has created a "young, chic, and cool" Islam among marginalized Muslims (Mushaben 2008, 508). The idea of a "Muslim cool" or a "cool Islam," which began in 2005 with Amel Boubekeur's short treatise, *Cool and Competitive: Muslim Culture in the West*, has occupied the discussions of young Muslims over the last decade. "Cool

Islam" has been conceptualized in a number of ways. First, it represents an alternative set of values that might not necessarily fit neatly into the traditional confines of religiosity as envisioned by moral entrepreneurs or even the state. In this sense, "cool Islam" is envisioned as a protest culture. Antiestablishment and innovative ways of reading religion into everyday lives resonate with the young and corroborate the many surveys of millennials that point toward a more open, liberal, and participatory form of piety. However, being liberal and open minded does not mean Muslims are leaving the teachings of Islam behind. On the contrary, it points to the increasing acceptance of plurality within the *ummah* and of various interpretations of the *deen*. The Arabic word *deen*, often defined as "religion," "faith," or even "a way of life," has become emblematic of Islamic hip-hop in the West as evident in the groups Deen Squad, Mujahideen Team, and Native Deen.

Second, and more specifically, "cool Islam" also refers to attempts to flaunt Islamic piety through performance and creative arts—music, dance, and fashion. In short, "cool Islam" means that Muslims can be pious and at the same time cosmopolitan and engaged in active citizenship. The younger generation has a more nuanced understanding of the Islamic concept of *aurah* (referring to parts of the body that needs to be covered) compared to the previous generation, who are more likely to be steeped in national and cultural baggage. This is especially evident in Muslim millennials, who are decoupling the religious instruction of the *aurah* from elements of Arabization or local indigenous traditions, allowing them to showcase their individuality. Hence, many are discovering that despite beliefs to the contrary, the religious mandate to cover body parts and not flaunt body shape does allow for experimentation in fashion. Jonathan (Bilal) Wilson (2012) contends that in terms of fashion, there are two ways young people are infusing their identity with popular culture while at the same time fulfilling their religious obligations. One way is by wearing a more customary Muslim dress with non-Islamic peripherals, such as pairing a long white robe with a baseball cap and trendy sneakers. Others choose to go the opposite route by donning a non-Islamic dress with Islamic peripherals—for example, by styling a mini skirt over jeans coupled with a headscarf with a dog tag saying, "Muslim and Proud." Hip-hop culture thus fits into both categories—pious and cool.

Shamim Miah and Virinder Kalra (2008, 22) argue in their article "Muslim Hip-Hop: Politicisation of Kool Islam" that hip-hop artists such as American group Native Deen have created a new phenomenon of "KOOL Islam, which is hip, upbeat, trendy and above all western." They also contend that the type of music by performers like the Soldiers of Allah from Los Angeles is "Kool" and rebellious. Soldiers of Allah's last album, called 1924, symbolizes the year the caliphate, or the Islamic state, was destroyed by Ataturk. Their tracks call for the unifying of the *ummah* under a caliphate system and glorify heroes in Islamic history such as Salaheddine, Khalid bin Walid, and Harun al-Rashid. In their heyday, the group gained popularity not just in the West but also in the Middle East and Southeast Asia. Although they released their last album before September 11, the group predictably gained notoriety after September 11 as debates on Islam entered more prominently into the public consciousness. Ziauddin Sardar (2006) contends that it is within hip-hop that cool Islam can be found as hip-hop provides the tools to project a politicoreligious message, an image of Islam as pragmatic and rational, and a view of Muslims as united, empowered, and harnessing their creativity to fight against imperialism.

Hence, Muslim hip-hop provides an effective point of unity for emerging Muslim communities in diaspora who, as expected, hail from diverse backgrounds. To test this theory, I began studying the Nordic Muslim hip-hop scene. I observed that the rise of hip-hop coincided with the increase in Muslim migration to Sweden, Norway, Denmark, and Finland over the last few decades. The Scandinavian region has seen an upsurge of Muslim hip-hop artists becoming international superstars, such as Maher Zain and the group Outlandish. In his study of Swedish Muslim hip-hop culture, Ackfeldt (2012) emphasizes the multidimensional aspects of Swedish Muslim hip-hop that are more crucially about performing and embodying religious beliefs rather than a platform for social activism or political commentary. This emphasis on the self allows for the possibility of a plurality of Muslim hip-hop and the cultivation of overarching messages of peace, responsibility, and living ethically. Ackfeldt calls it an *ethislamic* project that is directed toward the hip-hoppers themselves as well as serving as *da'wah* to the larger non-Muslim demography. The rise of Muslim hip-hop among the September 11 generation coincides with a significant shift in identity formation. Surveys such as those conducted by the Pew Research Center, for instance, show that unlike the previous generation, young Muslims in the West are more likely to identify themselves primarily as Muslims. Hence, it is not surprising that this new wave of religiosity and identity politics has seeped into popular culture.

Noteworthy is the fact that many Muslim hip-hop artists have said that using hip-hop as a form of *da'wah* has made them better Muslims and brought them closer to Allah. A profound experience is achieved through these songs— one that conveys a utopian and reified version of Islamic history and creates cultural styles for young Muslims to inject into their own activism. Hip-hop is brought closer to Islam through the salience of the *da'wah* agenda or via collaborations with *nasheed* artists. This strategy, however, tends to preclude Muslim hip-hop artists who prefer to present a more global outlook, desire to delve instead into social issues, or simply want to provide a form of halal entertainment while staying authentic to the pillars of hip-hop music. In the following paragraphs, I explore the other strategy Muslim hip-hoppers undertake to remain authentic to Islamic practice: using Islam to reinvent some of hip-hop's key features.

THE ISLAMIZING HIP-HOP PROJECT

While the infusion of hip-hop into *nasheed* can be achieved easily when couched in the *da'wah* agenda, Muslim hip-hop practitioners are criticized for practicing certain definitive elements of hip-hop as outlined in this section. This begs the question, expressed by hip-hoppers themselves in their search for authenticity, of whether Islam and hip-hop can co-exist.

The most highly contentious area is that of gender. As highlighted previously, the successful collaboration of Too Phat, Yasin, and Ahli Fiqir was conspicuous for the absence of Mawar Berduri (Thorny Rose), Ahli Fiqir's female member. Numerous female hip-hoppers thrive in the West, especially under the category of "hip-hop hijabis." These performers present themselves as equal spokespersons for Islam and Muslim issues and assert that their observance of hijab qualifies them to be in the public sphere. Hip-hop hijabis are not easily accepted by some Muslims who hold the view that the female voice and female public performance are *haram* (forbidden). Even among female fans, Islamic dress codes and the place of hip-hop hijabis in the genre have been widely debated. The documentary on the British hip-hop duo Poetic Pilgrimage, titled *Hip-Hop Hijabis*, ends with the two women sitting on the beach contemplating the authenticity of their craft. Poetic Pilgrimage's Sukina Owen-Douglas and Muneera Williams met in college and embraced Islam after being introduced to *The Autobiography of Malcolm X* in school. They want to demonstrate that Islam can coexist with Western culture and that there is a place for women in hip-hop music specifically and as vocal representatives of the *ummah* in general. Owen-Douglas sums it up by saying, "Hip-hop began as the voice of the underdog. . . . The voice of the ones whose story is never told, of those who are spoken about but not spoken to."[8] So salient are these discussions that the topic of gender deservedly forms a chapter of this book.

Contemporary young Muslims debate the hip-hop bodily regimen and issues of performativity. Critics have disparaged what they see as a heavy emphasis on "bling bling" (materialism) and "bagging honnies" (sexual relations with beautiful women) in hip-hop music and culture as concern with social causes such as rights and justice fades into the background. Practitioners themselves are wary of this trend. Poetic Pilgrimage explicitly describe themselves as "not a 'big blinging' group, we don't spend money on ourselves with flashy cars, and expensive items" (Khan 2011, 48). To varying degrees, the notion of bodily discipline is a strong feature of Muslim and Islamic hip-hop in contemporary society. For the most part, Muslim hip-hop practitioners strive to conform to a stricter body regimen than their non-Muslim counterparts. All-male Sunni Muslim groups such as the Brothahood, Mecca2Medina, and Native Deen perform with less aggressive gyrations, are modestly dressed when on stage, and are less likely to be "bling-blinged," display tattoos, remove a shirt during a gig, or pull a hand-on-the-crotch move.

This was apparent to me in the hip-hop performances I attended at the 2013 Muslim Day Parade held in the heart of Manhattan in New York City, which thousands of Muslims attended with their families. Hip-hop was the soundtrack of the parade. The Islamic lyrical and body discipline adhered to by Native Deen and Asim Sujud ensured that Muslims of all age groups could participate in a feel-good environment of ascetic discipline mixed with elements of fun and entertainment.

The parade also included a march, with protesters carrying the Rabia sign in honor of the hundreds of Egyptians who had been violently massacred a few months prior in the military coup staged by security forces against supporters of the Muslim Brotherhood. Kenneth Roth, the executive director of Human Rights Watch, was scathing in his analyses of the event: "In Rab'a Square, Egyptian security forces carried out one of the world's largest killings of demonstrators in a single day in recent history. . . . This wasn't merely a case of excessive force or poor training. It was a violent crackdown planned at the highest levels of the Egyptian government. Many of the same officials are still in power in Egypt, and have a lot to answer for."[9] Increasingly, family events like the Muslim Day Parade are places where young Muslims can come into contact with hip-hop and human rights activism with parental consent. This is not only a tool of the young; adults participate actively in socializing their offspring to the world of hip-hop as a viable platform for halal entertainment on one hand and *da'wah* and jihad on another.

Tattooing is another area where issues of hip-hop authenticity clash with Islamic piety. For young Muslims, the decision to tattoo their bodies comes with religious considerations (Kamaludeen 2016a). While the meaning attached to tattooing is often diverse, those who perceive tattooing as a "transgression" often do so by reason that there is the potential for contagion and contamination in breaking the skin of the body. Hence, numerous cultural barriers across religions have been constructed to proscribe and condemn tattooing. Muslims generally reject tattooing for similar reasons. Muslims believe that since God has made human beings perfect, it is a blasphemy to change the human form. The Qur'an, in An-Nisa 4:119, considers body modifications to be inspired by Satan, who "will command them (his devotees) to change what Allah has created." A number of specific *hadith* (narrations of the Prophet) have documented that the Prophet Muhammad cursed both the tattooer and the tattooed, thus placing tattooing squarely in the realm of deviant behavior. However, Muslims are divided between two dominant traditions—Sunni and Shiite. While Sunni Muslims are governed by the prohibition on tattooing, Shiite scholars (such as Ayatollah Sistani and Khamenei), who do not necessarily accept the traditional Sunni collections of *hadith*, have stated that there is no authoritative prohibition on tattoos.

Despite the overt prohibitions within the Sunni tradition, tattooing is undeniably gaining popularity among the young. While tattooing is typically an aspect of youth culture, it is also important to situate such body modifications within a consumer society. Young Muslims find themselves in a sociologically interesting position in that many of them have or are discovering a youthful, popular, and chic Islam that is a potent mixture of Muslim themes and global consumer culture. Tattoos in this regard are simultaneously rejected as *haram* and accepted as aspects of popular youth culture. For example, Australian rapper Matuse embodies the straddling of these seemingly conflicting identities. Matuse's Instagram page is infused with a flurry of hashtags such as #beardsandtattoos, #beardgang, #arabian, #king, #eastmeetswest, #international, #flow, #sydney, #travellingstranger, #thirdeyeking, #mirrah, #matuse, #misfit, #peace, #clothingline, #model, #inked, and #greenroom. A number of the hashtags read singularly and when taken as a collective are oxymoronic. For example, beards are seen as an overt Islamic identifier while tattoos and the concept of being inked are part of the profane, a trending global fashion industry that conflicts with the dominant interpretation of Islamic scholars. Projecting an East meets West international image but at the same time championing a local (Sydney) and ethnic (Arabian) identity positions Matuse as a self-proclaimed misfit. Put together, these hashtags reveal the desire of young Muslims to straddle multiple identities.

Despite these differences and challenges, the hip-hop bodily regimen allows Muslim hip-hoppers to remain authentic to both their Islamic and poetic affinities. Issues of accessorizing, body movements, and tattooing are more often couched as personal styles. The more important expectation for hip-hoppers in general is not whether they are tattooed or not but whether they resonate with the "street elite" because the "street," in all its nuances, is what hip-hop represents. I discuss in greater detail the Muslim hip-hoppers' projection of the "street" in the next section, but it is important to mention here the specific attempts by Muslim hip-hoppers to bring Islam back to the streets. This is done by incorporating references to Islamic history or heritage and addressing Muslim concerns. Maher Zain, hip-hop turned *nasheed* artist, in his song "As-salamu Alayka" (Peace be unto you), sings about his desire to walk "the streets of Medina" in the time of Prophet Muhammad, a time when the practice of Islam was the most puritan and authentic. Ahmed, a hip-hopper from Tunisia, emphasizes how hip-hop culture continues to respond to people's everyday lives, displacing the controversy surrounding the compatibility of hip-hop music with Islam. The rigor employed by many artists to keep their music real has undeniably led to its increasing acceptance in the Muslim world. If it is not already, hip-hop is fast becoming the most relevant musical genre of the new millennium. Ahmed succinctly encapsulates this as follows: "They hear their problems in this music, you understand? It is their lives in our tongues" (Shannahan and Hussain 2011, 42).

Although there are still young Muslims who embrace the street subculture of "gangsta hip-hop" and its accompaniments, like tattooing and gun violence, this is where many Muslim hip-hoppers draw the line. Even beyond Muslim communities, various grassroots movements have sprouted up to address the issue of gang violence, which is often closely knit with hip-hop. Anti-Racism Action Band (ARAB), a grassroots performing arts group based in Melbourne, has, since its inception in 2004, appropriated music to chip away at sociocultural barriers and battle anti-Muslim sentiment. The Australian government has recognized that young Muslims are frequent victims of verbal and physical abuse in the streets due to their religion. Accordingly, the government awarded Victoria Arabic Social Services a grant to raise the esteem of Muslim youth and combat youth gang culture. This model has also been replicated in Sydney, where hip-hop has been incorporated into other larger, more mainstream events. For example, the Sydney Writers Festival usually includes a number of hip-hop performances and projections.

Increasingly, hip-hop is being appropriated for motivational and even academic purposes, with the goal of keeping youth off the streets. I attended one such innovative event, sponsored by a hip-hop education think tank, called Legacy Building: Cultivating a Global Cipher from the Streets to the

Classroom at the Schomburg Center in Harlem, New York. I was struck by the energy and passion of artists such as Jasiri X and hip-hop scholars Jeff Chang, Bakari Kitwana, and Chris Emdin, who spoke convincingly about the merits of hip-hop pedagogy. Students from public schools who attended the program took to the stage to favorably describe their experience with educational hip-hop and the rewards they reaped. This pedagogical shift in the classroom is astutely explored in Low's (2011) book *Slam School: Learning through Conflict in the Hip-Hop and Spoken Word Classroom*. This aspect of progressive hip-hop that adopts culturally sensitive strategies to achieve academic results has not been adopted in learning institutions in Muslim classrooms. Despite the homological imagination, when it comes to formal learning, hip-hop pedagogy is still seen as inappropriate for the classroom.

Gangsta hip-hop's threat to religiosity has also led internationally renowned Islamic preachers like Nouman Ali Khan and Khalid Yasin to denounce hip-hop for its negative impact on young Muslims. Their sermons "Music and Hip-Hop in Islam"[10] and "Hip-Hop with Sheikh Khalid Yasin"[11] can be found on the Internet. A video entitled "Muslim Youth in Australia Documentary," released in 2008 by the Islamic Dawah Centre of Australia, cites hip-hop culture as a contributing factor to the social ills within the Sydney Muslim youth community.[12] According to Fadi Rahman, president of the Islamic Centre for Research: "You see hotted up cars, big jewellery, the toughness, the talking and haircuts. If you speak to any of these kids, they're into rap and all sorts of things coming from black American society. They're relating to being victimised just like the black Americans. Once you provide a person with such a mechanism, they're always on the attack. They think they're being victimised and that justifies why they get into trouble."[13] For some, this has led to a total rejection of hip-hop culture. In Sydney, grassroots activists campaigning against gang violence have called for the repudiation of hip-hop among young Muslims. Such campaigns rely on reputable and persuasive icons capable of changing young peoples' hearts and minds. Once touted as a music icon, Napoleon (a.k.a. Mutah Beale), a former colleague of slain gangsta rapper Tupac Shakur of the group Outlawz, has a popular following among the "Muslim gangs" of Western Sydney. Napoleon, who until 2005 was singing about praying while holding a loaded gun, has left the music industry out of his strong belief that hip-hop is not compatible with Islam. Since then, he has been traveling all over the world doing missionary work and giving talks to young people about Islam and the pitfalls of hip-hop culture. On one visit to Sydney in 2006, Napoleon advised young Muslims to resist the allure of the glorified image of hip-hop culture and refrain from engaging in a criminal lifestyle:

I come from the lifestyle where we was preaching gangsta music and also we was really doing most of that stuff. The kids on the street they want to go do it, they end up in jail, or killing someone, or on drugs, something like that.... There's people in my neighbourhood, they used to be criminals, they used to be bank robbers, they used to be killers. They became Muslim and nobody would even hear a cuss word coming out of their mouth.... Music glorifies everything that is totally against Islam. It glorifies lying, stealing, murder, raping. They're feeding this stuff to our kids. If you listen to this stuff, you get brainwashed into believing it.[14]

Former hip-hop stars such as Napoleon, Freeway, and Loon, once insiders in the industry who now live more austere lifestyles, provide a powerful narrative that complements the views of traditional scholars who are skeptical about the place of hip-hop in Islam. Napoleon, who runs Mug Ways Café in Saudi Arabia, now talks about his transition from #thuglife to #muglife, using the latter as a tagline for his business. He continues to speak about the evils of hip-hop culture today.

These turnarounds by some of Muslim hip-hop's biggest icons do not diminish the increasing trend of "hip-hop activism" among the September 11 generation as a collective. If anything, they demonstrate the genre's resilience (which goes beyond its artists) and the genre's critical engagement with current and former performers. It does not matter who says it. It is about what is being said. No figure thus far has become successful enough to create a personality cult. The incorporation of *nasheed* into hip-hop and the efforts to Islamize cultural icons in hip-hop culture have caused some Muslim youth who once considered music *haram* and un-Islamic to take a more sympathetic view of Muslim hip-hop groups. In a somewhat unexpected turn of events, the popularity of hip-hop has also led Muslim performers outside the genre to ride on its coattails. In 2016, Zayn Malik, known as Zayn, together with American hip-hop artists Chris Brown and Usher, released the remix version of the song "Back to Sleep." Zayn left the popular boy band One Direction in the aftermath of his #FreePalestine tweet in July 2014 during the height of the intense Israeli bombings of Gaza that killed 2,205 Palestinians, more than two-thirds of whom were civilians, and 71 Israelis, of which 93 percent were soldiers (Kamaludeen 2016b). His proclamation brought a torrent of abuse and death threats on social media, similar to the fate suffered by hip-hop icon Rihanna, who deleted her #FreePalestine tweet within eight minutes. Since his 2014 tweet, Zayn has been the subject of anti-Muslim attacks, including accusations that he has been engaging in "boy band jihad" and "pimping Islam" to his fans. His critics point to his Pakistani background, frequent sporting of the keffiyeh, social media tweets about his fasting during the Muslim holy month of Ramadan, and Arabic tattoos, all deemed dangerous proselytizing tools in an attempt to lead impressionable fans toward "One Direction: facing Mecca."[15]

Despite these massive undertakings to Islamize hip-hop cultural identifiers and the seeming achievements in mediating the tenuous relationship between hip-hop and Islam, challenges ensue for Muslim hip-hoppers on various fronts—from the conservative religious elites to the global hip-hop community and society at large. This is why some, like Swedish rapper Saul Abraham, express a desire to avoid being pigeonholed as a "Muslim hip-hopper" (Ackfeldt 2012). Taking on a religious master identity or being overly focused on da'wah can have consequences. First, the artist is confined to an Islamic audience and may end up performing only at religious gatherings and functions. There are various obstacles to taking this stance. Foremost is the issue of the acceptance of the hip-hop art form in conservative religious arenas. The artist's authenticity as a Muslim is often questioned, owing to his or her subscription to a Western liberal art form that comes with its own unique style. Second, when the message comes first and the musical aesthetics second, the craft suffers. In response to this, Jabbar and Ali, a.k.a. the Lead, out of New York City, seek to make "authentic and original music" (Fink 2012, 4) that sets them apart from what they perceive to be redundancy in much of contemporary hip-hop. Third, Saul Abraham finds it hypocritical that hip-hoppers claim to be creating music for the sake of Islam when many theological scholars contend that music is *haram*. Having come full circle in narrating the struggles of Muslim hip-hoppers to be authentic to their faith, I turn to other facets of the authenticity debate.

AUTHENTIC TO WHOM?

I started this chapter with the view that the quest for authenticity is central to hip-hop culture. Given that "indigenous" practitioners have to contend with the need to be authentic to "what hip-hop really is," it should be no surprise that Muslim hip-hoppers face an even greater challenge. Although Muslim hip-hoppers try to closely appropriate key hip-hop elements like articulating the sentiments of the street, capturing the feel of the underground, and speaking truth to power, much redefinition has to take place not only because of their Muslim identities but because of the contexts of their respective societies. The following section elaborates on these elements and other dimensions of authenticity.

Since the nascence of the genre in the streets of the Bronx, hip-hop culture has been harnessed globally as a powerful tool of social critique. Hip-hop culture has been synonymous with the notion of "the streets." Making references to the streets confers upon hip-hoppers a sense of street authenticity and the ruggedness and resistance that come along with it. It also connotes the ability to represent. Its legitimacy is drawn from its penchant to represent the common person and its unwavering affiliation to the marginalized. The conception of the streets is contrasted against that of the elites and their claims of the common people. Hence, if the street and its actors are real, then the elites are demonized as fake or out of touch with ordinary people. Cheryl Keyes vividly captured the symbolism of the street in *Rap Music and Street Consciousness* (2002). A significant part of the street approach to religion and spirituality is that an individual's relationship with God is largely personalized. The recognition that everyone has at one point been tainted by the streets ensures a more empathetic religiosity. Hence, since everyone has been exposed to the harsh realities of the street, human beings cannot be the arbiter. Only the divine can judge. This inclusive approach to piety allows the street to embrace with compassion those who society might cast away as being contaminated or contaminating. The ability to offer a voice to those who face social exclusion and to elucidate upon social issues, such as unemployment, crime, and lack of attention and support for young people, gives street piety its universal appeal. For young Muslims worldwide, this is a powerful idea.

References to the street used by Muslim hip-hop artists typically fall within several themes. First, a key street theme for hip-hoppers is the marginalized nature of their communities and the difficult lives they had to endure growing up. For example, Native Deen, with millions of viewers on YouTube, raps about "running streets carrying heat yo he aint into that," narrating the struggle for respectability and to make ends meet in the streets. In 2009, English rapper Ashley Chin, now known as Muslim Belal, released an album entitled *From the Streets to Islam* that addresses his adolescent years and his association with hip-hop. The usage of the word *street* here is akin to Elijah Anderson's (1999) famous "code of the street." It refers to the cultural adaptation of young people who live as outcasts in urban ghettos. Swedish-born white artist Senior-I, who came to Islam at the age of twenty, captures the predicaments of urban disenfranchised youth in his song "Street Anthem":

Walk it down with the gang show hype to fight
He didn't realise it might be his last night to life
Cos money, alcohol drugs, that's the game of streets

Snatchin' out the youngest ones, they get caught by police
Click clack bam lock you fit in
Played around in the streets got takin' event
In the background sounds of the mommas weeping and crying
Watching her son laying down and slowly dying

From this perspective, the streets can be seen as the low life, a life of sin, something from which Muslims should escape. In the track "Dawah" by Omar Esa and Muslim Belal, this point is again explicitly made: "What is the benefit of hanging in the streets, Acting bad like you wanna run the scene, You're getting nothing from that empty life you lead, Come to Islam you'll find your inner peace." Second, the streets signify the everyday life, the common, the ordinary, the very social norms that govern a society and not just the laws and regulations that reflect the desires of a particular strata of society. Luqman Rashad, the founder of MPAC, a group based in Chicago, alludes to how we can come to know a city and put a finger on the pulse of society by going out to the streets: "Chicago is hip-hop, its funny cause you will go out in the streets and see that everyone raps. Mashallah there is a lot of talent, as well as a lot of room for problems and beef. It's all about moving strategically and maintaining focus."[16]

This idea of the streets, however, turns Anderson's conception of a binary between a street worldview and a decent worldview on its head. Anderson sees the street and the decent as two integral components of society that coexist to socially organize the local community. The streets denote the informal rules regulating the dangerous inner-city life with the battle for respect at the center while the decent is more oriented toward the values of mainstream society. Living in the same ghetto, the street and the decent are both aware of the other's values, with individuals and families adjusting their behaviors accordingly to live symbiotically.

However, the hip-hop understanding of the street worldview does not exist in opposition to that of decent mainstream society. In hip-hop, the street worldview, with all its apparent messiness and rough realities, is the decent worldview, which provides a window into the realm of everyday life. In fact, beyond the issue of worldview, hip-hop activists themselves are not merely those of low economic backgrounds or literally "from the streets." Educated, middle-class youth also engage in hip-hop, indicating hip-hop as an inclusive platform that unites its practitioners on the basis of their passion for the genre and, at times, on the basis of their sense of shared persecution. Hip-hop groups like the Brothahood, for example, often share social media updates on their personal lives, such as news of marriage and fatherhood—affirming the normalcy, or "decency," of their lives. Hence, the street disposition or ruggedness portrayed by hip-hoppers does not necessarily stem from pathologically "deviant" behavior. Rather, it is more indicative of the show of resilience amid common adversity.

While the notion of the "underground" in hip-hop was historically related to gangsta hip-hop, this relation is being challenged even in the United States, where portraying hip-hop as synonymous with gang wars and violence (like in the *Empire* television series) has been written off as passé. A more expansive view of the "underground" includes any marginalized person within society, even someone from an economically stable background. Thomas Solomon's 2005 study of Turkish hip-hop reveals the centrality of the concept of the underground to notions of authenticity. The most apparent understanding of Turkish hip-hop as underground refers to the peripheralization of the genre from the mainstream industry. Much of the rap music that is produced does not find its way into commercialized markets but is instead distributed through websites or file transfer networks. In Turkey, record labels shun rap acts due to the censorship that has been meted out by the Turkish Ministry of Culture, which maintains a tight leash on material that is deemed to be antiestablishment, advocates for Kurdish rights, or contains vulgarities. Hip-hop gatherings, both formal and informal, thus have become crucial platforms to access the music. Turkish rappers have also imagined the term *underground* to describe the hardcore and uncompromising style and attitude they bring to their music. This may come in the form of refusing to concede their right to use profanities or even vandalizing public and private property with graffiti. Hence, the underground is defined by its marginality with regard to mainstream popular culture. What is interesting in Solomon's study is the assertion that the underground in the Turkish hip-hop scene is not linked to class and race. Hip-hop practitioners do not come from minority groups or underprivileged backgrounds but are often middle-class graduates with comfortable careers. Thus, street credibility and the ability to draw from a troubled past do not count for much.

The image of black masculinity also has an impact on the global hip-hop movement in its search for authenticity. The impact of Malcolm X on black Muslim youth cannot be emphasized enough. Hardly an interview with a Muslim hip-hop artist doing socially conscious music passes without reference to Malcolm X, the African American experience, and the need to abstract personal troubles to larger problems of societal structure. His appeal is amplified by the appropriation of his image as part of popular culture in a time when young people are besieged by information through print and digital media.

Paul Gilroy traced the diffusion of hip-hop culture in *The Black Atlantic*, observing: "Dislocated from their original conditions of existence, the sound tracks of this African American cultural broadcast fed a new metaphysics of blackness elaborated and enacted in Europe and elsewhere within the underground, alternative, public spaces constructed around an expressive culture that was dominated by music" (1993, 83). However, no one could have predicted the extent of the global proliferation of hip-hop culture forty years after its birth.

For many Muslim youth, the homological imagination, which includes the internalizing of common lived experiences of Muslim youth and African Americans (Kamaludeen 2012), has magnified the image of "black masculinity." By referencing piety in their lyrics, Muslim rappers such as Mos Def singing "Allah, the Lord of the worlds" and Nas singing "Been blessed with Allah's vision, strength and beauty" are paving the way for the "reconstruction of black masculinity"—something young people find appealing. In his study of revolutions and music, William Anselmi (2011) drew attention to the significance of US and French protest singers in Italy and concluded that imagination plays a pivotal role as a vehicle of change. Despite the global dispersion of Muslim hip-hop, groups of diverse ethnic origins routinely make reference to African American civil rights struggles in their lyrics. Fun-Da-Mental's "Wrath of the Black Man," a song conceived around a speech given by Malcolm X, is perhaps one of the most explicit. Singles such as this reinforce shared social conditions and highlight the unity between Muslims who live as minorities in the West and African Americans. Australian Muslim youth activists, for example, have expressed concern because young Muslims are not turning to Australian or even Lebanese or Islamic culture but are instead mimicking black rap culture.[17]

It is interesting to note how the symbiosis in the flow of ideas and shared imaginaries has eventually returned to their respective sources. Just as the NOI and the Five Percenters of the twentieth century drew from the cultural vocabulary and iconographies of Islam in innovative and hypermasculine ways to fight white supremacy, many young Muslims are now turning to the everyday lived struggles of African Americans for inspiration in their fight for social justice. Fueled by galvanizing figures such as Malcolm X and the lessons of the civil rights era, as well as by modern social movements like #BlackLivesMatter, hip-hop music thrives today.

To a degree, this imagination has led to an unproblematic internalization of black street culture among a section of young Muslims. Gangsta hip-hop, which has sprouted in urban ghettos and at the fringes of various global cities, presents one manifestation of this homological imagination. This popular subgenre of hip-hop culture is a source of moral panic for many media observers and members of the Muslim community. A variant of gangsta Muslim hip-hop often singled out as unsavory is that glorifying militancy and terrorist acts.

The track "Dirty Kuffar" (Dirty infidels), which was released in 2004 by the British Pakistani group Sheikh Terra and the Soul Salah Crew, is a case in point.

Proclaiming a "G-had," the video featured masked rappers carrying arms and the Qur'an while images of conflicts in Iraq and Chechnya and the twin towers attacks flashed in the background, with Osama portrayed as a lion. The song encouraged the killing of US military crusaders in Muslim lands and sending them to hell. The video also paid attention to the politics of race in the United States. Not unlike Malcolm X's criticisms of house Negroes, which influenced a host of gangsta rappers, such as KRS-One with his song "House Nigga," Sheikh Terra and the Soul Salah Crew called out Condoleezza Rice and Collin Powell for being slaves to their white masters. In many observable ways, Muslim hip-hop videos of this nature, with their heightened aggressiveness, hypermasculinity, and exalting of armed violence, replicate the gangsta hip-hop scene in the United States. Turning the debate on its head, KRS-One has shifted the gaze from the gangsta rap scene to the power holders, controversially referring to "The Star-Spangled Banner," the national anthem of the United States, as the first gangsta rap song in US history.[18] Muslim gangsta rappers such as Sheikh Terra and the Soul Salah Crew, through their own narrative, are also trying to reverse the gaze in their own works.

Interestingly, throughout many controversies, KRS-One's rap has always maintained strong religious elements. KRS-One's public image took an even more spectacular turn in 2009 when he published an eight-hundred-page book, entitled *The Gospel of Hip Hop*, in which he proclaimed that one hundred years from now, a new religion will eclipse all others. The *Guardian* promptly published an article with the subtitle: "Stand Aside Christianity, Islam and Judaism, a New Rap Religion Is Set to Take over the World and KRS-One Is Its Prophet."[19]

Even though September 11 was a definitive moment in terms of the enhanced scrutiny young Muslims experience and in terms of forming a shared identity among a generation, it does not negate the localized challenges members of the September 11 generation were already facing before the terrorist attacks. In that sense, too much can be made of explaining away instances like the "Dirty Kuffar" video in terms of fighting the war on terror and the toxic influence of gangsta hip-hop. Hip-hop scholar Tricia Rose asserts that there is something sinister about the conflation of hip-hop and Islamic terrorism and the failure to look at music as a mere platform to protest social ills that have already plagued the locality, not unlike rock culture in the past. She sees this as a long-term strategy of the Far Right to attach the "fear of infiltration, decline of society, and economic insecurity to black culture" (2008, 99) when, in actuality, in many instances, the September 11 incident was merely a catalyst for exposing and deepening preexisting cracks. Many studies conducted prior to and even on the eve of the attacks identified these social problems and the patterns that caused them.

Jessica Jacobson's (1998) study on religion and identity among young British Pakistanis found that a crucial aspect of the problem for a significant proportion of the respondents was an inability to define the British nation or British identity. It is difficult to reconcile the deluge of popular notions of "Britishness" when some interpretations of whiteness or what constitutes British heritage can be quite amorphous. This is compounded by the fact that British Pakistani youth themselves are ambivalent about their own identities. However, the awareness that many white Britons view British Pakistanis as immutably alien or foreign causes young people to realize that their Pakistani ethnicity is sui generis, not something they can freely influence. Both internally within the Pakistani community and externally within white Christian Britain, these modes of thinking perpetuate a sense of inevitability that ethnic affiliations still persist as the dominant identity. Jacobson asserts that the attractiveness of Islam as a marker of identity is that Islam provides welcomed certainties to these young people in a world full of ambiguities. According to Jacobson, Islam is also attractive in that it is seen as a barrier to the secularizing trends of the larger British society.

This situation is compounded by what Jo Goodey (2001) calls the criminalization of South Asian youth in Britain and what Claire Alexander (2000) exposes as mythology and mythmaking surrounding "the Asian Gang." Goodey's study demonstrates the difficult relationship between teenage boys and law enforcement, with the boys vocalizing their discontent at the way the police conduct themselves illuminating the hardened stereotypical behaviors on both sides. Since the events of September 11, there has also been a sharp increase in studies looking at the criminalization of migrant Muslim youth living as minorities in Western countries. Problems with identity formation, xenophobia, and perceived injustice at the hands of the agents of the state are only a few of the issues. In Europe, the situation is exacerbated not only by September 11 but, more recently, by events like Brexit and the rise of right-wing parties throughout Europe.

In a similar vein, *New York Times* columnist David Brooks lashed out at gangsta hip-hop and radical Islam as the twin causes of the problem. In his article "Gangsta, in French," Brooks discussed the influence of Osama bin Laden and Tupac Shakur on poor young Muslim men. In the aftermath of the Paris riots of November 2005, which raged for three weeks, he pointed to the rioters' immersion in hip-hop and rap culture and their replication of US ghetto gang culture as a form of global hegemonic resistance (Brooks 2005), basically insinuating that young people primarily envision their everyday lives as resembling the struggles of African American street culture. To be sure, Brooks has been roundly criticized for his anachronistic interpretation of French hip-hop, selective reading, and detachment from the ground.

French Muslim rapper Akhenaton argues that the conflation of rap and violence continues and even gained strength in the aftermath of the Charlie Hebdo attack in 2015 in which two brothers, Saïd and Chérif Kouachi, embarked on a shooting spree at the satirical newspaper in Paris in retaliation for the paper's repeated derogatory depictions of Islam and the Prophet Muhammad: "Every time we see a terrorist now we see pictures of him before, and of course he's rapping.... So people are like, "He used to rap, curses! First you rap and then you blow yourself up!" I think we're in a certain period now where we need to say it again—that hip-hop is a culture, hip-hop brought so much to the entire world and to society. When we talk about rap music in France people think it's all about delinquents, you know? We are creating things. There are these amazing performers, graffiti artists, rappers."[20]

However, it is important to realize that the kind of moral panic fostered by personalities such as Brooks stems from the fact that many people refuse to believe hip-hop is a legitimate music genre separate from the culture that is often, rightly or wrongly, associated with those who partake in the genre. To put it into perspective, even if this particular description of a much-maligned subculture within hip-hop holds true, it is important to situate it within the unique conditions of French society. Unlike the multiculturalism models of the United Kingdom and the United States, the French republican system does not confer the same rights and social status to minorities' ethnic, religious, and linguistic identities (Orlando 2003, 398). Hence, it is understandable that the music produced in France captures this angst as the struggle for young Muslims to express their identities is even fiercer given the structural impediments created by the state.

Despite overt African American influences within Muslim hip-hop, any idea that Muslim youth are simply mimicking US black culture—devoid of any direct mentorship by its "original" practitioners—has to be viewed critically. This perception generally can be attributed to the amount of exposure given by the media to "black" music and the glamourizing of the lifestyle in the music genre. However, to take such a reductionist approach in understanding Muslim youth consumption of hip-hop is to lose sight of the homological imagination that has emerged in the global conversations within the hip-hop *ummah*.

These conversations have definitely brought other dimensions of authenticity to the fore for consideration within the hip-hop *ummah*. Although "blackness" remains salient in much of Muslim hip-hop, the *ummah* is cognizant of alternative cultural repertoires—especially when representing their own.

Furthermore, most of the hip-hoppers I called "globalized Muslim youth" in my previous book project a very cosmopolitan outlook. Muslim hip-hoppers realize that they have to engage the wider society for social change to occur. This might make overt projections of certain identities that are not in sync with the larger community—whether "black masculinity" or even Islamic identity—counterproductive.

Asian Dub Foundation (ADF), a London-based rapcore outfit active since 1993, has managed to successfully fuse a variety of identities. The lead vocalist and Muslim member of the group, Saidullah "Deeder" Zaman, a.k.a. MC Master D, has an illustrious hip-hop background. He became interested in music at the tender age of six when he started break dancing and rapping with his sister. A year later, together with his elder brother, DJ Saifullah "Sam" Zaman, and fifteen-year-old MC Mushtaq (who later went on to become the lead rapper of Fun-Da-Mental), they formed the rap group State of Bengal. Sam Zaman, who passed away in 2015 from cardiac arrest, is noted for the creativity of his music, which is said to have influenced a wide spectrum of genres from Bollywood to the American rap scene.[21] He had several high-profile collaborations, including one with Afrika Bambaataa. Although ADF takes on a more South Asian than Muslim identity, and of late a more cosmopolitan disposition, they have consistently and vigorously raised issues affecting the local Muslim community.

Especially for Muslim hip-hoppers who live as ethnic minorities in their own countries, the strategy of catering only to their religious and racial demographic does not make economic sense. The debates on authenticity take an added dimension as they transgress not only the official language of hip-hop culture, which is Ebonics, but also sing in a language they do not use and barely comprehend. The predominantly Sinicized space in Singapore (Kamaludeen and Turner 2014) has led young Malay Muslim hip-hoppers to ply their craft in national Mandarin song competitions. Juz-B, a group formed in 2001, mesmerized audiences on the popular talent show *SuperBand* with their powerful renditions of Wang Lee Hom's songs.[22] Wang is Chinese American and lives in Taiwan. Juz-B's strategy to carve a name for themselves in the local scene was to first make a mark in the larger Chinese market. The group competed in an a cappella competition in Taiwan in 2005, where they managed to impress the judges with a Mandarin song and won four out of seven awards. According to the group leader of Juz-B, Khairul Afwan Bin Rohizan, "I remember we were standing in the queue at the first auditions. . . . People were staring and pointing at us, whispering, *"Zhe ge ma lai ren ah?"* (Mandarin for "Are they Malay?"). . . . It's really tough juggling that, along with arranging the songs a capella-style, and coordinating our dance moves. . . . We were touched when a few group members asked us whether we needed any help to translate the judges' comments or the song lists they give to us each week." The group was praised on their blog by fans for their immaculate singing. Jasmin Lim commented, "I am amazed with how well you guys sing, especially in Mandarin. The words are clear and the pronunciation is accurate." Despite this, the all-Malay group recounted the confusion they experienced in navigating an all-Mandarin competition and learning a new Mandarin song every week. Juz-B is not the only hip-hop group of Malay Muslim youth who face this predicament. Five out of the six members of QI:NOBE, a local hip-hop rock group, are also Malay (Rasul 2006): "When the judges are giving us comments, we just stand there and smile. . . . It's all plastic. Then we get Samuel (Lau, the group's lead singer) to translate for us" (QI:NOBE member Jeffrey Zauhari).[23]

While this example may be rather unique, it is inevitable that hip-hop culture takes on a somewhat "glocalized" form due to the sheer magnitude and rate at which Muslim youth globally are immersing themselves in and reproducing hip-hop culture. Tricia Rose (1994, 35) discusses the "cross-fertilization" of practices and the interplay of graffiti, rapping, and break dancing that have ensured stylistic continuity within hip-hop culture.

Indeed, this cross-fertilization has transcended the conventional boundaries of hip-hop to include folk elements and religious practices. Anthropologist Timothy Daniels likens the influence of *dangdut* in Indonesia to that of hip-hop in the United States. "Similar to rap music, which arose out of poor African American neighborhoods in the United States and stigmatized as low-class culture before becoming part of national pop culture, *dangdut*, long popular with *wong cilik* (J. common people), has become a national pop form popular with all social strata, rich, middle class, and poor" (2013, 167). The Indonesian Jogja Hiphop Foundation (JHF), founded in 2003, believes that traditional Javanese *wayang kulit* (shadow puppet theatre) and gamelan music form solid bases for hip-hop to build on because the alliterations and rhymes found in *wayang kulit* synchronize with the rapping and chiming of gamelan, fitting seamlessly into the breakbeats of hip-hop music. JHF's musical inspiration comes from a variety of diverse indigenous sources, including gamelan, local folktales, *shalawatan* (Muslim prayer recital), *dangdut* (Indonesian pop music), and *Jathilan* (a popular Javanese dance based on rhythmic-trance dance).

Last, just as many African American Muslim hip-hop artists have made the link between the poetic nature of hip-hop and the Qur'an (Kamaludeen 2012), many Muslim hip-hoppers tend to couch their craft within the rubric of the Islamic tradition (Alim 2006a; Mandaville 2009). Abdul Khabeer (2007) stresses that poetry has an exalted place in pre-Islamic Arabia that confers social status and symbolic power on its practitioners. A continuity of this long-standing tradition is found in the Qur'an, which is believed by Muslims of all ages to be a text of superior linguistic pedigree. In fact, Prophet Muhammad was reputed for his use of beautiful language as a missionizing tool. Seeking to emulate the Prophet, who is regarded as being perfectly endowed with the words to mesmerize his audiences, hip-hoppers utilize the rhymes and idioms of Islamic symbolism to engage with young people today. As former hip-hop artist Napoleon handsomely describes: "Moses was sent with magic, Jesus with medicine, and Muhammad with poetry" (Abdul Khabeer 2007, 130). The Qur'an, which contains a specific chapter on "The Poets," is seen as the pinnacle of literary prowess and was composed at a time when, in Arab society, the literati, poets, and orators were glorified. In chapter 17 verse 23, God throws down a challenge to the naysayers: "If mankind and the jinn [supernatural spirits] gathered in order to produce the like of this Qur'an, they could not produce the like of it, even if they were to each other assistants."[24]

East Asian hip-hopper Daddy Chang's conversion story includes first learning about Islam through black history and hip-hop and then September 11 before finally finding solace in the poetic message of the Qur'an, which he compares to the craft of conscious rappers. He talked about how the images of Middle Eastern Muslims as violent perpetrators of the twin towers attacks did not square with the narrative of Muslims he experienced in hip-hop:

> The Muslims I heard about from hiphop was always the ones who got oppressed first before fighting back, but thought if so, then it was a little extreme anyways. I thought that Malcolm X wouldn't have supported something like 911 so that atrocity probably wasn't really what Islam teaches people to do. It was for the first time I wanted to read what Islam really teaches [be]cause I was already at the stage of: TV tells 90 percent nonsense while everybody else and many white kids were dissing Hindus and picking on them for [being] Muslims. I read some of the teachings of Prophet Muhammad (Peace Be Upon Him) and re-confirmed my thoughts that the media was definitely 99 percent nonsense [be]cause all those teachings of Prophet (PBUH) was the most fair and reasonable person I have read out of all the other religious books. Don't get me wrong, I love teachings of Buddhism and Christianity as well, my mother herself is a Buddhist and I love the teachings of Buddhism but I felt it just is too saintly for regular human beings to absorb, I felt like his teachings should be for Angels to read or something, but I thought the teachings of Muhammad (PBUH) and his quotes were both real and spiritual comparing it to humans' condition and fits more for masses to practice and read.[25]

In this light, a number of Muslim hip-hoppers thus see themselves as progenies of the "Muhammadan mission" as they appropriate hip-hop to galvanize the concerns of urban minority Muslim youth living as part of the September 11 generation. The "poetic jihadis" (Kamaludeen 2012), to whom the next chapter is dedicated, emerged as a social group intertwined with the birth of versions of Islam that arose from a particular facet of protest culture.

Although most hip-hop of the September 11 generation derives its inspiration from American artists, which has led to a segment of hip-hoppers rhyming issues that are detached from their community, there have been attempts to synchronize the genre with local and Islamic traditions. Some have also likened rap to the ancient Syrian storytelling style of the *hakawati*, a term later popularized by Rabih Alameddine's 2008 book of the same name. A *hakawati* is someone who does the *Haka*, an Arabic term for telling or reporting that brings to life the *hikayah* (story). *Wati* denotes an expertise in a particular street art. The point of convergence with hip-hop and, more specifically, the rap style, is *hakawati*'s strong emphasis on the delivery of the narratives, the word play, rhythm, and poetry. As Alameddine eloquently states: "It's because you should know that, no matter how good a story is, there is more at stake in the telling" (2008, 96). The narrations are distinct in their colloquial style and are interwoven with rhymes and puns, and readers admire it not just for its story but its words.

In another example, some have argued that the act of rapping and the dynamic exchange reminiscent in rap battles parallel the thousand-year-old Levantine art of *zajal*. *Zajal* is a verse-repeating, chorus-based poetry that is half sung and half spoken. It is popular in Middle Eastern countries such as Algeria, Lebanon, Palestine, and Jordan where *zajjalins* can acquire quite high social status for their skills. It is often performed in the form of a debate where poets engage with one another in a show of improvisation abilities against the beats provided by percussive instruments. The human voice and the beat instruments symbolize the two oldest forms of musical instruments.

Similarly, Afghan duo 143 Band claims that rap music has a history of at least eight hundred years and originates with Jalaluddin Balkhi Rumi, a thirteenth-century poet and Islamic scholar. Rumi is believed to have come from the Balkh city of Khorasan, located in what would be Afghanistan today. 143 Band, who in 2014 was crowned Afghanistan's best rap artists at the Rumi world music awards, maintains that verses such as these are examples of the rap written by Rumi:

تو نه چنانى كه منم، من نه چنانم كه تويى   You are not who I am, I am not who you are,

تو نه بر آنى كه منم، من نه بر آنم كه تويى   You are not who I am, I am not who you are[26]

Rumi continues to be a compelling source of inspiration for hip-hop artists. In 2017, Brother Ali described his latest album, *All the Beauty in This Whole Life*, to *Billboard* by quoting Rumi, "I used to be clever so I wanted to change the world. . . . Now I'm wiser and I want to change myself."[27] He used this as an entry point to discuss contemporary social problems while infusing a sense of introspection into his own positionality as a Muslim American rapper. Baz Luhrmann's 2016 Netflix series *The Get Down*, a dramatization of the history of rap, features a graffiti artist who goes by the name of Rumi 411. In one powerful scene, the words of Rumi are seen emblazoned on a subway train in the South Bronx: "Where there is ruin, there is hope for a treasure."[28] Although there are many other current examples of Rumi respect, 2017 marked a significant tribute to the Persian poet. The entertainment world went wild when hip-hop's most famous couple, Jay-Z and Beyoncé, named their daughter Rumi, thus imprinting Rumi's place in the hip-hop hall of fame and cementing hip-hop's love affair with the literary genius.

In this chapter, I have broached an array of dimensions of authenticity that Muslim hip-hop practitioners defer to. Ranging from key hip-hop elements of the street, the underground, blackness, and speaking truth to power to styles derived from particular cultural repertoires such as regional or local identities as well as Muslim traditions based on the Qur'an or other traditional artistic forms, there are indeed a multitude of paths to authenticity. The highly diverse references to authenticity mean that the genre of Muslim hip-hop as a whole might not possess enough coherence to excite young Muslims collectively. Hence, it is little wonder that fan bases are often clustered around the lyrics and poetics of particular kinds of artists. Miah and Kalra (2008, 16) point to US-based groups such as Soldiers of Allah and Native Deen. These two groups serve distinct needs of the hip-hop *ummah*. While Soldiers of Allah emphasizes "politicized resistance with a particular objective in mind," Native Deen is more concerned with fostering a "spiritual, developmental and a personal-political message." Either way, Muslim hip-hoppers face tremendous challenges. On the one hand, they may be confronted by Muslims who feel they have overstepped the prescribed religious boundaries, and on the other, non-Muslims may feel alienated from the music due to its overt pronouncements of Islamic piety.

As part of managing the tensions between hip-hop and Islam, Muslim hip-hoppers frequently evoke their strong Muslim identity amid their detachment from both traditional culture and a highly misogynistic brand of hip-hop.[29] In an endeavor to represent a "real" and "authentic" Islam, a significant number of Muslim hip-hoppers have infused elements of *nasheed* and Islamic devotional music, coupled with the negation of the NOI and Five Percenter influences in early Muslim hip-hop music. At the same time, some Muslim hip-hoppers' engagement with Islam (through *nasheed*) has led them down different paths. The dilemma over the compatibility of Islam and hip-hop culture has led Muslim hip-hoppers like Maher Zain to shun the scene altogether or to make a transition to more devotional types of music. In 2017, after an illustrious twenty-year career, Outlandish broke up, with one of their singers, Waqas, moving on to release his *nasheed* album, *One Foot in the Sink, the Other on a Banana Peel*. As he stated, "It's a long title I know. The foot in the sink represents deen (creed or religion) and culture for me, during the act of doing Wudu (ritual washing to be performed in preparation for prayer and worship)—for a non-Muslim it probably looks strange and funny to see someone do this. The foot on a banana peel represents dunya, the world which is slippery, so it's a life-long battle to keep striking a perfect pose and maintaining a balance between the two."[30]

The title and photograph on the cover of his album unmistakably capture the predicament of the September 11 generation. The symbolism connotes that a practicing Muslim, depicted by a man taking ablution for prayers, is in a constant state of risk and instability. The album was well received by both critics and audiences for its ability to capture the lived realities of young Muslims in the West who are attempting to balance two unique cultures. Featuring collaborations with American hip-hop DJ turned imam, Suhaib Webb, and *nasheed* singer, Safe Adam, fans especially appreciate Waqas's intimate sharing of his own personal journey of straddling his ethnic Pakistani roots and his Danish homeland.

A number of artists have left the hip-hop scene altogether. In addition to Napoleon, Loon (now known as Amir Junaid Muhadith), formerly a successful recording artist from P. Diddy's Bad Boy Records who went on to found his own company, Boss Up Entertainment, gave up hip-hop in 2009 when he embraced Islam. Shortly thereafter, he began focusing his energies on giving *da'wah*. To this end, he appeared on global television networks like Aljazeera and went on a university tour, giving talks in disparate places from his hometown at Georgia State University to as far as the University of Queensland in Australia, where he shared about his past life as a hip-hopper and his journey to Islam. In 2013, Loon was arrested and sentenced to fourteen years in prison for allegedly being involved in a drug conspiracy prior to his conversion to Islam, a felony he has denied. Swedish rapper Ayo also decided to leave the music industry after his conversion to Islam in 1999 and his subsequent pilgrimage to Mecca, citing vices like drugs and alcohol that often accompany the hip-hop lifestyle.

Ironically, divergent and passionate quests for religious authenticity have resulted in the addition of layers of intricacies within the already complex world of Muslim hip-hop in which former hip-hoppers like Napoleon and

Loon compete for the attention of the September 11 generation with artists who have successfully fused *nasheed* with hip-hop, on the one hand, and others who exhibit a different understanding of authenticity, such as Matuse or even fictional characters like *Empire*'s Preacher Azal, on the other. For the everyday consumers of popular Muslim hip-hop, the entry of Muslim hip-hop jargon into the hip-hop landscape and the mutation of meanings as the terms travel across ethnic and geographic boundaries add to what Baudrillard has termed "a carnival of signs." This crucial consideration over authenticity will be taken up further in subsequent chapters.

NOTES

1. Joe Reid and Kevin O'Keeffe, "Is *Empire*'s Depiction of the Hip-Hop World Authentic?" *Atlantic*, January 29, 2015, https://www.theatlantic.com /entertainment/archive/2015/01/empire-episode-4-recap-false-imposition /384951/.

2. Louis Farrakhan, The Divine Destruction of America: Can She Avert It?", *The Final Call*, accessed March 15, 2018, https://www.finalcall.com/artman /publish/Minister_Louis_Farrakhan_9/article_7595.shtml.

3. Fatwa on Music by the Grand Mufti and Shaykh of Al-Azhar, translated from Arabic by Shaykh Michael Mumisa Alimiyya, https://islamictextinstitute .co.za/music-azhar-fatwa/; "Singing & Music: Islamic View," Islam Online Archive, accessed February 12, 2020, http://www.islamonline.net/servlet /Satellite?pagename=Islamonline-English-Ask_Scholar/FatwaE/FatwaE&cid =1119503544202.

4. "Muslim Queen," Deen Squad, accessed November 30, 2015, https://www .youtube.com/watch?v=yzDCOwjsH6o.

5. Joe Lee, "The Nasyid Evolution," *Malay Mail*, April 6, 2004.

6. The Night Pray Hiphop, "About," Facebook, December 5, 2010, https:// www.Facebook.com/thenightpray/info?tab=page_info.

7. Li Xueying, "Firm in Their Faith," *Straits Times*, July 16, 2005.

8. Kate Beaudoin, "7 Muslim Rappers Who Are Shattering Stereotypes about Islam," Mic, June 19, 2015, https://mic.com/articles/120901/7-muslim-rappers -who-embrace-their-faith-through-hip-hop#.NBZYqOKVQ.

9. Human Rights Watch, "Egypt: Rab'a Killings Likely Crimes against Humanity," August 12, 2014, https://www.hrw.org/news/2014/08/12/egypt -raba-killings-likely-crimes-against-humanity.

10. "Music and Hip Hop in Islam," darklight254, streamed live on August 16, 2009, YouTube video, 00:04:15, https://www.youtube.com/watch?v =yxI4JA7v_qo.

11. "Hip-Hop with Sheikh Khalid Yasin . . . FUNNY . . . ," Halal Sheikh, streamed live on July 28, 2011, YouTube video, 00:06:45, https://www.youtube .com/watch?v=fYqvly5OGUI&spfreload=1.

12. Islamic Dawah Centre of Australia, "Muslim Youth in Australia Documentary," IDCA Productions, January 4, 2008, http://www.tubeislam .com/video/2510/Muslim-Youth-in-Australia-Documentary.

13. Cameron Stewart and Amanda Hodge, "Isolated and Angry," *The Australian*, December 14, 2005.

14. Simon Kearney, "Give Up Your Guns or Face the Music," *The Australian*, July 1, 2006.

15. Pete Samson, "1D's Zayn Branded a 'Pimp' for Islam," *The Sun*, April 5, 2016, https://www.thesun.co.uk/archives/news/699475/1ds-zayn-branded -a-pimp-for-islam/.

16. Muslin Hip-Hop, MPAC interview, http://www.muslimhiphop.com /Stories/3._MPAC_Interview, accessed March 15, 2018.

17. Stewart and Hodge, "Isolated and Angry."

18. "KRS One [First Gangsta Rap Song Was 'Star Spangled Banner']," CoalMineMusic, streamed live on January 31, 2010, YouTube video, 00:01:32, https://www.youtube.com/watch?v=ali Qvpzhzkw.

19. Sean Michaels, "KRS-One Writes 'Gospel of Hip-Hop,'" *Guardian*, September 1, 2009, https://www.theguardian.com/music/2009/sep/01/krs-one -gospel-hip-hop.

20. Jeremy Allen, "Franco-Arabic Rappers in Paris," *FACT Magazine*, November 3, 2015, https://www.factmag.com/2015/11/03/franco-arabic -rappers-in-paris/.

21. Gautam Pemmaraju, "Sam Zaman, Pioneer of the Asian Underground, Influenced Everything from US Rap to Bollywood Beats," Scroll, May 23, 2015, https://scroll.in/article/729353/sam-zaman-pioneer-of-the-asian-underground -influenced-everything-from-us-rap-to-bollywood-beats.

22. "Fa Ru Xue – Juz-B @ Superband Season 1," JuzBchannel, streamed live on April 3, 2010, YouTube video, 00:01:30, http://www.youtube.com/watch?v =1G1LuBFXYcE; "Juz-B – Qing Fei De Yi 2005 @ TAIWAN," razaleigh, streamed live on August 18, 2006, YouTube video, 00:02:19, http://www.youtube .com/watch?v=WjN_xGIbfGU&feature=related.

23. Juliana June, "Mandarin Also Can, Mah! All-Malay Group Performs Chinese Songs with Aplomb at Channel U's Band Search," *Today*, May 29, 2006.

24. Quranic Arabic Corpus, http://corpus.quran.com/translation. jsp?chapter=17&verse=88.

25. Wang Daiyu, "Islam in China Interview with Daddy Chang," *Islam in China Project*, May 10, 2015, http://islaminchina.info/islam-in-china -interview-with-daddy-chang/.

26. Farid Shefayi interview for Star Educational Services, "Music with a Message—Musicians on a Mission: An Interview with Paradise and Diverse from 143 Band," May 25, 2016, https://www.facebook.com /stareducationalsocietyafg/posts/music-with-a-message-musicians-on-a -missionan-interview-with-paradise-and-divers/1073855796019706/.

27. Andres Tardio, "Brother Ali Talks Donald Trump, Injustice & Creating 'All the Beauty in This Whole Life,'" *Billboard*, March 27, 2017, https://www .billboard.com/articles/columns/hip-hop/7736708/brother-ali-donald-trump -injustice-all-the-beauty-in-this-whole-life-album.

28. Part 1, Episode 1, "Where There Is Ruin, There Is Hope for a Treasure," from *The Get Down*, https://www.netflix.com/sg/title/80025601.

29. Neda Ulaby, "Brother Ali: An Honest Act of Worship," NPR, October 5, 2009, https://www.npr.org/templates/story/story.php?storyId=113504052; see also Roose (2016).

30. New Asian Post, "Pakistani Rapper Waqas releases 'One Foot in the Sink . . . ,' Out Now," June 5, 2017, https://www.newasianpost.com/pakistani -rapper-waqas-releases-one-foot-sink-now/?print=print.

—ɯ—

IT IS . . . A PROBLEM OF HUMAN RIGHTS

IN 2013, YASIIN BEY, ALSO known as Mos Def, one of the world's most famous Muslim hip-hop artists, in collaboration with Reprieve, a human rights organization, uploaded a video of himself being voluntarily subjected to the same force-feeding procedure that prisoners on hunger strikes at the Guantanamo Bay prison had undergone daily since September 11. The clip, about four minutes long, shows the rapper, clad in an oversized bright orange jumpsuit, being chained around the wrists and ankles to a medical chair. As the video continues, Bey squirms and sputters as doctors insert more than a meter of feeding tube into his nose, throat, and stomach. The video, directed by an award-winning filmmaker, ends with Bey, in obvious trauma, begging the doctors to stop. Bey's gruesome demonstration was the subject of much public debate. While many praised Bey's moral courage and his endeavor to raise awareness about force-feeding, which the United Nations Commission on Human Rights considers to be torture, a great number of his critics questioned his loyalty to the United States, his country of birth. The video has since gone viral on YouTube and has been viewed more than eight million times.

Mos Def's fight for the rights of his Muslim brethren has been decades in the making. In the year 2000, he conducted a concert to benefit Mumia Abu-Jamal, former member of the Black Panther Party and journalist whom the *New York Times* described as "perhaps the world's best-known death-row inmate."[1] Abu-Jamal was alleged to have been involved in the 1982 murder of a police officer and has been embroiled in a protracted court battle spanning three decades. In 2012, his death sentence was reduced to a sentence of life imprisonment. In 2006, a short trilogy of Abu-Jamal's prison notes was published under the titles,

"A Rap Thing," "On Rapping Rap," and "Hip-Hop or Homeland Security." He argues that the three vices of violence, misogyny, and materialism associated with rap music are inherently American rather than black as "America is easily one of the most violent nations on earth, and has a barely suppressed hatred of women. Materialism is almost a pre-eminent American trait" (2006, 25). Abu-Jamal's life story inspired the music of many rock bands and hip-hop acts, such as KRS-One, Snoop Dogg, Jurassic 5, and Immortal Technique. With his iconic signature, "From Death Row—This is Mumia Abu-Jamal," he even made an appearance in Immortal Techniques' album *Revolutionary Volume 2*, where he orated "Hip-Hop or Homeland Security," emphasizing the absence of security within the hip-hop generation, whom he claims grew up betrayed, feared, and destined for a life of incarceration.

Mos Def puts it plainly in an interview with Ali Asadullah: "If Islam's sole interest is the welfare of mankind, then Islam is the strongest advocate of human rights anywhere on Earth. . . . It's about speaking out against oppression wherever you can. If that's gonna be in Bosnia or Kosovo or Chechnya or places where Muslims are being persecuted; or if it's gonna be in Sierra Leone or Colombia—you know, if people's basic human rights are being abused and violated, then Islam has an interest in speaking out against it, because we're charged to be the leaders of humanity."[2] The conviction that Islam's concern for human rights extends beyond merely safeguarding the interests of the Muslim *ummah* drives many hip-hop artists. In the aftermath of Hurricane Katrina, Mos Def released a song called "Katrina Clap," chastising the Bush administration's handling of the disaster, that he performed from the back of a truck at the curb of Radio City Music Hall for an appreciative crowd. Despite having a permit for the public performance, Mos Def was swiftly arrested. The activism of those who have had brushes with the law is vividly discussed in Paul Butler's *Let's Get Free: A Hip-Hop Theory of Justice* (2010), which captures the ways hip-hop artists have narrated their skirmishes with the criminal justice system. It documents the active citizenship exhibited by the hip-hop community, not just by criticizing the system but also making suggestions on how it can be improved.

In 2006, Mos Def appeared in a documentary that explores issues of crime and poverty in the City of God, a ghetto in Brazil's Rio de Janeiro. Over the years, he has publicly broached many explosive topics, including racist attitudes toward African Americans, the danger of nuclear weapons, and the mainstream media's depiction of "Islamic terrorism." His music, while not devotional in the conventional sense, is driven by Islamic beliefs such as the need to respect and protect the basic human rights of all and to speak out against cruelty and oppression as God's vicegerent on earth.

Legal scholar SpearIt, in his article "Sonic Jihad: Muslim Hip-Hop in the Age of Mass Incarceration" (2016), contends that although hip-hop has had a long history of critiquing the criminal justice system, specifically the police and prisons, the most stinging critiques against legal institutions are often made by artists associated with Islam. This is evident in various charts of the best hip-hop tracks on prison life, of which about half are dominated by acts associated with Islam.[3] This long history of Muslim engagement with the American criminal justice system is exemplified by NOI's manifesto, published in 1965, called "The Muslim Program." The group lists this important creed as part of ten Muslim wants: "We want freedom for all Believers of Islam now held in federal prisons. We want freedom for all black men and women now under death sentence in innumerable prisons in the North as well as the South."[4]

This cause is pursued in graphic fashion in Lupe Fiasco's "Prisoner 1 & 2," one of the most iconic prison rap songs. The track, which runs for about eight and a half minutes, starts with a collect call from prison, an example of just one of the many ways private and public businesses benefit from high incarceration rates. Quadir Lateef, Lupe Fiasco's compatriot who left Howard University to pursue a career in rap, also addresses these "big money" schemes in his track "En Garde," calling prison the new slavery. In "Prisoner 1 & 2," Lupe deconstructs life in a carceral state, including the meting out of long sentences and the role of religion in helping people survive life behind bars. Although the charts show that hip-hoppers affiliated with Islam have long been at the forefront of these debates, living under heightened securitization as part of the September 11 generation ensures this trend will continue. Less than a year after Mos Def, a US citizen, released his video on the torture at Guantanamo Bay, he was denied entry into the United States for immigration and legal reasons.

Hip-hop and the prison system share more similarities than one would think. The age of mass incarceration and hip-hop culture both came into prominence in the 1970s, after the civil rights movement, growing side by side to become multibillion-dollar industries in their own rights. And, of course, many from the hip-hop generation have been incarcerated in increasing numbers, which has motivated the production of songs that tackle this harsh reality. SpearIt traces Muslim empathy for inmates to the theology and history of Islam itself, which not only encourages the fair treatment of prisoners but also sanctions freeing prisoners who have been rehabilitated. The Prophet advocated for the release of non-Muslim prisoners in exchange for teaching Muslims how to read. Some groups have taken this to its extreme, making possible the emergence of what SpearIt considers to be radical strands of Muslim hip-hop, like Latino rap groups Mujahideen Team and Immortal Technique, who lay down narratives such as prison breaks and calls to arms in their songs.

Taken at face value, Mujahideen Team's 2005 album *Clash of Civilizations*, a play on Samuel Huntington's famous thesis in which he points to Islam as a major threat in a global culture war, appears to mark this self-fulfilling prophecy. However, much of the anger of the tracks, with their talk of "out of the prisons, out of the slave plantation" ("Welcome Home") and how the projects are "the breeding ground for prison industrial enslavement" ("So Clear"), can be attributed to the continued victimization of minority groups at the hands of the criminal justice system.

EXPANDING BLACK LIVES MATTER

Inspired by African American hip-hoppers such as Mos Def and Lupe, Muslim hip-hoppers consider their Islamic identity as a mandate to push for issues of social justice through socially conscious hip-hop. Muslim hip-hop is increasingly characterized by young Muslims from various ethnic backgrounds pronouncing their identities while espousing local and global messages of justice and equality in solidarity with their Muslim brethren. Muslim hip-hop therefore serves as an important platform for human rights activism, especially amid the backdrop of global anti-Islamophobic mobilization.

This is true regardless of religious worldview. The human rights dimension serves as a common ground for lyrical or performative collaborations even with non-Muslim hip-hoppers. However, most pertinently, Muslims who do not consider themselves "religious" do not shy away from the genre. The right to represent Islamic-inspired or Muslim-driven hip-hop is claimed by Muslim hip-hop practitioners of various orientations—practicing or not, Sunni or Shiite, NOI or Five Percenters. Omar Musa, a Malaysian Australian rapper who has released three hip-hop albums and won the Australian Poetry Slam and the Indian Ocean Poetry Slam in 2008 and 2009, stated that part of the allure of hip-hop to him as a young male living in a downtrodden neighborhood was precisely "the Islamic thing in it. . . . I was brought up very religious. I don't consider myself religious anymore, but my stuff is influenced by these ecstatic illuminations I'm trying to get to. So, it definitely still informs my writing. And even my style of performing for that matter" (Mordue 2014).

Awate, a twenty-five-year-old Saudi-born, London-based hip-hopper of Eritrean descent, similarly draws from his Islamic background to push for social justice. An accomplished hip-hopper in his own right, Awate has received praise from superstars Mos Def and Lowkey, although his highest commendation came from two of the most well-known hip-hop moguls. Jay-Z declared that Awate "can really spit" while Kanye West called his rhymes "amazing," admitting, "I didn't know people in the UK could rhyme like that."[5] Awate went on tour and opened for Lowkey from 2008 to 2012. The common ground that inspires many hip-hoppers is their collective fates of living as minorities in the West. Awate rhymes about his multiple identities of being black, African, working class, Muslim, and a refugee. As such, his songs are often directed at the imbalanced policies of the state and the institutionalized and everyday discrimination faced by those who live at the margins of society. One of the issues Awate is passionate about is the overpolicing of ethnic minorities, an issue that finds resonance among those living in many global cities (Kamaludeen 2018b).

Of course, this theme is all too familiar in the United States. The #BlackLivesMatter movement was originally conceived in 2012 in the aftermath of the acquittal of George Zimmerman, a white Florida neighborhood-watch volunteer who was tried for the murder of Trayvon Martin, a seventeen-year-old African American. The movement, which is now national in scale and even includes a chapter in Toronto, Canada, has expanded its mission to address racism in all its manifestations. #BlackLivesMatter has had significant backing from the American hip-hop community and its Muslim members. This is vividly captured in the Game's heavy-hitting song "Don't Shoot," which was released in August 2014 shortly after the Michael Brown shooting. Featuring an all-star cast including DJ Khaled, Rick Ross, Diddy, and Swizz Beatz, among others, "Don't Shoot" highlights police brutality, racism, and inequality in the United States. It also pays homage to Michael Brown, Emmett Till, Ezell Ford, Trayvon Martin, and Sean Bell.

Some have taken a broader approach to the senseless killings. In fact, DJ Khaled, a Palestinian MC who considers himself a devout Muslim, rebranded himself from his original moniker, Arab Attack, out of consideration for all the lives lost: "I dropped it because, after the whole 9/11 thing, you know I'm not one of those ignorant people. I'm a positive person. 'Arab Attack' was mainly used for music, like we attack you with music, but when 9/11 happened, I said, you know what, I'm not gonna use that name no more. It wasn't respectful to the people that went through some stuff."[6] Since the Arab Attack name would have attracted controversy and definitely would not have been good for business, dropping it was a logical decision. While many hip-hop stars have alluded more broadly to the black struggle for rights, there are others who dissect, blow-by-blow, key events that have shaped the collective conscience of the movement. For instance, the song "I Am Troy Davis (T.R.O.Y.)," by Jasiri X of the NOI, focuses on the execution of Troy Davis, an African American man whose conviction for the murder of a police officer was based on flimsy and contradictory evidence, including the testimony of prosecution witnesses who later stated they had been coerced by police. "Jordan Miles," another impassioned Jasiri X song, concerns the brutal beating of eighteen-year-old Jordan Miles, who was attacked by undercover police officers while walking to his grandmother's house.

Through the Internet, the epidemic of police brutality directed at African Americans in the United States is now more visible than ever, which has motivated Muslim hip-hoppers in the United Kingdom to support the #BlackLivesMatter movement. For instance, London Muslim rapper TekMill, following Awate's criticism of police misconduct, posted a message on his Facebook account, "You trust police, i trust Allah."[7] The overrepresentation of Muslims in United Kingdom prisons has been the subject of much discussion. A 2015 BBC report entitled "Why the Surge in Muslim Prisoners?" addresses the issue head on. There were 5,502 inmates in England and Wales in 2002 who identified themselves as Muslims, but by 2014 this number had exploded to 12,225. While overall prison numbers increased by about 20 percent during this period, incarceration rates for Muslims jumped by 122 percent. According to the 2001 census, Muslims make up 3 percent of the general population, with the number increasing slightly to 4.8 percent ten years later. On the other hand, Muslim recidivism rates were 36 percent, which is lower than the rest of the population at 45 percent (Shaw 2015). Many academic studies have pointed to the discrimination faced by Muslim men in prison and in the streets post–September 11 (Beckford, Joly, and Khosrokhavar 2005; Marranci 2009). This dire social reality facing young Muslims with regard to the criminal justice system is amplified for migrant Muslim rappers, who feel especially marginalized in the United Kingdom after having been part of the privileged majority group in their countries of origin.

Muslim hip-hop practitioners also partake in the discourse of human rights by challenging prevailing definitions and pushing boundaries for inclusion. In this case, Muslim hip-hoppers outside the United States sometimes express frustration with what they perceive as a double standard when it comes to the #BlackLivesMatter movement's selective championing of human rights. In essence, Muslims who are doubly marginalized because of their racial and religious identities feel excluded by the #BlackLivesMatter movement. The main point of contention revolves around the meaning of "blackness," which can be perceived as partial to the United States, or more specifically the African American experience, and as such precludes Muslims in general or groups like South Asians from being under its banner. This frustration is articulated by

Awate's fellow London artist Maya Arulpragasam, who goes by the acronym M.I.A.:

> It's interesting that in America the problem you're allowed to talk about is Black Lives Matter. It's not a new thing to me—it's what Lauryn Hill was saying in the 1990s, or Public Enemy in the 1980s. Is Beyoncé or Kendrick Lamar going to say Muslim Lives Matter? Or Syrian Lives Matter? Or this kid in Pakistan matters? That's a more interesting question. And you cannot ask it on a song that's on Apple, you cannot ask it on an American TV programme, you cannot create that tag on Twitter, Michelle Obama is not going to hump you back.[8]

Although she is not Muslim, M.I.A.'s statement strikes a chord with many in the hip-hop *ummah* who feel that statements such as these cannot be made publicly even by the most influential in the industry. In the secular fundamentalist environment that has pervaded many cosmopolitan cities today, it is easier to speak about racial discrimination than to speak about Islamophobia. Despite the presence of Islam in black history and hip-hop culture, not many artists are willing to risk public disapproval. In response to her statements, M.I.A. was accused by black rapper Azealia Banks of being antiblack while benefitting from the culture.[9] One response to M.I.A.'s question as to why non-Muslim hip-hop heavyweights are not speaking up more for Muslims of the September 11 generation is, to put it crudely, that it does not affect them. According to Lawrence Krisna Parker, a.k.a. KRS-One:

> I was asked about why hip hop has not engaged the current situation more (meaning 9/11), my response was "because it does not affect us, or at least we don't perceive that it affects us, 9/11 happened to them." . . . I continued to say; "9/11 affected them down the block; the rich, the powerful those that are oppressing us as a culture. Sony, RCA or BMG, Universal, the radio stations, Clear Channel, Viacom with BET and MTV, those are our oppressors, those are the people that we're trying to overcome in hip hop everyday, this is a daily thing." We cheered when 9/11 happened in New York and say that proudly here. Because when they were down at the trade center we were getting hit over the head by cops, told that we can't come in this building, hustled down to the train station because of the way we dressed and talked, and so on, we were racially profiled. So, when the planes hit the building we were like, "mmmm, justice."[10]

Despite this sentiment, KRS-One declared decades ago that he was going to harness the power of hip-hop as a "revolutionary tool for changing the structure of racist America" (Cheney 2005, 90). He finally released an album in 2010 called *It's All Good* that specifically addressed the realities of the war on terror in Muslim countries like Iraq, Iran, Afghanistan, and Pakistan. The provocative track "Real Terrorism" highlights US-sponsored terrorism, including the extermination of Native Americans during the United States' founding, the bombing of Japanese civilians during World War II, and the current killing of civilians in connection with the "war on terror." The song asks which is the real terrorism—the United States' actions or September 11. Shortly after "Real Terrorism" was released, it was banned by YouTube, purportedly for its graphic war images. In response to the YouTube ban, KRS-One's collaborator Greenie stated: "The song tells the truth about the United States, its massacres, and the terrorist acts our government has committed around the world. The photos used in the video are just actual historic records and are important educational materials for all to see. I am shocked that YouTube allows silliness, sex, and pop rap—but not this important material."[11]

In an effort to be included in the movement to champion the lives of marginalized Muslim communities, #MuslimLivesMatter was created. The #MuslimLivesMatter hashtag, which had been trending since 2014, gained momentum in 2015 after three Muslim college students were shot in the head in their home near the University of North Carolina in Chapel Hill by a forty-six-year-old white man. Autopsies showed that the two girls had been murdered execution style, with the gun pointed to the head, after the husband of one of the girls had opened the door to the gunman's knocking. Outraged Muslims all over the world, including American Muslim community leaders Linda Sarsour, who cochaired the 2017 Women's March, and Yasir Qadhi, Muslim scholar and dean at the Islamic Seminary of America, took to social media with the hashtag. Chapel Hill's mayor, Mark Kleinschmidt, released a statement in the aftermath of the tragedy in support of the #MuslimLivesMatter movement, proclaiming that "Chapel Hill is a place for everyone, a place where Muslim lives matter."[12]

Sarsour, who was named one of *Time* magazine's one hundred most influential people following the march, is a strong proponent of the #BlackLivesMatter movement. She has been working hard to bring the two struggles together and has been reaching out to other marginalized communities to form solidarity groups. A hijabi of Palestinian origin, she is not seen as particularly religious or conventional either within and outside the Muslim community, as acknowledged by her mentor, Imam Talib Abdur Rashid of the Mosque of Islamic Brotherhood, Inc., a Harlem-based mosque that is a lineal descendant of the Muslim Mosque, Inc. founded by Malcolm X. The imam, however, qualified this by saying that the values Sarsour stands for—social justice and the sacredness of life—are at the heart of religious practice.[13] Imam Talib himself is a mentor to the hip-hop generation and an avid supporter of the #BlackLivesMatter movement. Nicknamed the "hip-hop imam," his mosque was featured in the *New Muslim Cool* (2009) documentary that examined the life of Puerto Rican American rapper Hamza Pérez.

There are difficult conversations to be had about the place of other struggles within the #BlackLivesMatter movement given the complex and interweaving global situation. On the one hand, to insist that #BlackLivesMatter broaden its mission to embrace other grievances might suggest that those who make this request do not fully understand the breadth and depth of the African American experience, which includes a history of slavery, segregation, and police and other forms of institutional brutality that are particular to their community. Meanwhile, there are minority groups who feel that the movement is too limiting and that conversations need to be broadened as they, too, deserve to feel safe in their own country. To this end, and seeing their struggles as similar, in line with the mantra of "Muslims are the new blacks" in the post-9/11 age of securitization, young Muslims, through their appropriation of hip-hop culture, are broadening the mission of the #BlackLivesMatter movement to include other ethnic minorities. Artists like Awate attempt to close the gap between #BlackLivesMatter and #MuslimLivesMatter by highlighting the history of Muslim subjugation under colonial rule and its enduring impact on the psyche of its people today. His work often focuses on his experiences in the United Kingdom, which also has a history of slavery, oppression, and racism, and addresses the everyday negative stereotyping of Muslims and their struggle for safety and equality. As he stated:

> I wrote "Fever" as a kind of triumphant ode to surviving in this city. In London . . . the city is full of pressures weighing down on you and people can't talk to each other. The school steals your history and raises you to have no pride in your identity. The police prey on you and make you fear stepping out of the dwelling you can't afford. But nonetheless, people survive. We remember our history and greatness and I like writing quite tongue in cheek critiques about the powerful. I came here as an Eritrean refugee, already in diaspora, born in Saudi Arabia and was always made to feel like an outsider. My perspective is different as I see the ridiculous everywhere.[14]

The rapper recounted how school grounds in London have become the site of ethnic prejudices as even preschoolers act on the biases passed on by their parents. He has received death threats and has been criticized as racist, a label he vehemently denies, for publicly speaking out about the past transgressions of the British Empire and issues of ethnic inequality. He argued that high-lighting the inconstancies inherent in the idea of multiculturalism, which is compounded by a narrow definition of Britishness, does not make him a bigot:

> If you're saying ban Burka's [sic] because Muslim women are oppressed, try and look at your own Patriarchy in your own country first, and don't talk on behalf of someone by thinking they're voiceless, when they have a voice, and the whole reason why they have become voiceless is because you're speaking on behalf of them! ... Why are white people on the news talking on the behalf of Muslim women and saying "aww they're so oppressed and voiceless?" Why did you take the call? When they booked you why didn't you take the initiative, and get someone who is Muslim and can talk from experience!![15]

In essence, hip-hoppers are regularly building bridges between communities by seeking out common struggles and, more importantly, a shared humanity. Recent burgeoning work explores the affiliation between music and human rights (Dixon 2002; Fischlin and Heble 2003). In what is perhaps the most comprehensive work to date, Ian Peddie, editor of the two-volume book *Popular Music and Human Rights* (2011), brings together specialists from the fields of punk rock, blues, heavy metal, and folk music. The studies trace and accentuate the centrality of social movements and protest traditions within popular music. Departing from the traditional study of human rights that focuses primarily on the perspectives of formal organizations and institutions, the writers instead examine the cultural responses of musicians to address the issues that besiege their societies through their art. Conspicuously, however, hip-hop is only mentioned in passing and is not included among the impressive list of genres that have contributed to the push for human rights. Collectively, work in the fields of Islamic studies and music studies demonstrates the cogency of both religion's and popular music's responses to issues of human rights. Against the backdrop of these developments, it is timely that we examine the hip-hop activism of young Muslims in urban settings and how these ideals are operationalized in everyday life.

The attractiveness of the human rights discourse within hip-hop music is one of the main reasons for the genre's global appeal. Even if issues like Islamophobia and the marginalization of Muslim youth seem particular to the predicaments faced by this social group, the appropriation of hip-hop as a vehicle to advance human rights is not new. It is not confined within the Muslim hip-hop *ummah*, and Muslim hip-hoppers do not rap merely for the rights of Muslims. Kumasi, a hip-hop artist from Compton, for example, strongly believes interest in human rights was embedded in the genre from its infancy. As Marcyliena Morgan argues in *The Real Hiphop: Battling for Knowledge, Power, and Respect in the LA Underground*, within hip-hop lyrics, it is Islam and Rastafarianism that symbolize independent political thought and challenge racism and class privilege (2009, 174).

The development of hip-hop as a platform to voice issues of social justice has given rise to a globalized social group I call the "poetic jihadis." This strand within the hip-hop community infuses the genre with Islamic symbolisms to galvanize the concerns of urban minority Muslim youth living as part of the September 11 generation.

FROM CIVIL RIGHTS TO HUMAN RIGHTS

Many have attested to the ability of hip-hop to document the social realities of the everyday life. Nowhere is this point more provocatively made than in Todd Boyd's *The New H.N.I.C.: The Death of Civil Rights and the Reign of Hip-Hop* (2002, 12), where he states that "although I would never encourage anyone to ignore one's history, I would suggest that you might get a better read of what's going in the world of Black people today by listening to DMX on It's Dark and Hell Is Hot than by listening to repeated broadcasts of Martin Luther King speeches."

One of the remarkable characteristics of hip-hop culture is its ability to elevate discussions, especially those on race and institutionalized discrimination. In this regard, hip-hop provides a platform to abstract one's predicaments from the self to the group, the native to the diaspora, the national to the global, and civil rights to human rights. Particularly, the expansion of civil rights to human rights is universally empowering in that it is founded on the premise that all people possess basic fundamental rights. Civil rights groups recognize that their struggles are inherently limiting as citizens are left vulnerable to the state's definition for its people. A discourse on civil rights tends to leave its activists having to grapple with what it means to be a citizen of a particular country—may it be an American Muslim or an Indonesian Muslim or a Muslim living as a majority or minority in a society. Therefore, as part of the larger historical process, civil rights groups have been reframing their demands to those of human rights, allowing narratives to be internationalized and transnational solidarities to be formed. In his book *The New H.N.I.C.* (which stands for Head Niggas in Charge), Todd Boyd (2002, 150–51) controversially proclaimed that the civil rights era "has passed" and has now been taken over by a more embracing hip-hop culture.

Quadir Lateef's track "H.N.I.C." (Hip Hop Needs Immense Change), a reinvention of the popular phrase, is at once a criticism of the current state of the industry and a plea to bring back hip-hop's passion and social conscious-ness. Through conscious hip-hop, the struggle for human rights among young Muslims of the September 11 generation is conflated with the symbolic status of the civil rights movement and African Americans' current struggle. Malcolm X's "*jihad* of words" (Floyd-Thomas 2003), which he successfully employed as a compelling "political and religious strategy" (Turner 2003) during his time, is reborn in today's Muslim hip-hop vernacular. Malcolm X's direct and confrontational style, and his description of race relations in the United States as an American Nightmare compared to his counterpart Martin Luther King Jr.'s more utopian narrative of an American Dream, captured the imagination of the hip-hop community, who appreciated his ability to "keep it real." In 1964, shortly after leaving the NOI, Malcolm X made a pilgrimage to Mecca and traveled to West Africa, where he was inspired to form the Organization of Afro-American Unity (OAAU) in Ghana. OAAU was a pan-African organ-ization whose mission was to fight for African American rights and to promote cooperation among Africans and people of African descent in the Americas. In a speech given before the OAAU in July 1964, Malcolm X sought to enlist the help of independent African nations by highlighting the unity of human struggles across cultures: "Your problems will never be fully solved until and unless ours are solved. You will never be fully respected until and unless we are also respected. You will never be recognized as free human beings until and unless we are also recognized and treated as human beings. Our problem is your problem. It is not a Negro problem, nor an American problem. This is a world problem; a problem for humanity. It is not a problem of *civil rights* but a problem of *human rights*" (emphasis added).[16]

The shift from civil rights to human rights advocated by Malcolm X has also been wholeheartedly embraced by the hip-hop community. Whether it is in the form of imbuing the genre with the mellower Islamic *nasheed* or the more aggressive gangsta variant, hip-hop has given urban Muslim minority youth a way to access the African American experience and a language of human rights. As hip-hop originally symbolized the civil rights movement and its at-tempt to empower people by speaking the truth about the African American experience, its music as well as the accompaniments of its culture confer a sym-bolic status to its practitioners. The prominent visibility of African American youth in popular culture and in the media, especially the depiction of young African American males, reverberates with the sense of marginalization felt by young Muslims. These images are further reinforced by what is perceived as a prejudiced criminal justice system and the concerns of living in an age of Islamophobia.

Kitwana contends that at the rate that young people are absorbing hip-hop culture globally, "these movements may be the catalysts necessary to jump-start an international human rights movement in this generation, a movement with the potential to parallel if not surpass yesterday's civil rights successes" (2005, 11). Not only have hip-hop practitioners imagined their local predicaments along the lines of the African American struggle, as is evident in many of their songs, but they have done so in their own unique style. Shamim Miah, who has been working with young people in Oldham, England, breaks it down by saying: "It is important to realise that hip-hop refers only to the musical genre, not mainstream culture filled with sex, drugs and violence" (cited in Sardar 2006). But despite these glocalized forms and the deconstruction of hip-hop culture amid conversations with other customs and traditions, the message of human rights and the centrality of the African American struggle for equality remain at the heart of the inspiration for many hip-hop artists globally.

Beyond Islamic symbolisms, global Muslim hip-hop culture also must be seen as a social movement that aims to uphold the tenets of multicultural living. Consequently, the reactions of governments to their local Muslim youth should be understood within the context of young Muslims increasingly reinterpreting their everyday concerns into a problem of human rights.

ASSERTING HUMAN RIGHTS IN ISLAM

It is of little wonder that the roots of Islam in hip-hop are so diverse, vibrant, and innovative. Hip-hop was born at a time of diverse religious reawakening, and many fought to have their religious freedoms protected by international laws. Effective lobbying culminated in the International Covenant on Civil and Political Rights being adopted by the United Nations General Assembly in 1966 and finally implemented a decade later. According to the treaty, "Everyone shall have the right to freedom of thought, conscience and religion. This right shall include freedom to have or to adopt a religion or belief of his choice, and freedom, either individually or in community with others and in public or private, to manifest his religion or belief in worship, observance, practice and teaching. No one shall be subject to coercion which would impair his freedom to have or to adopt a religion or belief of his choice."[17]

There has been much debate on whether Islam is capable of accommodating and advancing human rights (An-Na'im 1990; Dwyer 1991; Tibi 1994; Mayer

1995; Dalacoura 2007; Bielefeldt 2000; Sachedina 2009; Emon, Ellis, and Glahn 2012). Scholars have turned to the writings of both classical Islamic thinkers and contemporary reformers in noting the role of Islam throughout history in advocating human rights. Some scholars promote a return to classical Islamic thought, arguing that Islam flourished because the religion brought with it a bill of rights from the outset. They argue that Islam elevated the status of women and to a significant degree emancipated the poor and other groups who existed then at the peripheries of society. Others contend that the religion must be reformed to address more modern concerns. Advocates of this believe that religion has to be contextualized to fit contemporary needs and that Islam should be compatible with the dominant ideologies of today—liberal democracy and capitalism.

Yet others advocate for a synthesis of the two approaches, insisting that the argument might not necessarily be one at the expense of the other. They call for a parallel system where Muslims subscribe to sharia as well as civil laws. In this formulation, the former is often compartmentalized to the sphere of the personal, governing aspects such as marriage, divorce, inheritance, and death, while the latter manages the public domains, including the workplace and fulfilling the obligations of citizenship, such as compulsory schooling and conscription. By examining the United Nations records from 1946 to 1966, Susan Waltz (2004) debunks the myth that the Muslim world did not participate in the global human rights discussions after World War II and into the Cold War era. She charted the contributions of delegations from Syria, Egypt, Iraq, and Pakistan, among others, in contributing to the advancement of religious freedom, gender equality, and social justice. She also pointed out that countries like Morocco, Libya, Iraq, and Pakistan had female representatives in their respective United Nations delegations. While the roles played by Muslim states should not be exaggerated, they should also not be neglected. The vitality of these discussions has resulted in the inclusion of university courses on Islam and human rights in the West.

Away from the ivory towers of higher learning, although not totally removed from it, hip-hoppers like Jasiri X, Omar Offendum, and Anaya Alimah McMurray prove that the topic of the relationship between human rights and Islam is omnipresent among Muslim hip-hop practitioners. The struggle for human rights among Muslim hip-hoppers is not merely external. As much as hip-hop is appropriated to articulate discontent against the balance of power in international politics, the treatment of governments toward their Muslim populace, and the predicaments of being marginalized as part of a minority population,

Muslim hip-hoppers also face challenges within the Muslim community by virtue of being young and artistic, and females have even greater objections to overcome. This was one of the main themes of the documentary *Deen Tight*. In the film, many Muslim hip-hoppers, such as Anas Canon, the brother of famous international Muslim preacher Usama Canon, talked candidly about the social stigma they face within certain segments of the Muslim community for their position as hip-hop artists.

Historically, there has been significant criticism of the hip-hop industry from within Muslim religious circles, but since September 11, a number of high-profile religious leaders, including Usama Canon, have come out in defense of the hip-hop community: "Let's be honest, when we do this thing called community we put our own twist on it. And the twist I put on it is a northern Californian, mixed kid who comes from a hip-hop, reggae, hacky-sacking, boogie-boarding background. . . . Hey, bro, call it what you want to, and if that's what Cali Islam is then we accept."[18]

Embracing his hip-hop background as a badge of honor and projecting a kind of *Californian Islam*, as he terms it, that is welcoming and nonjudgmental, Usama Canon has been influential in shaping the dispositions of a new generation of Muslim hip-hop artists. As the founding director of Ta'leef Collective, which loosely translates as "the coming together of many things," Canon's lectures are often punctuated with hip-hop references. Brother Ali, rapper and vocal supporter of the hip-hop industry, contemplated leaving his music and devoting his life to the study of religion until Canon advised him against it. Brother Ali, a white albino blind rapper who converted to Islam at the age of fifteen, fondly remembers Usama's advice: "Who's going to serve your fans while you're gone? Only you can do that."[19] Brother Ali, who credits the stylish preacher for making him embrace his role as a hip-hop artist, composed a track for Canon entitled "Uncle Usi Taught Me" on his latest album, *All the Beauty in This Whole Life*. In 2016, Ta'leef Collective expanded from California to Chicago, where Canon is also the spiritual leader of the Inner-City Muslim Action Network, which hosts the hugely popular recurring international hip-hop festival Takin' It to the Streets. The 2016 event included many famous artists, such as Rakim, Brother Ali, and Malaysia's Yuna, and incorporated an MC workshop by Canadian Iraqi rapper Narcicyst and British Palestinian Shadia Mansour, widely known as "the first lady of Arabic hiphop."[20] The event was heartily supported by many prominent Muslim preachers because it remained true to the Inner-City Muslim Action Network's mission of reaching out to at-risk youth and the underprivileged through sponsoring art that is spiritually rooted, spatially relevant, and socially conscious.

One renowned Islamic preacher who attended the event and has had a long affinity with hip-hop is Imam Suhaib Webb. William Suhaib Webb was a hip-hop DJ himself before embracing Islam. Webb studied Islam at the prestigious Al-Azhar University in Cairo and went on to become the imam of the Islamic Society of Boston Cultural Center, a position he held until 2013. In a Facebook post in 2011, he argued that Muslims are the sole community that turns its back on its cultural icons, those charismatic leaders with the greatest cultural capital, such as artists like Mos Def, whom he lovingly refers to as Brother Yasin. Suhaib Webb, who admitted to having held harsh views toward hip-hop in the past, has since toned down his views, claiming that he "would rather be with a sincere, vulnerable struggler, than a fake Saint."[21] However, not all struggles are easy to overcome. Some are harder to fight, even when couched within the domain of human rights. One example is gender equality. Anaya Alimah McMurray wrote of how artists like herself, Eve, and Erykah Badu "exercise agency, creating new meanings and interesting spaces of resistance through mixing faith and hip-hop culture" (2008, 75–76). In asserting the equal position of women in hip-hop culture specifically and in society in general, she laments the intense scrutiny and double standards exacted upon female Muslim hip-hop artists. For example, alluding to some of the promiscuous messages in Mos Def's song "Ms. Fat Booty," she proclaims that "it is not as if I think these activities and/or lyrics make these men any less Muslim; however, I do know that a Muslim woman who is explicit about her religious beliefs could not take a similar approach without more backlash from Muslim communities" (2008, 89). Similarly, members of Poetic Pilgrimage, stars of the 2015 documentary *Hip-Hop Hijabis*, also seek to promote women's rights within Muslim communities. The struggle to fight sexism within Muslim communities is not limited to the efforts of female hip-hoppers. In the words of Abstract Vision/Humanity from their track "(H)Islam":

Many ignorant fools from far and wide
feel that oppression is how one should reside
seclusion of women and false interpretations
lead to the destruction of many nations
They believe they're exclusively correct
rape their women and slash their necks
a "democracy" simultaneously livin' the ways of hypocrisy
a false recognition of the female rights
Islamic ways are far far more contrite

Two American Pakistani boys collaborated to produce this track, contending that hip-hop provides the means for them to persuade members of their community to tackle the issue of gender bias (Nijhon 2008, 86). The music of Abstract Vision/Humanity and Poetic Pilgrimage seeks to address patriarchal conceptions within the hip-hop world and combat "notions of cultural interpretations of Islam."[22] Even though both male and female hip-hoppers today have come out strongly in defense of Muslim women, the ability to speak up for the latter often comes at a price, especially when it is women doing the talking. This will be discussed in more depth in the next chapter.

The complex nature of this struggle for justice within the Muslim hip-hop *ummah* also includes some practitioners attempting to maintain their right to reread mainstream Islam. The influence of the NOI and the Five Percenters on hip-hop culture has been so profound that Harry Allen, an influential commentator, called Islam the unofficial religion of hip-hop (1991, 48). What is less discussed, though, is the move away from the regulation and dogmatization of organized religion as evident in hip-hop culture. It is not merely about switching from one form of structured religion (the dominant example being Sunni and Shiite Islam) to another (as seen in the NOI and Five Percenters' orientations). A segment of Muslim hip-hoppers call for not only a reinterpretation but also an individualization of religion. Anaya posits that her categorizations of Muslims are examples of her "agency in new meaning-making that is a result of my own cultural experiences. These categories are not intended to be static. Instead they represent my particular worldview, a unique lens to contribute to the multiple perspectives impacting discourses on Islam" (McMurray 2008, 91). This manifestation of piety, often referred to as New Age spiritualty, is not founded on formal organizations but on individual personal experiences with "the divine" (however defined), which allows people to determine their own path in the religious marketplace. The individualization thesis has become increasingly popular among sociologists of religion. Proponents of this theory contend that orthodox religion will give way to increasing subjectivity characterized by its personal, syncretic, and deregulated nature.

I pointed out in my book *Digital Culture and Religion in Asia* that the growing significance of "new media Islam," which has become more potent since the establishment of Facebook (2004) and YouTube (2005), has had profound effects on the younger generation. At the elementary level, Islam becomes a "religion online" where the fundamental teachings of the faith are uploaded unto the virtual sphere. Additionally, it is now also engaged as an "online religion" whereby religion, by its very being on the Internet, is reconstituted. These interactions with digital culture and its actors thus alter the Muslim sense of self, the configurations of solidarity groups, the social networks that are possible, the authority relationships among adherents, and even state-society dealings (Han and Kamaludeen 2016). Given the youthful demography of many Muslim populations and the increasing religious consciousness of Muslims the world over, these social processes are not only going to be heightened but are also likely to become more complex and nuanced. Hence, Islam is being read in a more in-depth manner in unprecedented numbers owing to its pervasive online presence, and it is repeatedly being reread through the lens of modern identities and newly found cultures.

The very notion of individualization of religion syncs with the conception of jihad in Islam. Often misunderstood as referring to a holy war, jihad, as many Muslim scholars have explained, means "struggle" or "striving," and the foremost form of jihad relates to one's personal improvements before moving on to intermediate spheres of influence and eventually the larger society. Therefore, it is not uncommon to hear Muslim hip-hoppers couching their craft within their personal struggles and a desire to elevate the status of those with similar predicaments. Their purpose (their jihad), their method (their artistic narratives or "poetics"), and their typically socially marginalized backgrounds all fuse into a formidable social identity, which I discuss at length in the following section.

POETIC JIHAD: HUMAN RIGHTS FROM THE STREETS

Many hip-hop documentaries have been produced post–September 11 that provide an insight into how young Muslims are grappling with their everyday lives and using music as not just an outlet to vent their frustrations but also a platform to effect social change. *Slingshot Hip Hop* (2008), *New Muslim Cool* (2009), *Deen Tight* (2011), and *Hip Hop Hijabis* (2015) all capture the powerful messages that the hip-hop ummah is trying to express. Kumasi from Black Wall Street states in *Deen Tight*:[23]

> I say cos them blacks got to strap . . . pop
> And they shoot Mexicans once again or somethin'
> I woke up 5 o'clock slot early in the morning
> 5 o'clock same time somebody selling that crack
> Crack crack black black
> Couldn't understand my man . . . so I started rapping
> I put it down pick back up my pen
> Blacks and Mexican we could be the same gang
> Blacks and brown boy that seem to be the same thin'
> I rap for that cat that ain't got no water
> The orphan whose pops died has no father

I rap for the guy who's homeless no shelter
I rap for the young man insist who's a failure
For the woman who is a broad for the cat who is a dog
For the earth that is full of the smog
I rap for the H2O to be perceived as clear instead of a glass full of ink
I rap cos poetry in Quran I rap cos the songs also rhymed
I rap . . . I don't know, I just rap. That's what I do. I rap.
And that's that. Kumasi . . . Praise God. Alhamdulillah.

Kumasi, who believes that it is a social duty to use his musical success to engender humanitarian works, states: "A day that goes by and you were not able to help someone is a day wasted."[24] His impromptu rap cited here demonstrates the potency of hip-hop as a freestyle, spontaneous culture that can be harnessed to address issues of human rights. The activism of many Muslim hip-hop groups goes beyond advancing the issue of human rights within the Muslim community. Hip-hoppers present a global message and a cosmopolitan stance that is occasionally embodied in performance, such as through dress. In a 2008 Islamic concert in Sydney, one of the singers from the Brothahood came on stage wearing a skullcap, zikr beads, jeans, and a "Free Burma" T-shirt, a comment on the humanitarian crisis facing the tens of thousands of Burmese refugees who were fleeing from the authoritarian military junta.

Issues of racism, rights, and Islam form the cornerstone of Muslim hip-hop music (Gazzah 2008; Solomon 2011). It is convenient to see human rights activism within hip-hop music as subversive as it is necessarily an act of speaking truths to create power. Many hip-hop artists explicitly talk about their music's potential to subvert the state as well as its deviance. As a medium, it is increasingly exploited from the Middle East to Latin America to Africa. As a case in point, X Plastaz, a Tanzanian outfit, declares: "We talk about things that happen in everyday life, good and bad things like war and disease. We also talk about human rights. We rap about these matters to educate others to come to the rescue of the destitute. Another topic we've addressed is AIDS" (Lemelle 2006). While the use of music as a medium of expression is hardly a novelty, Muslim hip-hop sets itself apart due to its emphasis on the poetic element of the craft.

The undermining of human rights and diminishing social space for meaningful discussions even in Western liberal democracies calls for a critical examination of culture (Hutnyk 2011, 51–66). Citing Muslim hip-hop group Fun-Da-Mental, John Hutnyk feels that examining "difficult" music allows listeners a window into human rights transgressions. To be sure, hip-hop's social commentary and antagonistic style offer ideal platforms to articulate public misconceptions of Islam as well as the everyday injustices Muslims face locally and globally. These causes manifest in the music of many Muslim hip-hop activists, and human rights activism is the reason some are doing hip-hop. Iron Sheikh, for instance, is an "activist first, then an MC. I got back into producing hip-hop as an alternative way to communicate the messages and ideas I work with" and "if it weren't for the politics, I wouldn't be doing it" (Maira 2008, 183).

Young Muslims who are deprived of basic rights of citizenship and access to resources in their countries of birth are also fighting a generational battle. Although the elders still hold the thresholds of power that govern the community, they are increasingly challenged by a more educated youth population. Globally, better educated and more youthful religious imams (Islamic clerics) or *ustaz* (Islamic teachers) are taking the helm of various mosques. Tensions within the Muslim community centering on generational gaps had already appeared prior to September 11. This younger second generation, whose migrant parents struggled with language and culture, speaks the language of their host country and can easily connect with the larger non-Muslim population through dialogue, sports, and music. It has been documented that urban Muslim youth in Germany see themselves as "genuine Berliners" and do not want to be restrained and pigeonholed in an insular homogenic social group. A poll of Turkish boys and girls in Kreuzberg schools revealed that 60 and 56 percent of them respectively identify themselves primarily as Berliners. They clamor for a deculturalization of religion and an overlapping of subcultures, an integration of popular culture with a segregation of the sexes. While wanting to blend into the urban lifestyle, they still hold on to their rituals of intimacy; as it has been put, "they not only want to remain, they also want to remain different" (Mushaben 2008, 521). With the growing discourse of human rights in popular culture in the West, young Muslims envision their civic participation as a way of integrating into mainstream society.

Staring Islamophobia in its face, young Muslim hip-hop practitioners have decided to take on a heightened Muslim identity. Facing the perpetrators of their everyday oppression and distorted representation in the media, they take it upon themselves to regain their pride and redefine their image. Young people often relate to the continuous turmoil in the Muslim world as if it were their own. Fending off criticisms from parental, religious, and institutional authorities as well as other cultural gatekeepers, young Muslims hone their craft and take it to unprecedented levels of popularity and influence. Young Muslims' newfound confidence in straddling piety and popular culture is best captured by one of their hip-hop icons, NOI star Rakim: "I applied it and I love what I live and I live Islam so I applied it to everything I do. I applied it to my rhymes and I felt that I wanted the people to know what I knew. I felt that I was put here for that purpose and I just want to fulfill my legacy as far as being a conscious rapper and putting the word that I felt the streets needed to hear out there."[25]

This political consciousness and sense of social justice account for the poetic jihadis' success in reaching out even to those who were not originally attracted to the music. This strand within hip-hop culture bridges the generational gap. Even if the elders have not started moving to the aesthetics of hip-hop music, they are compelled to take notice of its increasing significance. Ibn Thabit, a Libyan hip-hopper, reflects: "There has been a huge demand for revolutionary music, and people are recognizing hip-hop as an important medium of expression. . . . Before the Libyan revolution, hip-hop was almost like a punk movement, a way to (anger) your parents . . . once the uprisings began, even grandmothers were thanking me for what I was doing."[26] A BBC piece entitled "Syria Conflict Finds a Voice in Hip-Hop" reported on an atypical hip-hop concert in Beirut where "most of the unsmiling crowd was sitting at tables, and not a single person was dancing," with one of the young Syrians in the crowd commenting, "I don't like the music, but I like the words. I am Syrian. I feel the words. The lyrics really express my feelings. We aren't dancing because we are listening to the lyrics."[27] The political turmoil in Syria has nurtured a fertile ground for conscious hip-hop to blossom, with groups like LaTlateh thriving because they are capturing the pulse of the streets (Mohajer and Rajpar 2012). Blogger Nour Al-Ali puts it aptly: "You may begin with swaying to the beat, but you will, as I, sigh at the end of the song because it reflects a reality ignored by mainstream media. They do not speak of news as statistics or whatnot, no; they speak of how they, as citizens, are living in Syria are thinking and feeling."[28]

Hip-hop is also an important arena for anti-Islamophobic mobilization in many parts of the world. This is even more significant given the violence against minority Muslim populations who live as relatively new migrants in many cosmopolitan cities. In the United States, for example, Human Rights Watch reported that Muslim hate crimes increased by an unprecedented 1,700 percent after September 11. The passing of the Patriot Act a month after September 11 institutionalized discrimination against Muslims, whose legal rights were diminished amid an increase in intense surveillance by the state. As Miguel d'Souza (quoted in Maxwell 2003, 115) perceptively puts it, "Hip-hop's movement has come out of the ranks of suburban and migrant youth whose dissatisfaction with the isolation of suburban living, unemployment, racism and the Anglo-Saxon dominance . . . to identify with similar sentiments coming from African-American rap."

In addition to expressing their everyday religiosity, Muslim hip-hop groups exert their rights to citizenship and highlight internal problems within their society. Australian Muslim hip-hop group the Brothahood deploys their music as an attempt "to break down stereotypes and barriers that we face as Muslims" and appeals to the similar ancestry everyone shares regardless of religion or religious orientation.[29] As stated in their track "The Silent Truth":

> From beer I refrain, prayers I maintain
> Can't get on a plane without copping all the blame
> People can't you see that we are all the same
> Children of Adam but playing the blame game
> It's a shame, and that's the damn well truth
> If I hear another word I'm going to cut your ass loose
> News got you scared that I'm going to knock out your tooth
> So gullible, you believe in mother goose
> How cute, but that doesn't make it right
> Australia is mine too so I'm going to put up a fight
> You want to send me back? Yo send me back where?
> Australia is the place where I let down my hair
> you don't care, but that's in your nature
> they find an excuse they can to rate and then hate you

Through tracks such as "The Silent Truth," the Brothahood articulates issues related to migration, xenophobia, media prejudice, Islamophobia, and the deleterious treatment Muslims experience under the claim of national security that makes their integration as citizens in Australia difficult. This is also the case of Muslim hip-hoppers in the UK and France. In his reading of the UK's Fun-Da-Mental and France's IAM (Imperial Asiatic Man), Ted Swedenburg (2002, 16) states that "in both countries Muslims are attempting to construct cultural, social and political spaces for themselves as ethnic groups (of sorts), and are massively involved in anti-racist mobilisations against white supremacy." Although not overtly laden with Islamic content, IAM's tracks contain references to the harsh reality of being Muslim in France. In their song "Nés sous la même étoile" (Born under the same star), the group raps about the injustice of poverty and a sister being mocked for wearing the Islamic veil. In "Pain au Chocolat," IAM alludes to the rampant stereotyping of Muslims as terrorists. Elsewhere, Swedenburg puts forth that "Fun-Da-Mental's expressions of pride in Islam appealed to Muslim youth who had been raised on British popular culture yet also felt wounded by British Islamophobia" (2001, 58).

By contrast, Muslim hip-hoppers living in majority Muslim countries, such as in Southeast Asia, the Middle East, and North Africa, experience much less social marginalization and stigmatization as a consequence of their religious identity. In these parts of the world, Muslim hip-hop groups forefront other aspects of human rights. The Indonesian outfit JHF, for example, focuses their lyrics on the internal problems of their country. They emphasize social issues and rap about poverty and youth. A number of their songs have become anthems to fight corruption, chanted at street protests and political rallies. The music video of their emblematic song, "Jogja Istimewa" (Jogja is Special), depicts compelling scenes with the group seen participating in these rallies, rapping in full voice.

For diasporic youth living as minorities, having hyphenated identities often gives rise to more complex narratives about their sense of belonging and their allegiances. This evolution seems even more inevitable given that many Muslim hip-hop artists live in diaspora. Their ability to deconstruct and transform their hyphenated identities into liquid identities that transcend national boundaries and tribal affiliations places them at the forefront of Muslim conscious rap. Juan Flores (2000), in his book *From Bomba to Hip-Hop: Puerto Rican Culture and Latino Identity*, highlights the power of hip-hop culture to reassemble identity in order to create a space in which a unique sense of self can arise, one that is able to transcend ethnic and national boundaries.

In the words of Omar Offendum, a Syrian American who was born in the Middle East but then migrated to the United States: "I believe it is more important for us to participate in the hip-hop culture and not get focused on 'I am Arab' because that can only get you so far. You want to have a universal message that all human beings can relate to and find something that they can unite around. That is how I do my music. So, while it is really important to represent myself, my people, my history and my culture, I do that in an effort to unite people, instead of telling people 'I am this' or 'I am that.'"[30] Offendum released his first solo album, provocatively titled *SyrianamericanA*, in 2010. In his album, he problematizes his hyphenated identity and place in the polarized world. He dedicated the song "Superhero" to the young people fighting for justice and freedom in the Arab world:

> Look up in the Sky
> It's a Bird
> It's a Plane
> It's an Arab Superhero & He Came to Bring Change
> Unite the Divided & Free 'em' from the Chains
> Of the Tyrants Who Reign in Vain & Pain

While he tapped on his Arab identity as a unifying force, Omar also appropriated the imagery of the "superhero," which is undoubtedly American. He later collaborated with Canada's Ayah and Narcicyst for a song called "#Jan25" to show solidarity with the demonstrators of the Egyptian revolution. He cited the song as evidence for how the revolution has captured the imagination of the young and the "spirit of resistance" it has come to symbolize, not only for the citizens of Egypt but for all those who are oppressed globally.

Another hip-hop artist who engages in an intricate weaving of "flexible citizenship" (Ong 1999) is Daddy Chang. Chang is a Taiwanese Muslim with Canadian citizenship who raps for China. Although he is renowned for his vocal Islamic messages in his songs "Jihad," "Free Palestine," and "Never Alone," he also penned a prayer song for Japan in the aftermath of the 2011 Tohoku/Sendai earthquake:

> My neighbors, I am praying for you,
> I hope in the future we will no longer compare ourselves over our position
>   in Asia
> Right now you are weak, so I will put aside arguing about history for now
> Though it doesn't mean I will no longer be against having been attacked
>
> Some cash, wrapped in a Muslim letter,
> And sent to the [Taiwan] Tzu Chi Foundation
> Of course, my donation to Yunnan province was 10x and up!
> Because blood is thicker than water, this is principle.
>
> It is not courage, this is a kind of human morality
> Let all my fellow countrymen who disagree come and curse me
> But I have the responsibility, to raise mankind's character!
> As a Chinese person, I represent the Chinese in wishing the best for
>   the Japanese!
>
> Because the facts of history has given us scars,
> But the lesson of scars does not mean China can lose its mind,
> This tsunami, has killed many of our neighbors
> And the bodies of many family members for many families are unable
>   to be buried
>
> Just like the tragedy we ourselves have also had in history
> Refugees and ruins and the like are all grievances we too have had
> But always holding a grudge is not what Confucius taught
> I sincerely hope that repaying evil with good has effectiveness in bringing peace
>
> In the past I cursed those who admired Japan as traitors,
> But much of their culture, is indeed worth respecting
> Like the rare hope and order maintained by the people after the disaster
> This is worth us learning from

While Chang evokes particular identity markers such as Asian, Muslim, Taiwanese, Chinese, and Confucian, he also appeals to human morality by calling for solidarity among the East Asian Confucian states and urging young people to put aside the grievances of the previous generations. Grappling with issues of power and hegemony, new-generation rappers like Chang embody a more neighborly and panregional disposition while still being rooted to their primary identities. Acknowledging that he still remembers the lessons from history and that his loyalty is to the Chinese people does not stop him from empathizing with his Japanese neighbors in their time of crisis.

However, solidarities formed across cultural blocs are not to be solely attributed to hip-hop. Studies of youth culture in the East Asian bloc have pointed to a convergence of experience within the region. There is an amorphous cultural flow among countries in the East Asian region resulting in alternating and multiple nodes of cultural power that siphon in the nascence of a pan–East Asian youth culture. Trends toward a pan-Asian youth culture are perhaps best described by the creation and influence of Taiwan's youth drama *Meteor Garden (Liuxing Huayuan)*, an inventive adaptation of the Japanese comic series *Hana yori dango* about the lives of high school students. The drama is retold in a Taiwanese setting and features the popular Taiwanese group F4, which has a large following among East Asian youth. Not surprisingly, the program also has been very successful in China. The economic boom in Japan followed by the rise of the four Asian tigers (Hong Kong, South Korea, Taiwan, and Singapore) and the rise of China have brought about the necessary technological developments and level of affluence among East Asian youth to afford them with greater autonomy and freedom of expression.

Similar themes can also be found in the many works on South Asian or Desi hip-hop (Nair and Balaji 2008; Sharma 2010). As a collective, millennials embracing hip-hop are fighting against the rigidity of ethnic identity formation seen in hegemonic Desiness, hegemonic Chineseness, hegemonic Arabness, and so on. Seen in this way, it is not so much that hip-hoppers are driven by a desire to emulate African Americans but rather by the aspiration to adopt the most potent popular cultural force of their time. As such, these acts are the responses of a generation who are more literate and educated and who are determined to put their own imprint on the construction of self. Whether these constructions are theirs or those they have been led to believe are their own is another matter altogether. What is certain, however, is that the younger generation is not satisfied with merely ingesting a hereditary culture, which many of them understand involves invented traditions anyway.

A comparative study of 102 diasporic Bangladeshi Muslims in the United States and the United Kingdom ages eighteen to sixty-four revealed an upsurge of a revivalist Islam based on what Kibria (2008, 243) calls "a fundamentalist model of Muslim identity and practice" and the adoption of "Muslim" as a public identity. The growth of this "new Islam" among diasporic youth is fueled by a feeling of entrenched cultural and political alienation and a yearning to be detached from Bangladesh. According to the study, one of the reasons young people seek to detach from Bengali Islam is that it sanctions social inequalities reminiscent of the sociocultural norms of contemporary Bangladesh and is *unreflexive* and *routinized* in character. This is as opposed to the "self-conscious spirit of devotion necessary to the belief and practice of true Islam" (Kibria 2008, 254).

This is not to say that young Muslims have no interest in discussing issues of ethnicity or in speaking directly to those with whom they share a common heritage. Notwithstanding the global influence of hip-hop and its human rights dimension, we still witness, within the Muslim hip-hop *ummah*, the trend of speaking to one's own cultural bloc to uplift and empower them, be it the broader Arab, Chinese, or Malay worlds. This happens despite many artists physically living in the diaspora and at times having limited ability to transcend language barriers. Nonetheless, hip-hop empowers individuals, like Daddy Chang, to speak freely against the opinion of the majority, but, more importantly, it provides the medium to reach their audiences. Omar Offendum expresses his passion for human rights not only through his performances in numerous countries but also through the public talk circuits. He has been a guest lecturer at some of the most notable universities in the world, including Harvard, MIT, University of Pennsylvania, Trinity College, University of Texas, Stanford, Qatar Education City, New York University (Abu Dhabi), and the American University of Beirut.[31] Through these narratives, Muslim hip-hop practitioners offer alternative repertoires for resistance based on their respective cultures, effectively provincializing semblances of the African American experience, even though the goal for human rights remains intact.

What most Muslim hop-hop practitioners globally have in common, however, is using human rights as the premise to raise awareness about the struggles in the Muslim world. Especially after September 11, the London hip-hop group ADF has publicly objected to the caricaturing of Muslims in mainstream media and the demonizing of migrants, as well as pointed to the adverse effects of the war on terror on the local Muslim community, including the surveillance and raids of their sacred spaces. In the aftermath of the raid of the North London Finsbury Park Mosque in 2003, an ADF member slammed the incursion as "another part of the build-up of hysteria as a means of rallying people for war. . . . There are seeds being planted in people's minds that Islam equals fundamentalism. It's like saying all Christians have something to do with extreme Christianity. I'm not a supporter of fundamentalism from any doctrine."[32] In 2011, ADF railed against British prime minister David Cameron's accusation that the country's policies on multiculturalism were inviting terrorists into the United Kingdom. ADF contended that this rhetoric pandered to the Far Right, and the group urged the government to pay attention to "Muslim grievances" such as the destruction of Iraq based on false intelligence concerning weapons of mass destruction, the Palestinian predicament, and the United States' funding of proxy wars in Afghanistan.

The fight against the polemics of the Far Right has become a staple of Muslim rappers in Continental Europe and increasingly in the United States since Donald Trump has taken it upon himself to retweet the anti-Islamic propaganda of the Far Right to his forty million followers. Leading the charge is Medine Zaouiche from France, whose first solo album, 11 Septembre, takes a critical look at the treatment of Muslims after September 11. An article published by the *Guardian* in June 2016 entitled "The French Hip-Hop Stars Fighting the Far Right" named Medine as one of the flag-bearers of the movement.[33] For nearly two decades, he has worked tirelessly at countering Islamophobic ideologues. Just a year after his album dropped, he published an article in *Time* magazine entitled "How Much More French Can I Be?" lamenting the othering of people of color and the continual questioning of their national allegiance. Medine's rap is interwoven with messages about the fates of the destitute, migrants, and Muslims in Europe. Despite his efforts to uplift his fellow Muslims, in 2015, Medine's own view of life in France was grim: "The Muslim community over the last 10 years has been demonized particularly. It was difficult for a young Muslim guy from the banlieues to get on before, and after Charlie Hebdo it has become impossible. It's been like being in prison this last decade."[34] Unfortunately, the misery described by Medine is all too familiar to young Muslims in France who are trying to carve an identity for themselves amid relentless assaults from the Far Right.

Beyond national concerns, the Palestinian struggle for self-determination has become a major rallying cry for Muslim hip-hoppers. Many established or up-and-coming Muslim hip-hopper either have a song about Palestine or make references to the politics of dispossession in the third holiest land in Islam. Yaseen Qasem (a.k.a. I-Voice or Invincible Voice), who in 2009 left the Bourj el-Barajneh Palestinian camp in the outskirts of Beirut for Canada, highlighted the centrality of Palestine in the Muslim hip-hop imaginary, remarking, "Nas said, 'Hip-hop is dead,'" referring to Nas's provocative album that he released in 2006. "We say, 'Hip-hop is not dead. It just moved to Palestine.'"[35]

Not just verbal *mujahidins* (Alim 2006a), groups like the Brothahood also engage in operationalizing Islam. In March and July 2009, they performed in two Free Gaza concerts for the benefit of the Palestinians. In addition to donating 100 percent of their proceeds from the concert to the Palestinians, the Brothahood also performed their latest pro-Palestinian track, "Act on It," for the first time. The Palestinian American duo Hammer Bros, in their pro-intifada song "Free Palestine," which shares the same title as the track by British MC Ambassador, raps about the Palestinians' "right of return," linking it to injustices around the world, and not being "blinded by incidents like this, one of the reasons that the Bros have the mic in fist!" Pakistani American group Aman sings about "being Muslim Robin Hoods fighting for justice in a foreign land" in their song "Arabian Knights." Maher Zain also released a song called "Palestine Will Be Free" in 2009. Poetic Pilgrimage lent a female voice to the conflict in their track "Silence Is Consent," which focuses on a number of Muslim leaders whom they allege are turning a blind eye to the problem and inflicting shame on the *ummah*. Their track starts with an instruction from the Prophet: "The leader of the people serves the people."

Hip-hop groups from Palestine receive added attention within the hip-hop *ummah* and among scholars of Muslim hip-hop. David McDonald's brilliant study of Palestinian hip-hop in *My Voice Is My Weapon: Music, Nationalism, and the Poetics of Palestinian Resistance* (2013) reveals the power of the message of young hip-hoppers and the degree of the homological imagination among consumers of Muslim hip-hop. Because of the potency of hip-hop rhythms, moves, and crowd/performer rituals, even in crowds unfamiliar with the ins and outs of hip-hop music, there is monumental potential for resonance with the audience. McDonald attributes this level of popularity to hip-hop's "subaltern power of empowered resistance" as enshrined in the life work of Tupac Shakur, one of young Palestinian hip-hoppers' biggest idols: "Tupac's subaltern posture of empowered resistance against racism and dispossession resonates with these young Palestinian rappers to the extent that Tupac might assume the politicized identity of a Palestinian *shahīd*: a martyr for the cause of self-determination. Tupac, according to such criteria, is Palestinian" (2013, 20–21).

Da Arabian MCs (DAM) of Lod, Israel, the most famous Palestinian hip-hop group in the world, has been the subject of much scholarly writing and a feature-length documentary called *Slingshot Hip Hop*. DAM is composed of brothers Tamer and Suhell Nafar and their friend Mahmoud Jreri. The trio projects a strong Palestinian identity in their songs, rapping about having been "Born Here," a twist on a popular Israeli Zionist song of the same name, and being a "Stranger in My Own Country," venting their feelings as targeted citizens despite making up a fifth of the country's population. They draw inspiration from Tupac Shakur, noting that Tupac's depiction of aggression and crime in the ghettos reverberated with their experiences back home. Part of the group's popularity stems from their multicultural outlook, rapping in both Hebrew and Arabic and conversing in English. The group was dubbed "the spokesman of a new generation" by *Le Monde*, a major French newspaper.[36]

Examining human rights activism among Muslim hip-hop practitioners enables us to explore the relationship between Islam and human rights in a more nuanced and sophisticated way. It is becoming clear that Muslim rappers are increasingly delivering global messages with universal applicability that address "non-Muslim" issues as well as those affecting the Muslim *ummah*. In so doing, young Muslim hip-hoppers are able to transcend their personal misfortunes and locate themselves within a larger global context. Not only can we see the us-versus-them rhetoric that is often caricatured as defining the September 11 generation, capturing the angst of young Muslims who rant against greater securitization and foreign involvement in the domestic policies of Muslim lands, but we also witness human rights activism within Muslim communities. The September 11 generation's rereading of religion allows us to view intrareligion contestations from a clash *within* civilizations (Senghaas 2002) perspective rather than a Huntingtonian clash *of* civilizations. Hip-hop affords the space to broach taboo topics such as heresy, gender, and sexuality. In short, young Muslims are continually challenging their positions as active participants in the global community and within the Muslim *ummah* itself.

Hip-hop allows its Muslim practitioners to transcend differences in Islamic orientations through its socially conscious agenda. Richard Turner (2006), whose study concerns male Muslim youth who are influenced by rap music, dubbed hip-hop as North America's foremost youth culture and shows how young men are converting to Islam as a result of hip-hop's long flirtation with the religion. Common's memoir, *One Day It'll All Make Sense* (2012), a *New York Times* best seller and lauded by Maya Angelou and NOI's leader, Louis Farrakhan, among others, provides an insider perspective into the solidarity within the American Muslim hip-hop circuit across different Islamic orientations. Young Muslims consider Muslim rappers such as Common, Talib Kweli, Hitek, the Roots, and Wu Tang Clan to be role models for spiritually and politically conscious black youth. According to Turner, rap music transcends the "oppositional subcultural music" stereotype for youth who seek to make sense of "the ultimate spiritual and political concerns in their lives." These identities have since become "paradigms for global Muslim youth" (2006, 41).

In essence, hip-hop as appropriated by the poetic jihadis is an attempt to reconcile two apparently irreconcilable cultures, Islam and hip-hop. It is a rebellion against both the exaltation of misogynous and Afrocentric themes in hip-hop and the conservativeness of Islamic music such as the *nasheed*. As hip-hop culture undergoes an Islamization process when appropriated by this segment of Muslim youth, the lyrics remain devotional, although they also incorporate a heavy dose of social reality.

This discussion of hip-hop and human rights serves as the launching pad from which to proceed to the next chapters. The manifestation of hip-hop culture among urban minority youth is also a response to a dialectical relationship with moral entrepreneurs who attempt to manage young people through music as youth attempt to advance their human rights activism through hip-hop. In the next chapter, I explore how performative hip-hop serves as a response to the traditional disciplined bodies of "Islamic music."

NOTES

1. Sara Rimer, "Death Sentence Overturned in 1981 Killing of Officer," *New York Times*, December 19, 2001, https://www.nytimes.com/2001/12/19/us/death-sentence-overturned-in-1981-killing-of-officer.html.

2. "You're Gonna Serve Somebody," beliefnet, accessed February 12, 2020, http://www.beliefnet.com/Entertainment/Music/2001/04/Youre-Gonna-Serve-Somebody.aspx?p=2.

3. Anthony Obst, "I Ain't Goin' Back: The Best Prison Raps; The 25 Realest Rap Songs," *Rebull Music Academy*, April 29, 2013, https://daily.redbullmusicacademy.com/2013/04/prison-raps-feature.

4. The Muslim Program, "What the Muslims Want," NationofIslam.org, https://www.noi.org/muslim-program/.

5. http://awatewillmakeyourlifebetter.com; Hammer & Tongue Hackney September, Facebook, September 6, 2016, https://www.facebook.com/events/hammer-tongue-hackney/hammer-tongue-hackney-september/285305711843234/.

6. Amos Barshad, "Khaled: The Heeb Interview," HeeB, April 15, 2008, http://heebmagazine.com/dj-khaled-the-_heeb_-interview/3152.

7. TekMill, Facebook, July 9, 2016, https://www.facebook.com/search/top/?q=TekMill%20trust%20Allah&epa=SEARCH_BOX.

8. Richard Godwin, "Single Mother, Refugee, Campaigner and Controversialist: Meet M.I.A," *Evening Standard*, April 21, 2016, https://www.standard.co.uk/lifestyle/esmagazine/single-mother-refugee-campaigner-and-controversialist-meet-mia-a3228831.html.

9. Beatrice Hazlehurst, "Azealia Banks Takes Aim at M.I.A, Calls Her 'Anti-Black,'" *Paper*, August 30, 2017, http://www.papermag.com/azealia-banks-takes-aim-at-m-i-a-calls-her-anti-black-6-2479545107.html.

10. Sky Obercam, "KRS-One's 'Real Terrorism' Video Banned on YouTube," *TheGrio*, September 12, 2011, https://thegrio.com/2011/09/12/krs-ones-real-terrorism-video-banned-on-/.

11. "KRS-One's 'Real Terrorism' Video Banned by YouTube [Video]," Hiphopwired, September 12, 2011, https://hiphopwired.com/114447/krs-ones-real-terrorism-video-banned-by-youtube-video/.

12. Kevin Sullivan, Mark Berman, and Sarah Kaplan, "Three Muslims Killed in Shooting Near UNC; Police, Family Argue over Motive," *Washington Post*, February 12, 2015, https://www.washingtonpost.com/news/post-nation/wp/2015/02/11/three-killed-in-shooting-near-university-of-north-carolina/.

13. Alan Feuer, "Linda Sarsour Is a Brooklyn Homegirl in a Hijab," *New York Times*, August 7, 2015, https://www.nytimes.com/2015/08/09/nyregion/linda-sarsour-is-a-brooklyn-homegirl-in-a-hijab.html.

14. Killakam, "Eritrean Rapper Awate Sees London through the Lens of an African Immigrant In 'Fever,'" *Okayafrica*, September 29, 2015. Awate, "Fever," https://www.youtube.com/watch?v=KvBWfb7UBKo.

15. Tashan, "Awate: The 'Wide Awake' Rapper," *Cre8ingvision*, July 27, 2014, http://www.dehai.org/archives/dehai_news_archive/2014/nov/0109.html.

16. Malcolm X (1965), 75. Abayomi Azikiwe, "Malcolm X and Global Black Struggle," *Workers World*, February 19, 2014, https://www.workers.org/2014/02/13105/.

17. "International Covenant on Civil and Political Rights," General Assembly of the United Nations, December 19, 1966, https://treaties.un.org/doc/publication/unts/volume%20999/volume-999-i-14668-english.pdf.

18. Leila Fadel, "An American Muslim Preacher Faces His Own Mortality," *NPR*, January 10, 2018, https://www.npr.org/2018/01/10/576469015/an-american-muslim-preacher-faces-his-own-mortality.

19. Fadel, "American Muslim Preacher."

20. Jon Donnison, "Meet the First Lady of Arabic HipHop," BBC News, September 7, 2010, https://www.bbc.com/news/av/world-middle-east-11214039/meet-the-first-lady-of-arabic-hiphop.

21. Suhaib Webb, Facebook, August 3, 2015, https://www.facebook.com/suhaib.webb/posts/10153470302688080/.

22. Sharrae, "'Hip Hop Hijabis': Catching Up with Muneera of Poetic Pilgrimage," patheos, April 15, 2013, http://www.patheos.com/blogs/mmw/2013/04/hip-hop-hijabis-catching-up-with-muneera-of-poetic-pilgrimage/.

23. Mustafa Davis, *Deen Tight* (documentary, 2010, Cinemotion Media), https://vimeo.com/27049587.

24. Rap Eden, forum, accessed February 8, 2018, http://www.muslimhiphop.com/Hip-Hop/Kumasi.

25. "An Interview with the Lyrical Legend Rakim," Finalcall.com, last updated April 18, 2009, http://www.finalcall.com/artman/publish/Entertainment_News_5/An_interview_with_the_lyrical_legend_Rakim.shtml.

26. Naomi Westland, "Rappers Provide Anthems for the Arab Spring," *USA Today*, May 23, 2012, https://hiphopdiplomacy.wordpress.com/2012/05/23/anthems-for-arab-spring/.

27. "Syria Conflict Finds a Voice in Hip-Hop," BBC, August 4, 2012, https://www.bbc.com/news/world-middle-east-19017267.

28. "Hip-Hop & Rap from Syria: LaTlaTeh," Nour Al-Ali (blog), August 25, 2012.

29. "Brother Ali, 'Shadows on the Sun' 15th Anniversary Tour," MuslimHipHop.com, September 22, 2018, http://www.muslimhiphop.com/index.php?p=Stories/11._The_Brothahood_Interview.

30. Hass Dennaoui, "Omar Offendum: Uniting People through Hip-Hop," *Arab News*, December 8, 2010, https://www.arabnews.com/node/362469.

31. "Hip-Hop Artist Omar Offendum Makes Canadian Debut at TPFF Launch," Palestine News Network, April 13, 2011, https://www.thefreelibrary.com/Hip+Hop+Artist+Omar+Offendum+Makes+Canadian+Debut+at+TPFF+Launch-a0253907485.

32. Paul Lester, "Rappers with a Cause," *Guardian*, January 24, 2003, https://www.theguardian.com/music/2003/jan/24/artsfeatures.

33. Iman Amrani, "The French Hip-Hop Stars Fighting the Far Right," *Guardian*, June 10, 2016, https://www.theguardian.com/music/2016/jun/10/kalash-nekfeu-and-the-french-rappers-fighting-racism.

34. Jeremy Allen, "Franco-Arabic Rappers in Paris," Fact, November 3, 2015, http://www.factmag.com/2015/11/03/franco-arabic-rappers-in-paris/.

35. May Jeong, "Multi-Culti Toronto Is a Draw for Global Hip-Hop Ingenues," *Globe and Mail*, October 28, 2011, https://www.theglobeandmail.com/news/toronto/multi-culti-toronto-is-a-draw-for-global-hip-hop-ingenues/article559527/.

36. DAM official band page, YouTube, https://www.youtube.com/user/dam1st/about.

—ʍ—

SHE REPPIN' ISLAM AND SHE GIVES IT A MEANING

IN CONJUNCTION WITH THE 2017 International Women's Day, Mona Haydar, a heavily pregnant twenty-eight-year-old seminary student born to Syrian immigrants living in Flint, Michigan, dropped her first rap video entitled "Hijabi—Wrap My Hijab." The video was released to serve as an anthem to empower Muslim women and showcase those who don the hijab in a positive light. The track—which features women from diverse backgrounds wearing different styles of hijab, from the "hoodjab," a style associated with the Afrodiasporic tradition, to more conventional ways of wrapping—was so successful that Mona and her crew released a "Wrap My Hijab" dance tutorial a few months later after she had given birth. The YouTube video has since garnered more than seven million views and almost thirty-two thousand comments of a very polarized nature.

> All around the world
> Love women every shading
> be so liberated
> All around the world
> Love women every shading
> power run deep
> So even if you hate it
> I still wrap my hijab
> Wrap my hijab
> Wrap my hijab
> Wrap, wrap my hijab

The play on words of *wrap* and *rap* in the hook of the song cements the spirit of defiance in observing the hijab, not only by *wrapping* themselves with the hijab despite the stigma faced by larger society but by utilizing *rap* as a tool of resistance. Mona alludes to "Me and my hijabi ladies, We was born in the eighties," hence rallying around a common generation of Muslim women who are "takin' back the misnomers" and "teleportin' through trauma." These women, who came of age and transitioned into adulthood in the immediate post–September 11 era, face similar issues and challenges. The song discusses the demonizing of Muslim women—tackling, head on, the pervasive view of the hijab as a primary symbol of female oppression. In an interview, she shared her experience of a man suggesting she was "hiding something" under her pregnancy bump and wanting to rip off her hijab.[1] If there is ever a need to confirm such sentiments of disgust for hijab-adorning women, one need only look through the top comments for the video, which are dominated by dispositions of a similar ilk. In 2018, four of the top five comments are:

1. Does anyone in the comments section realize why women wear hijabs in the middle east? Oh. yeah, if they don't, they get stoned (1,041 likes)
2. Islam is not a religion of peace. -There are only 2 genders. Feminism is cancer. (846 likes)
3. i still wrap my oppreression [*sic*] wrap my oppression wrap wrap my oppression (217 likes)
4. Why don't you go back to Syria & wrap about your hijab? Since you know, Islam is very empowering and all? (199 likes)

Mona turns this narrative on its head, contending that she advocates a "feminist planet." She condemns the schizophrenic exoticizing and orientalizing gaze toward Muslim women, hinting at some people's obsession with female tresses and erotic imagination of the hidden beauty of hijabi women. By advocating her brand of feminism, Mona and her friends offer a powerful critique of feminist orientalism that seeks to situate the Islamic veil squarely within the ambit of patriarchy and oppression. In academia, scholars like Lila Abu-Lughod, who famously asked the question, "Do Muslim Women Need Saving?" (2013), have fought this strand of Western imperialist thought. The hip-hop hijabis have taken the debate to a new front by challenging this form of colonial racism in popular culture. As Mona mentioned in an interview, beyond the message of wrapping one's hijab, the song is really about bringing awareness to the dark sides of "colourism" and advocating for "the empowerment of women."[2]

Mona's combative language nonetheless does not reflect her life's activism. An initiative she and her husband started called #AskAMuslim, which involves offering free donuts and coffee to attract members of the public into interacting with them, has gained traction among American Muslims and non-Muslims alike. However, non-Muslims who are not persuaded by the video's message and her overall activism to shatter the Western perception of oppressed hijab wearers continue to draw attention to the gross mistreatment and punishment of women who have chosen not to wear the hijab in some Muslim countries and within communities in Western countries. They insist that women's liberation is governed by the very Western democracies they are living in, instead of the culture they represent. To the undiscerning eyes, these criticisms seem right on point. While Mona Haydar's song and video put her in a positive light in many mainstream online news channels like the BBC, NPR, and Buzzfeed, she admitted that "there has been a lot of backlash,"[3] including within the Muslim community itself. The main criticisms by Muslims center on the permissibility of music in Islam and the acceptability of female performance in public. In short, many argue that the video is not a representation of Islam.

Integral to the debate on the body and performativity is the question of the relationship between Islam and gender—more specifically, the contestation over the female form. Additionally, the controversy surrounding the very involvement of Muslim women in hip-hop and the existence of eminent and emerging artists such as Miss Undastood, Soosan Firooz, Mona Haydar, and Poetic Pilgrimage gives rise to broader issues of gender, hip-hop, and Islam.

REPPIN' ISLAM—OR NOT?

Performance, especially the management of the body, is an area of contention in Muslim hip-hop and a source of disagreement and polarization among hip-hop practitioners. Many Muslim hip-hoppers at some juncture will have to address concerns about reconciling their piety with their craft. These tensions are encapsulated in the comment by hip-hop journalist Adisa Banjoko:

> Our deen is not meant to be rocked! . . . I see these so-called Muslim sistas wearing a hijab and then a boostier, or a hijab with their belly-button sticking out. You don't put on a hijab and try to rock it! Or these brothers wearing Allah tattoos, or big medallions with Allah's name—Allah is not to be bling-blinged![4]

The fact that the Muslim body becomes a site of moral judgment leads to the demonizing of the performative aspects of hip-hop music, particularly the sexualized or violent body associated with particular dance moves but also the unruly crowds during public performances. In this regard, hip-hop is a response to the disciplining of the body within the context of traditional Islamic music. These social developments will be contextualized against significant attempts by Muslim hip-hoppers to Islamize hip-hop performance.

The hijab is central to the identities of many female Muslim hip-hoppers. It is not merely a prop or a fashion accessory because donning the hijab has been part of many artists' daily lives and is not undertaken for purposes of their hip-hop "acts." Miss Undastood, an African American hijabi and a native New Yorker, is one of the most prominent female Muslim hip-hoppers. After embracing Islam in 2001, she has been branded the first lady of Muslim hip-hop in the years following her conversion. The poor quality of existing Islamic music was one of the key motivating factors for Miss Undastood's artistic endeavors. She states, "So much Muslim music has no flow or it mixes Islam with outside influence. . . . And some of it is corny. Like [the group] Allah's Army. I played it one time and never played it again."[5] In 2002, she released her first album, entitled *Dunya or Deen*, which is Arabic for "World or Faith." She practically released the album on her own, selling it on the Internet to increasing numbers of Islamic hip-hop enthusiasts. In 2003, at the tender age of nineteen, her lyrical prowess saw her crowned the first woman to win the Battle Champions, a prestigious hip-hop accolade in New York City. Her uniqueness as a Muslim female hip-hopper quickly got her noticed in the mainstream media, although she was ultimately signed by Dawa Media, a popular Muslim label founded by London hip-hop outfit Mecca2Medina.

Miss Undastood, who was on a television show called *Cover Girl: Young Women's Lives after 9/11*, raps about a multitude of issues pertaining to gender and Islam. As a hijabi, she exhibits a heightened consciousness about the way she presents herself. Her songs discuss her decision to wear the hijab and the tendency to reduce women to an article of clothing. In her track "Hijab Is the One Thing," she stresses that "just because I cover don't mean I'm more righteous / Just because she doesn't, don't mean she's less pious."

In donning the hijab, these women inevitably act as ambassadors to their faiths. As Miss Undastood expressed in an interview in 2007: "I want to be a voice for Muslim women . . . a voice for the woman's perspective in Islam."[6] Part of the allure of Miss Undastood is her courage to tackle tough topics, such as polygamy, interreligious couples, and gender roles, that are often problematic for non-Muslims and at times considered taboo by segments of the Muslim population. In "Co-wife," she raps freely about the benefits of polygamous relationships for women: "She don't want to be bothered 24/7 anyway / She doesn't have to cook and clean every day." At the same time, she chastises Muslim men who abuse the polygamy provision in Islam: "Why take 2 or 3 when you know you ain't got it? / Keep 'em on welfare and living in the projects."

Ironically, the involvement of female hip-hoppers and their pursuit of representing Islam are factious issues in the Muslim hip-hop scene. While their male counterparts also face the fundamental question on the compatibility of hip-hop and Islam, criticisms of female hip-hoppers are even more severe. Muneera Williams, of the UK hip-hop group Poetic Pilgrimage, agrees that wearing more conventional attire such as the hijab when performing often does little to appease critics. Many of the critics' grievances have to do with Muslim women being involved in "this type of music." According to Muneera:

> I personally want to wear the hijab but that's got nothing to do with what you think of me onstage or how you think I should look. That's between me and my Lord and it should be the same with Deeyah. But when we perform as Poetic Pilgrimage we face people who say: "You're a Muslim, you're wearing the *hijab* and you're mixing your religion with this type of music. How dare you?" Whichever direction we turn in, there will be someone with something to say. . . . Those opinions are not necessarily the majority, they're just the more vocal opinions, often expressed by the people who own the mosques and the publishing companies. They feel this gives them the right to shout louder than anybody else.[7]

Speaking up comes at a high price for female Muslim rappers. Miss Undastood recounted the abuse she received from men as well as women, saying, "Some guys don't appreciate the whole feminist empowerment thing I'm doing. . . . I sold a CD to a woman's husband and she got angry my face was on the cover."[8] She confessed that she might have to stop rapping if she wants to get married because "some men are intimidated by a strong Muslim woman . . . and they don't like the idea of a woman being so public." Others, like Indian hip-hopper Sufia Asraf, who is known back home as the former "burqa rapper," have expressed similar sentiments. While the challenges faced by female hip-hoppers in some conservative Muslim majority countries are undeniably harsher, the burden of hyphenating *hip-hop* and *Muslim* has become too much for some to bear. Despite her initial successes, Miss Undastood, who has endured relentless criticism, even abuse, by audience members at her shows, recently expressed that she no longer wishes to carry the torch of the Muslim identity: "I'm trying to get out of 'Muslim Music' and make something for everybody and now, you know, some people they really don't know how to embrace that. I'm done being a poster girl for Islam. I don't want that to be on my shoulders anymore."[9]

While Miss Undastood might have been motivated by the need to capture a wider market, others have shown clearer signs of conflict with their Muslim identity. Grammy Award–nominated singer and songwriter and poet Maimouna Youssef (Mumu Fresh) admits to staying out of the "Muslim circle" despite being brought up in an Islamic environment and having Muslim friends because she was overwhelmed by the notion that Muslim women are not supposed to put themselves out in public. When asked about how she reconciles her craft with her Islamic identity, she said, "I am good with God, me and God are so good . . . and so I just deal with it like that. I know that my music, it can be sensual because I am a sensual being . . . but it is also very spiritual."[10] When asked the same, Algerian-born Canadian songwriter and rapper Meryem Saci—who struggled with not being allowed to sing while she was growing up, which led her to "question a lot of things about the religion"—asserts that "Islam is a very strong piece of my identity but it is not my full identity. And I am not an ambassador of Muslim women because I am not your average type of woman. . . . I am a representative of a human being that is seeking their own truth."[11]

The ability to transcend one's own people in a migrant community under siege can be difficult, especially for women. Jasmin Zine's twin study of Muslim girls' experiences with racism, Islamophobia, and peer pressure, as well as how they reconcile their gender, race, and piety in Canadian schools, is illuminative. In the first study (2001), Zine demonstrated that the students resisted assimilation by establishing a strong network with other Muslims, in and out of school, who share their beliefs and rituals. These networks allow Muslim students to preserve their identity and act as safe havens against the cultural other. Her other work (2006) focuses on how Muslim girls construct their sense of self within an Islamic worldview. They are caught between their community's patriarchal regulations of the body and the prejudice and Islamophobia of the larger society. As such, those who fall outside the perimeters of communal and societal norms risk being ostracized from both sides and therefore seek to create a third space where they can straddle both identities. This encapsulates Meryem's hesitance at being seen as a representative of Muslim women.

Although the tide may be turning, these challenges perpetuate an environment of men speaking on behalf of the women in Muslim hip-hop. Addressing the British South Asian community, the group ADF, in their track "Tu Meri" (You're mine), urged their listeners to see women as equals, singing, "Standing together side by side, I'm not your shadow but I could be your guide. . . . Asian sisters shouldn't hear slackness, But conscious lyrics like Sounds of Blackness, Asian brothers come listen to me, Respect your sisters if you wanna be free." It is noteworthy to reflect on the falsetto utilized by Master D to front the female voice in this track. Ashley Dawson's (2002) interpretation of this act as speaking against "the fundamentalist Islamic notion of woman as man's shadow" is specious given that the notion has no bearing in Islam, although Sardar (2013) argued for it metaphorically, contending that Muslim men, specifically South Asian Muslim men, have long cast a shadow over the development of their counterparts. However, what is intriguing is the subtle yet subversive way Master D broke into a female voice midtrack in this hypermasculine genre. At the same time, he deconstructed notions of masculinity within hip-hop. Singing in falsetto presents a creative way for male hip-hop groups to project a female voice into their music without inviting the controversy of including a female hip-hopper. This technique of singing is a common feature in traditional South Asian songs.

Part of the rejection of female musicians as representatives of Islam stems from the debate over the hijab itself. While most commonly construed as a covering for the head worn by Muslim women, in Islamic practice it has a wider understanding and application. First, hijab is not a requirement only for women. Men are also required to cover parts of their bodies out of modesty, albeit in slightly different forms. A commonly accepted understanding is the coverage of the areas between the navel and the knee, as well as the prohibition from wearing silk clothing and gold ornaments. For women, loose-fitting clothes of nontranslucent materials are needed in order to conceal the shape of their bodies. Second, hijab also entails codes of male-female interactions such that both are mutually responsible for creating a healthy social environment for respectful interactions. And, most important, these prescriptions are for the sole purpose of serving God, not for elevating one gender above the other. As stated in the Qur'an 24:30–31, "Tell believing men to lower their eyes and guard their modesty. That will be purer for them. Allah is aware of what they do. And tell the believing women to lower their eyes, and guard their modesty, and that they display not their ornaments except what appears of them. And that they draw their veils over their bosoms and display not their ornaments except to their husbands, their brothers. . . . And repent to Allah, all of you O believers, that you may succeed."

The place of Muslim women in music when men are in the audience is therefore contentious when set against these requirements. Muslim women are not expected to shun the public sphere altogether. Indeed, women in the time of Prophet Muhammad not only had a strong presence but could gain prominence in society. Since September 11 there has been an influx of hijabi hip-hoppers, who adhere to a strict dress code, entering the industry, although critics of female Muslim hip-hoppers believe hijab is not adequately observed due to the presentation of the female bodies and voices in the presence of the male gaze.

Concern over the (mis)representation of the hijab comes from both men and women alike. Indeed, many negative social media comments by Muslim women show their displeasure at what they deem to be men bringing excessive attention to the female body forms and movements. In response to these uninvited attentions, which at times call for their own homogenizing interpretations of the hijab, female Muslim hip-hoppers like Poetic Pilgrimage and Mona Haydar have taken different paths, moving away from a "unilateral" view of the hijab. On the one hand, Muneera from Poetic Pilgrimage called for an individualization of how she should be allowed to interpret the hijab, as "it was between me and my Lord." On the other hand, Mona Haydar demonstrated that there is diversity even in the adorning of the hijab. Her video's representation of Muslim women donning different hijab styles—including exposure of the hair and even necks of some performers—showcased the cosmopolitan nature of urban Islam.

Besides challenging the limits of performance for the Muslim body, Mona's video also has the added dimension of embracing women of different body types—as personified by the expectant Mona herself. Many Hollywood celebrities have taken up the agenda against body shaming, advocating for varied notions of a perfect woman's body. Beyoncé, Kim Kardashian, and others have increasingly glamourized images of expectant bodies in popular culture. As if offering herself as the "Muslim face" of this cause, Mona's video is therefore a significant departure from many other Muslim hip-hop videos, even those celebrating the position of Muslim women, which tend to showcase unmarried women almost exclusively. Not surprisingly, her image does not sit well, even among her female audience. Women who commented on the singer's pregnancy and her belly rubbing in the video said these images were simply weird. Mona said in an interview, "The fact that a pregnant woman is in a music video was just shocking for a lot of people. . . . And I found it really disturbing that people were so shocked. Often, people had more to say about me rubbing my belly than about the actual content."[12]

Mona Haydar, however, takes this backlash in stride, saying that diversity of opinions is what enriches Islamic culture. Many also threw their weight behind Mona's cause and challenged the naysayers in the Muslim and non-Muslim communities alike, taking on cultural gatekeepers along the way. As stated by one Alia Azmi in her comment on Mona's YouTube video:

But I didn't get an impression she or any of those girls are saying "this is Islam" or "this is a valid interpretation of *hijab*" etc. As far as I can see they are just saying this is me/us, this is what we're doing, what we're going to keep on doing. Ok we might view their interpretation as wrong but if anything it's still a very minor dismeanor. It gets to me when people treat "women sins" as so much more serious than other sins. Never heard people getting excited over how all these Muslim footballers are exposing their awrah as they play, even the Saudi team.[13]

Alia's comment is representative of the arguments used by Mona's supporters to dispel her critics. The first approach debunks the illegitimacy of her actions outright, arguing that there is nothing that transgresses Islamic belief. The second point of view contextualizes her actions by arguing for a plurality in terms of interpreting the religion and its rituals. The third acknowledges that her actions might have transgressed the tenets of the religion but that it is a minor transgression and a smaller evil given the greater good of fighting Islamophobia in today's toxic climate. The last strategy calls out the androcentric stance as well as the double standards of her detractors, claiming that Muslims especially are harsher toward their womenfolk. As Alia Azmi mentioned in her commentary, there was not so much as a murmur, even among Saudi Arabians, when men from the Saudi soccer team were deemed not appropriately clothed by the standards of their ultraconservative kingdom. On the contrary, in a country where soccer is a national sport, albeit only for men, clothing is not an issue because pride in their team as a regional powerhouse and occasionally qualifying for the World Cup prevails over piety.

HIJAB (COUNTER)CULTURE

The shifting boundaries in framing hijab give birth to a counterculture of empowering women that takes place on many fronts. Internet forum pages and social media provide fertile ground for alternative voices to those of religious and cultural gatekeepers. This is part of a wider development. Global fashion houses investing heavily in fresh fashion designers creating new Muslim styles have helped nurture a new Muslim girl culture known as the hijabsters. In 2015, Japanese clothing company Uniqlo announced it had teamed up with popular designer and blogger Hana Tajima to launch a modest wear collection that will include stylish hijabs and inner AIRism hijabs. Some sources cite Tajima, a British Japanese fashion designer who converted to Islam in 2007 and subsequently began modeling her new hijab-based style online, as being a primary source of the hijabster cultural movement. A *New York Times* article published in 2014 declared Yunalis Zarai, a.k.a. Yuna, twenty-nine-year-old award-winning Malaysian pop star and the face of Uniqlo's Hana Tajima hijab collection, the new poster girl for hijabsters.[14]

Yuna, dubbed by *Billboard* magazine as a protégé of hip-hop superstar Pharrell, admits to being inspired "by the growing numbers of young women dressed like her everywhere, not just in Kuala Lumpur, but in cities from Chicago to Cairo," and she simply said, "What we wear is our own choice, how we cover up. . . . Personally, I found a balance." Many might feel her hijab wearing comes naturally since she is from a Muslim-majority country. However, Yuna discloses that initially she was seen as an outsider, even within her country's entertainment industry, as she struggled with her identity as a hijabi. Even in Malaysia, not unlike the United States, "women singers are seen as sexy here— you have to let your hair out and be beautiful." Yuna's strategy in the early part of her career was to hide her body, preferring to bask in the aura of mystery she created for herself: "I didn't put up a proper photo of myself—it was cropped, up until my nose. People didn't know what I looked like until my first show. They were shocked in the beginning, but they accepted me."[15] The upside of this approach was that it allowed listeners to warm up to her as an artist first as she distinguished herself with her unique sounds.

Yuna, who released a song called "Crush" with hip-hop icon Usher in 2016, was again faced with the hijab conundrum upon her transition to the West. "You should let your hair out," she reflected on those who want her to unveil herself, "you shouldn't be oppressed—you're not in Malaysia anymore. You should show your curves and be proud of it. But I am proud—it's my choice to cover up my body. I'm not oppressed—I'm free."[16] Her move to the United States in 2011 was a success, symbolically represented by the first single of her new album, which was entirely shot on the steps of the Los Angeles City Hall, etching her onto the city's cosmopolitan landscape (Williams and Kamaludeen 2017).

Developments toward making the hijab fashionable are still frowned upon by certain segments of society. Nonetheless, it has won over certain cultural gatekeepers in a bid to rally the community around positive and uplifting images of the young. The entertainer-hijabster archetype has proven a winning formula even among political elites in Muslim-dominated countries, which are keen to co-opt their fresh and cool image. Back home, Datuk Mas Ermieyati Samsudin, the chair of the women's youth wing of the United Malays National Organisation (UMNO), Malaysia's largest political party, in 2014 called on young women in the country to emulate Yuna: "Let us take the example of

Yuna, who always covers herself and is a 'hijabster,' and is a strong influence on teenagers and youth today.... Although she sings pop songs, she also promotes Islam through her personality and appearance.... In fact, Yuna's impact has encouraged many other new-age female artistes to wear the headscarf even though they are not singing nasyid."[17] A clear example of the intricate relationship between youth cultures, social identities, and mediated relations with authority can be gleaned from the state's release of a music video by Yuna for its "Visit Malaysia 2014" campaign.

The hijabster movement brings fresh appeal to the connection between hip-hop and hijab. The globality of these elements among the Muslim community is explicitly embodied in Deen Squad's track "Cover Girl." The song title, which alludes to the hijab as a head covering, is reminiscent of the CoverGirl cosmetics brand, which has a long list of celebrity ambassadors to appeal to the younger generation and represents a wholesome "girl-next-door" look. In this video, however, the hijab is the adornment, the "crown" and source of strength. The launch of "Cover Girl" on International Women's Day featured over thirty "hijabi role models" from countries ranging from the United States to Oman, Australia, Egypt, Thailand, and Malaysia in a celebration of individuality as well as nationality. The footage shows confident young Muslim women in their element who are not to be messed with singing along to the hook of the track, "She be rockin' that hijab," an indirect challenge to Adisa Banjoko's advice to Muslim women, "You don't put on a *hijab* and try to rock it!" The hijab, in this instance, is an expression of the observance of faith, a show of style and strength, the pursuit of dreams, and even the achievement of success.

Given the tenuous nature of the involvement of Muslim (especially female) youth in hip-hop, young Muslims are constantly rereading their relationship with hip-hop culture and what it means to be a hip-hop artist. In many Western societies, in particular, Muslim girls have long realized that framing the hijab as an act of choice empowers them to engage in issues of civil liberties in solidarity with their fellow citizens. Translating this to the genre, many songs in Muslim hip-hop take the position of defending and empowering female adherents. This is not surprising given that women are more frequently the victims of some of the most vicious hate crimes in societies. In many reports on crimes in which Islamophobia is the primary motive, women have more often than not been the victims.

Inevitably, many of the songs referring to Muslim women allude to the difficulties of wearing the hijab in Western cultures. Without a doubt, the hijab has been singled out as the most controversial Islamic identity marker in many secular societies. Although there are gradations of how different communities approach the hijab, as Christian Joppke (2009) demonstrated in his comparative study of France, Germany, and Britain, Muslim women in many Western societies struggle to justify their decisions to adorn the hijab under the coercive gaze of mainstream society and even some political leaders. In March 2016, Laurence Rossignol, France's minister for women's rights, caused a global scandal when she compared hijabis to "American negroes who were in favour of slavery."[18] She chastised fashion corporations Dolce & Gabbana, H & M, and Marks & Spencer for their Islamic fashion lines, calling them "irresponsible" and engaged in "promoting the confinement of women's bodies." Within several weeks, tens of thousands of outraged people signed an online petition calling for her to be punished. Faced with intense criticism from the general public, Rossignol backpedaled and ascribed her comments to a "slip of the tongue" while standing by her point of view. This episode is just one of the more high-profile cases that reflect the gaze 3ILM refers to in their song "Queen of the Land," with the lyrics, "They say the way you dress makes you un-liberated." "Queens of Islam," a song by MPAC, a Chicago-based group, continues this narrative by rapping, "I know it's tough for you, they always callin you names. . . . Just because you dress different don't mean you gotta feel bad. . . . I hear you women are oppressed, what they talkin about."

This is not an entirely Western phenomenon. Even in Southeast Asia, where the bulk of Muslims live, the hijab has been banned from various public spaces, such as schools, in countries like Singapore and Thailand, where Muslims are the minority. As a consequence, Muslim women who wear the hijab are doubly vulnerable and have been at the receiving end of numerous forms of discrimination, from unfair treatment at the workplace to downright physical attacks.

Asserting that individual success and identity can be conflated with a national identity, the "Cover Girl" track weaves the hijabi icons into national landscapes by having the female role models pose in front of their countries' most recognizable landmarks, such as the Eiffel Tower in Paris and the Sydney Opera House. The Canadian flag was featured at two points—once by one of the women and again by the singers themselves at the end of the song:

> To all my sisters in the place, with style and faith
> Allow me to say, you shine when you're miles away
> They better say SALAMS if they cross your way
> Or I'mma show 'em who's boss today (Hey, hey!) . . .
> Why you're messing with the righteous sisters?
> Why you acting like the head-scarf
> Wasn't worn by the Jews and Christians?

... She rock that head-scarf like the Mother of Jesus ...
Cover girls got dreams with no limits
That's why Ibtihaj done made it in the Olympics
And she braver and a lot more
Women in the prophet's days even fought wars
She striving, she keep believing
She rock that head-scarf like the Mother of Jesus
And that's her freedom. She knows her reason
She reppin' Islam and she gives it a meaning
AMEEN!

The track is a liberation anthem of sorts coupled with images of modern, fashionable hijabis who embrace hijab as an act of piety and at the same time flaunt their independence and freedom. Targeting a youthful audience, "Cover Girl is about hijab empowerment, it's to uplift the spirit of our sisters all around the world internationally," Karter Zaher of Deen Squad explained to Al Arabiya.[19] Recognizing that head covering is also a tradition in Judaism and Christianity, Deen Squad creatively challenges discriminatory views toward Muslim women who cover their heads by incorporating references to the Mother of Jesus as a covered pious woman. In so doing, they have also garnered a non-Muslim following.

Deen Squad's "Cover Girl" video unapologetically seeks to deconstruct long-standing stereotypes associated with hijabi women. First, it reconfigures the concept of beauty as being associated with showing more skin. Many of the fifty-two icons featured in the video are from the fashion industry—models, designers, and bloggers. Second, it dispels the notion that Muslim women are oppressed and only deserving of roles in the private sphere, away from the public eye. The video showcases powerful hijabi women in diverse jobs and features a doctor, a personal trainer, a nurse, and the CEO of a television channel. This point is made even stronger by the video's inclusion of several female athletes and fitness coaches, a terrain generally seen as taboo for Muslim women. And, as an extension of this point, the taekwondo coach, the boxer, and the fencer all assert their right to engage in contact sports as religiously observant women, and, no less important, they demonstrate that their hijab is not a hindrance to excellence in these domains. Ibtihaj Muhammad, the first Muslim American Olympian to don the hijab while competing, was given special mention in the lyrics. Collectively, the "Cover Girls" are seen as bosses who deserve to be respected (symbolized by the greeting of *salam*) and can take on their adversaries because they are empowered.

MUSLIM HIP-HOP AND THE MUSLIM QUEENS

The tremendous challenges faced by female Muslim hip-hoppers make it even more pertinent to study the role of male hip-hoppers who channel the voices of female hip-hoppers and other female Muslims. On the surface, this endeavor of men representing Muslim women might seem misplaced due to the misogynistic tendencies that exist in mainstream hip-hop. To the contrary, however, numerous hip-hop tracks refer to Muslim women as "queens." The place of women in Islam has always been mired in controversy. For instance, Fatima Mernissi's influential book *The Forgotten Queens of Islam* (1993) argues that talking about dominant women in Islam can be difficult because of the patriarchy that has existed in Muslim societies for hundreds of years. This is despite the Qur'an relating many stories of strong women; one particular story vividly documents the Queen of Sheba (Balqis) and her correspondence with Solomon. In the Qur'an, the Queen of Sheba was the epitome of an influential ruler; she was distinguished by her acute intelligence and enlightened form of leadership, lording over a sprawling and flourishing kingdom in what would today be Yemen, Somalia, and Ethiopia. Mernissi contends that male leaders who recognized women for their talents were often demonized and that their contributions have been stripped from the pages of history. The situation is further complicated when the fate of the female protagonists are considered tarnished by their socioeconomic class or involvement in the entertainment industry. Mernissi provides the example of a slave singer named Hababah and her relationship with Yazid II, the Umayyad caliph who ruled from 720–24. The episode is seen as a stereotypical tale of a dangerous courtesan who brought about the demise of a man of stature due to the latter's obsession with women and song.

Hence the conflation of contemporary Muslim women with the image of the Queen of Sheba is a strategic and powerful one. It goes beyond superficial comparisons and speaks to the gender role of modern Muslim women. Contrary to some conservative views that disfavor placing women in leadership positions, the overwhelming evocations of the Muslim queen in Muslim hip-hop situate women squarely against this tradition. Not only are women capable of being effective rulers of men, like the Queen of Sheba, but they are able to do this as individuals and not because they are married to a successful partner. Seen in this light, contemporary Muslim hip-hop can act as a counterculture that routinely normalizes the notion of the strong Muslim women. The queen is a metaphor that depicts Muslim women as powerful and given an exalted position ordained by God. In a conversation with Rami Nashashibi (2011, 153), the executive director of Chicago-based Inner-City Muslim Action Network, Isam from Outlandish explained, "We just felt so many of our sisters were being beat down by the circumstances and we wanted to do something that would tell them they are queens and we know we need to do more to be there for them in their struggle but this was a little something we felt we could do."

Some tracks, like "Aicha" by Outlandish, which has been viewed about forty-five million times on YouTube, go further and even exoticize the Muslim female. The song describes her as a shining star, likening her movement to the breeze. Picking up on the dominant queen metaphor, the track starts with "so sweet so beautiful / everyday like a queen on her throne." The album, *Bread & Barrels of Water*, was released in 2002, with the track "Aicha" achieving phenomenal success in Europe. It topped the charts in Germany, Romania, Sweden, and Switzerland and reached number two in Holland while peaking at number three in both Austria and Norway. In the United Kingdom, it even inspired a musical among Muslim teenagers, who appropriated the character of Aicha to present a counterdiscourse to the pejorative depiction of Muslim women as oppressed and powerless in the Western mainstream media. Miah and Kalra (2008, 13) contend that the musical articulates ideas of gender equality and portrays Aicha as a "strong, dynamic, trendy, colourful and a confident *muslimah*." Hence, the depiction of Aicha also responds to two other disparate camps. First, it criticizes the misogynistic objectification of women in hip-hop music, and, second, it offers a challenge to conservative moral missionaries within the Muslim community. Caught between these camps, students, both male and female, test the confines of accepted Islamic behavior in their local communities.

However, in many of these songs, queens are seen as being under threat from mainstream society. One such narrative is evident in a track by 3ILM, a group of five Muslim men hailing from Tampa, Florida, who got together in 2006. In their track "Queen of the Land," they discuss how women are objectified under society's "look, glare and stare," a gaze that comes with a value judgment, often a damning one, that is externally imposed. The song acknowledges that hijab-wearing women represent Islam—"you rep for the Deen"—owing to their conspicuous look and laments the stripping of the Muslim female voice in favor of an assumption that women who adorn the hijab are oppressed and somehow coerced into dressing in a certain way. Instead, the group contends that women are the "front runners in leading the Islamic cause": it is the female voice that should be heeded as a lesson and a guide in rationalizing their choice of attire.[20]

Be that as it may, the tendency persists for male hip-hop artists to fall into the trap of misogyny, even the very people who have advocated otherwise. Despite the overt and overwhelming support for Muslim women in Muslim hip-hop, some of the songs are criticized for their unsavory depictions of women. The track "Muslim Queen" by Deen Squad took the Internet by storm, generating passionate debates about the intersections among religion, music, gender, and authenticity. Part of the controversy is the song's adoption of Fety Wap's hit "Trap Queen," which is about life in a crack house. Interestingly, rappers like MC Lyte have called Fety Wap a feminist, and "Trap Queen" has been lauded for being an egalitarian ode to his partner in crime. The "Muslim Queen" music video has already been viewed more than three million times on You-Tube and has elicited a few thousand comments. The entire music video is set outside a mosque, with the top comment on YouTube stating, "imagine the imam of that mosque coming out and telling them off. lol :]." Others took issue with what they felt were lyrics that were misogynistic and patriarchal:

> She's so good with her business
> My modern day Kadijah
> No more drama when we living
> Not the same, she's so different
> The day that we get married she'll be mama in the kitchen

These lines came under fire for giving a false impression of Islam since the Prophet resisted a gendered division of labor in the household. Many also pointed to the Prophet's wife, Khadijah, as in the lyrics of Deen Squad, as an example of a successful businesswoman who was not confined to the boundaries of the household.

While it is never possible to fully excavate the intentions driving artistic works, these contradictions may be partly understood from the perspective of wanting to conform to the authenticity of the original hip-hop tracks they covered. This is evident in Deen Squad's subsequent song, "Jannah" (Heaven), which took the beats from Desiigner's track "Panda." While making a play on its lyrics—a common feature in sampling hip-hop songs—the duo was mired in more controversy, with their video attracting more than ten thousand comments on their Facebook and YouTube accounts. In the words of their song "Jannah":

> You got broads in Atlanta, I got many wives in jannah
> Did it all for the ajer, bismillah fix my intentions
> 72 wifeys that is why I be headed to jannah
> All I just wanted was Jannah, so I'm saying bun jahannam
> 72 chillin' hoor al Ayn women
> Halal money, get it

We go to Saudi, spend it
And this goes to all of my Akhi's, to the sisters the realest hijabis
Falasteenis and straight Pakistanis, all my Arabs and killa Afghanis . . .

I got broads up in jannah, I'm praying Allah gives me answers
72 in the after, Allah is the best of the planners
Feeling like Adam, my wifey my only companion
I did it all for ajer, I did all for ajer
All of the deeds are granted, all of the seeds are planted
ain't no more weeds in the garden, all of the hearts have been softened
Beautiful wives in Jannah, I pray that we make it to jannah
Family you should remember, to follow the holy commandments

Deen Squad started their song with, "You got broads in Atlanta / I got many
wives in Jannah," an obvious response to Desiigner's "Panda" hook, "I got
broads in Atlanta / Twistin' dope, lean, and the Fanta." Deen Squad's "Jannah" went on to rap about "72 wifeys / that's why I be headed to Jannah,"
which raised the ire of many of their listeners. Some pointed out that the idea
of the seventy-two virgins in heaven is a myth in Islam based on an inauthen-
tic hadith that should not be trusted. Many commentators ranted against the
objectification of women and the primacy of sex as the main reason to aspire
to go to heaven.

Besides the issue of lyrical structure, the borrowing of jargons from mainstream hip-hop led to controversy for Deen Squad. The usage of the word
broad, in particular, earned the wrath of many for its derogatory connotations.
The *Urban Dictionary* situates the term between *lady* and *bitch* in the spectrum
of respectable names for a woman. The word is believed to have originated in
the 1930s as a reference to female hips, which are wider than those of males.[21]
The heavy criticism the group received for that track contrasts with its shout-
outs of solidarity with Muslim women, with verses dedicating the song "to
the sisters the realest hijabis" and "my wifey my only companion." The song
signs off with the sermon of a popular US preacher, Nouman Ali Khan, who
runs the Bayyinah Institute in Texas. The track drew so much flak that Deen
Squad released a new version of the song with a fresh music video, removing
the section on the sermon and any references to the seventy-two wives or the
Muslim broad. They were replaced with the phrases, "I got my wife up in Jannah," "Palaces Golden, You see me Im ballin in jannah," "Wine Rivers Chillin,"
and "Turning up."

In addition to the artists' personal responses to fiascos such as the prior
example, another point of reflection concerns the representation of women
in the industry. Although women are represented, they are predominantly

represented by men. In their song "1-800-Muslims," New York City's Jabba-ruddin and Ali Umar, known as the Lead, acknowledge this and have called for women to represent themselves: "Me as a guy don't know what you've been through. Men wanna talk even though you don't speak." While Muslim hip-hoppers like Poetic Pilgrimage, Sista Keilana, and Mona Haydar have responded to such calls to lend a female perspective, they are also sometimes criticized in ways mainstream hip-hoppers had probably not anticipated given the host of female rappers in the industry. Within the history of hip-hop itself have been a long line of women who fought for female empowerment through music. In fact, the symbol of the queen or the queen mother, who raps about women's strength, inner-city concerns, and issues of piety, has contributed to hip-hop's effervescence since the early days. Women who were part of Af-rika Bambaataa's Zulu Nation, such as Queen Lisa and Queen Kenya, took on the queen moniker, although it must be said that rapper-turned-movie-star Dana Owens, a.k.a. Queen Latifah, arguably gave the hip-hop queen symbol its international fame (Keyes 2017). It has been well-documented that Owens received her Arabic name Latifah, which means gentle and kind, from her Mus-lim cousin when she was eight. Even though other artists might not necessarily adopt *queen* as a part of their stage name, ethnomusicologist Cheryl Keyes (2017) argues that many female acts, like Sista Soulja, who is affiliated with Public Enemy, and Khalilah-Azraa Vieira, a.k.a. Ladybug Mecca of Digable Planet, explicitly present the Afrocentric queen mother image.

The widespread influence of the NOI and the Five Percenters in the US context and the adherents' claims to Islam add to the complexity of discuss-ing Muslim hip-hop and who speaks for Islam, especially when broaching representations of religion and gender. Anaya McMurray (2008) feels that nonmainstream black Muslim women like her, Erykah Badu, and Eve are carving spaces of resistance not just in hip-hop music in general but also in the niche market of Muslim hip-hop. Anaya writes that their images chal-lenge the misrepresentation that all Muslim women are Middle Eastern, that Muslim women cover at all times, and that they don't have the freedom to pursue careers in music and entertainment. She acknowledges that dialogues on women's participation in music go beyond discussions of hip-hop. They take on power matrices in the community and has to contend with the different social groups they are a part of, be they religious, racial, or social.

Although hip-hop scholars have argued that references to Islam can be found from hip-hop's beginning, Malcolm X aside, there are very few tracks relating to other Muslim icons. Tracks concerning female figures are almost nonexistent. Increasingly, owing to the overlapping identities of blackness and

Islam, the battle to represent Muslim women in hip-hop music and to recount their struggles is no longer the exclusive dominion of male Muslim rappers, female Muslim rappers, or even Muslim rappers in general. Female rapper Rapsody's critically acclaimed 2014 track "Betty Shabazz" is thus a welcomed and much celebrated addition as one of the very few rap songs pertaining to an important Muslim woman. She shifts the gaze from Malcolm X to his wife, reclaiming the much downplayed but important place of women in the struggle for civil rights. Raised as a Jehovah's Witness, Rapsody's music video shows rows of strong black women wearing white headscarves interspersed with images of herself walking in a church.

In an interview with *Ebony* magazine, she lamented the hypersexualized images of female hip-hoppers in the industry:

> When you think about the female artist today, you're supposed to be sexy. You're not supposed to rap about messages or current events. It's always supposed to be about your body or what you can do sexually for a man. It's really disheartening for that idea to be put out, especially when you have young girls that look up to that. It affects how they think and how they perceive what a female is supposed to look like and how they're supposed to speak. . . . 9th and I have always talked about this from day one. Before anything got rolling, I remember he and a friend of his sat down and told me that the first thing that you have to do is define your line. What line are you not willing to cross? What are you *not* willing to compromise yourself for? It was always the music. I didn't want to sell myself short and put sex or my image above the music. Because the music is the most important thing.[22]

Rapsody also took aim at critiques of female hip-hoppers, declaring, "I'm ignoring all that female rapper shit is ignorant / competing with every MC / come step if you want to see."[23] Her prior track, "Coconut Oil," also demonstrates her solidarity with the Muslim community:

> Arab? Muslims? All of um my cousins
> Beauty brown skin might Bomb on a nigga
> Ain't nothing to do wit Qurans
> Ramadan for the figures
> Cheddar Come night we all eat together.

Rapsody consistently downplays the divisions between racial and religious identity in favor of advancing the female voice in the rap scene. Rapsody's struggle to disassociate from the hypersexualized image of hip-hop culture, and its objectification of women, strikes a chord with many female Muslim hip-hoppers, especially in conservative Southeast Asia. According to Shakirah,

cofounder of www.sghiphop.com in Singapore: "I don't believe in conform-
ing to what TV says hip-hop is about. . . . Hip-hop is a very misunderstood art
form, often highlighted in the media as a form of threat or negativity. But vice
can be found everywhere, it doesn't take hip-hop to promote violence, sex or
drugs. . . . Hip-hop culture is merely an art form to be appreciated, especially
for those with talent and passion. I'm a practising Muslim and hip-hop has not
done anything to change that."[24]

Shakirah, at twenty-two years of age, was performing gigs in Singapore and
Malaysia, organizing hip-hop events, and operating a hip-hop store called The
Cube. However, her fascination with hip-hop did not extend to the fashion
associated with it or the lifestyle many would affiliate with hip-hop artists.
Instead, she avoided body-hugging tops in exchange for long-sleeved shirts,
slacks, and the hijab and maintained a clean and pious outlook. As a leader in
the Singapore hip-hop movement, she thus served as a guide to other consumers of the subculture on the possibilities of reimagining hip-hop within the
Muslim context in which she lived.

WOMEN RAPPIN' IN EXTREME CONDITIONS

It is conspicuous that of the more than four dozen hijabi role models showcased
in Deen Squad's "Cover Girl" track, there are none from countries undergoing
civil war or extreme economic strife, such as Iraq, Syria, and Afghanistan. This is
not because these women do not exist. Indeed, the hip-hop *ummah* has enveloped
even these countries, and many acts operate in these very harsh environments.

Soosan Firooz, who broke into the scene in 2012 at the age of twenty-three,
is largely touted as the first female solo rapper in Afghanistan. The country,
long besieged by war and internal strife, is experiencing among the harshest
conditions according to today's global indexes. The United Nations 2019 Human Development Index, which ranks countries according to income, life
expectancy, and education, lists Afghanistan at 170 out of 189 countries. To
compound matters, a 2020 study by the World Justice Project measuring in-
dicators such as constraints on government power, corruption, transparency,
fundamental rights, order, and security as well as civil, criminal, and informal
justice named Afghanistan as one of the worst countries. The ultraconservative regime presiding over the country, which has become one of the epicen-
ters of the war on terror since September 11, has ensured that women do not
play much of a role in the public sphere. It is against this dire sociopolitical
backdrop that we are witnessing the rise of female rappers. Soosan's songs are
a direct critique of the fate of women in her homeland and contain specific

condemnations of violence against women. In the words of her song "Naqisul Aql" (Deficient-in-mind):

> Woman is not only a body, or a single body part
> So you can kill her, whenever you like to
> If women have defective brains
> So do your wife, your sister, and your mother too have defective brains

Soosan, who also performs to sustain her family, insists that her raps are inspired by the tragic conditions of women and girls in her country and the devastation of war. She revealed in an interview: "The people who threaten me say they will kidnap my brother or they will kidnap me, or assault me, or throw acid at me. And I thank them for it because their threats motivate me to work even harder."[25] Many prominent female Afghan entertainers have been maimed or killed for not backing down. In 2012 alone, a number of actresses were attacked in the capital city of Kabul. Sonya Sarwari was the victim of an acid attack after an awards show. Benafsha was fatally knifed when she and two other actresses, sisters Areza and Tamana, were ambushed by six men while on their way to a bakery.

Soosan's songs are not only about recounting the pains of living in her country but also about the discrimination she faced as a refugee in other Muslim countries. To escape the civil war back home, her family fled first to Pakistan and then to Iran. In a song called "Our Neighbors," she describes how she lived as a social outcast in these countries and was routinely subjected to taunts such as "go back, you dirty Afghan." She recounts: "I remember I was waiting in a queue to get bread from the bakery. We gave the baker the money but he didn't give me the bread. People in the queue were hitting the Afghan kids. Through rapping, I could describe the problems I was going through, and also the problems we face today in our society."[26] Despite the rather abject conditions, Soosan, who was featured on MTV's *Rebel Music* in 2015, foresees hope for the future. Even though some strongly resent what she is doing, Soosan acknowledges that the conditions in her country have changed enough, epitomized by the fall of the Taliban, to allow her space to hone her craft that was not there just a few years ago. This can be seen in the growing support she receives, especially among the youth: "One day I was walking down the street and I saw three schoolgirls at the bus station. One of them walked up to me and asked me whether I was the female rapper. When I told them I was, they hugged me and told me that I was their idol."[27]

Another female rapper who is optimistic about the Afghan rap scene is Paradise Sorouri, a model, manager, and women's rights activist. She performs with her partner, Diverse, a former computer science lecturer from Afghanistan's Herat University, where they met when Paradise was working in the university's administrative department before forming 143 Band. The numeral "143" denotes the number of letters in "I Love You," symbolizing their romantic relationship. Growing up in Iran as refugees before relocating to Kabul and identifying themselves as "pure Afghan," the duo has been writing music since 2008. The choice to do hip-hop was a pragmatic one attributed to several positives they see within the genre. The wordy nature of the songs allows them to pack a lot of messages, or even a complete story, into a song, which they claim a pop song is not able to do. The colloquial character of hip-hop music and its conversational style also enable the pair to speak directly to their audience and increase the power of their messages.

Similar to Soosan Firoz's "Naqisul Aql," the themes of 143 Band's songs center on women's issues such as the right to an education. Their 2013 track "Nalestan" is dedicated to Paradise's cousin, who set herself on fire to protest an early marriage. The duo came up with the first hip-hop protest song in Afghanistan, "Faryad e Zan" (A woman's voice), which attracted a lot of buzz from the media. The track riles against the commoditization of women and, more specifically, the crimes against women committed in the name of honor: "Don't be wife to a man who set you on fire! Don't be that man's Honor!" According to 143 Band: "It is obvious that there are a lot of men, especially *Mullahs*, who are doing whatever they want and label it Islamic. I am not judging Islam. I am saying that there are a lot of bad Muslims. If helping women to be empowered is Satanic, then what it is called to rape a seven-year-old girl in a *Masjid*? People say whatever they want to stop us. We have received a lot of death threats and we still continue what we wanted to do!"[28] Paradise concedes that even though the lives of women have changed since the Taliban regime, as seen in the number of girls attending university and participating in public life, the social impact of the Taliban's rule might prove more lasting. She estimates a mere 5 percent of women are able to go to work and provide for their children.[29] The struggles of Soosan Firoz and 143 Band have also opened the gates for other female rappers to break into the scene.

The flip side to this type of discrimination among Muslims in dire environments has been studied by Isoke (2015), who explored the world of female rappers in glitzy Dubai. Isoke discovered that the notion of blackness, and the embracing of blackness as an identity marker and source of solidarity for women of color, has encouraged many young women to affiliate themselves with hip-hop culture. Much of this is caused by discrimination of Muslims by Muslims themselves. Discrimination and bullying of darker-complexioned

Muslims by lighter-skinned Muslims in school has led some women to embrace African American music. African American music, thus, affirms "Sudanese" identity, for example. What is interesting is that the younger generation reported experiencing a new form of racism. A respondent in the study recounted how racism has changed drastically for those of her age group. Children of mixed parentage or from African countries spoke of the racism they were subjected to by Arabs in cosmopolitan Dubai. Blackness thus has become a metaphor for those who feel estranged from the social and political order of the day and provides ammunition to articulate a language of resistance to being treated as second-class citizens in a city where migrants form an overwhelming majority. Emiratis are a mere 7 percent of the population, and only 11 percent of noncitizen migrant workers come from Arab countries.

THE CONTINUING STRUGGLE FOR HIP-HOP

Some scholars have argued that the advent of black nationalism and black religion has exalted the position of women in society. However, given that black nationalism and black religion predate hip-hop culture, the patriarchy and misogyny inherent in the industry must come from outside these intertwining movements. Indeed, there have been studies that show how record labels profit from replenishing the bad boy image of their artists by selling sex and violence. Sharpley-Whiting's book *Pimps Up, Ho's Down: Hip Hop's Hold on Young Black Women* (2007) vividly describes the unsavoriness of contemporary hip-hop culture, where women are objectified and fetishized as strippers and porn stars. However, certain strains of hip-hop forbid vulgar and lewd representations of women. For example, the NOI and Five Percenters were known to be respectful of black women. Busta Rhymes raps in his track "One," in which he collaborated with Erykah Badu, "Yes y'all my beautiful Mother Earth, respect her to the max." Similarly, Wu Tang Clan's "Wu Revolution" chastises the misogyny within the African American community: "I'm callin' my black woman a bitch, I'm callin' my people all kinds of things they are not, I'm lost brother, can you help me?" Brand Nubian's track "Sincerely" includes a list of promises to make life better for womenfolk—love, education, protection—and also apologizes for past transgressions.

Notwithstanding, Lakeyta Bonnette (2015) posits in *Pulse of the People: Political Rap Music and Black Politics* that hip-hop's intimate relationship with black nationalist movements like the Five Percenters and the NOI ensured that ideas of the subservience of women entered the post–civil rights era, even in groups lauded for their highly positive lyrics. She discusses Lord

Jamar from the group Brand Nubian, who, in his track "Supreme Mathematics" from *The 5% Album*, sing about women being secondary to men yet very important for purposes of child-rearing: "Wisdom is the wise words spoken by the wise Black man Who is God" is followed by "Wisdom is symbolic to the Black woman Secondary, but, most necessary, to bring forth the seed of life." Women are commonly referred to as wisdom in Five Percenter "Supreme Mathematics." The lyrics appear to suggest that wisdom is of a lesser value to women than their reproductive roles. Bonnette also accuses NOI's Public Enemy of promoting sexism "under the guise of 'uplifting the race'"(2015, 97). Citing their song "She Watch Channel Zero?" she takes the group to task for not only stereotyping women as solely responsible for bringing up children but also for insinuating that women do not have jobs and are not able to distinguish between fantasy and reality, thus cementing the superiority of men.

It is not uncommon for young women of the September 11 generation to hold critical views of hip-hop culture, which has brought the discourse to the next level. Despite the dominant trend of portraying women in a positive light, as seen in the numerous songs referring to Muslim women as queens and fighting for women's causes, controversies emerge when women enter the hip-hop scene and express a desire to articulate these concerns themselves. The performances of women such as Mona Haydar and Miss Undastood have reignited debates on long-standing issues concerning the place of music in Islam, the place of women in Islamic entertainment, and the place of women in hip-hop culture in general.

The notorious reputation the subculture has gained for itself acts as an impediment for young Muslim women broaching the scene. Although these women have gone to great pains to disrupt the patriarchy and misogyny within hip-hop, by reason of their involvement alone, Muslim women have been subjected to similar hip-hop gazes by both men and women. There is no doubt that Muslim women like Mona, Soosan Firooz, and Poetic Pilgrimage are expanding hip-hop's portrayal of beauty, sexuality, and the work done by women and raising the conversations about these issues to a new level. Not only are women struggling against the hip-hop movement itself to improve the image of hip-hop and open up new spaces and styles that resonate with women, but they must also battle cultural and religious gatekeepers who question their place in the entertainment industry.

Tricia Rose (2008) has argued in *The Hip Hop Wars* that the worldwide commercial success of certain interpretations of hip-hop has resulted in the crystallization of a stereotypical view of black life; the most pervasive images, no doubt, are the aggressive, criminal black man and the promiscuous, naive black woman. This is also a theme picked up by Molefi Asante's *It's Bigger than Hip-Hop* (2008). Asante goes further by contending that the reductionist manner in which hip-hop presents itself runs the risk of isolating itself from the very people it seeks to represent—the black kids themselves. Given these grim analyses of the state of commercialized hip-hop, a mimicking of the black struggle through its consumption as a commodity sets itself up for a distorted adaptation from the start. While there are problematic adaptations of hip-hop among any culture or background, as I have and will continue to demonstrate in this book, globalized young Muslims have appropriated hip-hop culture in sophisticated and calculated ways.

NOTES

1. "Secret Life of Muslims: Sebastian Robins and Mona Haydar," *USA Today*, streamed live on April 24, 2017, YouTube video, 00:4:25, https://www.youtube.com/watch?v=vGX8VRJzTLk.

2. Trystan Young, "Hijabi Rapper Mona Haydar: 'There's Been a Lot of Backlash,'" *BBC News*, April 5, 2017, https://www.bbc.com/news/av/world-us-canada-39509711/hijabi-rapper-mona-haydar-there-s-been-a-lot-of-backlash.

3. Young, "Hijabi Rapper Mona Haydar."

4. Cited in Hisham Aidi, "'Let Us Be Moors': Islam, Race and 'Connected Histories,'" *Middle East Research and Information Project* 229 (Winter 2003), https://merip.org/2003/12/let-us-be-moors/.

5. Kristen V. Brown, "The Message: A Brooklyn Rapper Speaks Volumes about Women in Islam," *Street Level*, Arthur L. Carter Journalism Institute at New York University, Fall 2007, https://nyujournalismprojects.org/streetlevel/fall-2007/brown-missundastood/3/index.html.

6. Brown, "The Message."

7. Vic Motune, "Sing Out Sisters," *New Statesman*, July 10, 2008, http://www.newstatesman.com/music/2008/07/female-artists-muslim-women.

8. Brown, "The Message."

9. "Muslim. Woman. Hip Hop. Artist." *Islamic Monthly*, January 13, 2015, https://www.theislamicmonthly.com/muslim-woman-hip-hop-artist/.

10. "Muslim. Woman. Hip-Hop. Artist."

11. "Muslim. Woman. Hip-Hop. Artist."

12. Noor Wazwaz, "Hijabi Artist Channels Beyoncé for Debut of Her 'Resistance Music' and Video," NPR, April 23, 2017, https://www.npr.org/sections/codeswitch/2017/04/23/522189436/hijabi-artist-channels-beyonc-for-debut-of-her-resistance-music-and-video.

13. Comment on Mona Haydar, "Hijabi (Wrap My Hijab)," YouTube, accessed March 26, 2018, https://www.youtube.com/watch?v=XOX9O_kVPeo.

14. Chen May Yee, "A Malaysian Pop Star Clad in Skinny Jeans and a Hijab," *New York Times*, October 13, 2014, https://www.nytimes.com/2014/10/14/arts /international/yuna-has-become-poster-girl-for-young-hijabsters.html.

15. Steven J. Horowitz, "Pharrell Protege Yuna Talks Being Muslim in Music: 'It's My Choice to Cover Up My Body. I'm Not Oppressed—I'm Free,'" *Billboard*, April 22, 2016, https://www.billboard.com/articles/news/magazine -feature /7341537/yuna-interview-pharrell-williams-usher-muslim-faith -new-album.

16. Horowitz, "Pharrell Protege Yuna."

17. Akil Yunus, "Young Malay Women Can Emulate Yuna, Says Puteri Umno," *The Star*, November 26, 2014, https://www.thestar.com.my/news /nation/2014/11/26/umno-agm-puteri-yuna.

18. France 24, "French Minister: Muslim Women Who Wear Veils Like 'Negroes' Supporting Slavery," March 30, 2016, https://www.france24.com /en/20160330-french-minister-muslim-women-who-wear-veils-like-pro-slavery -negroes.

19. Rua'a Alameri, "Islamic Hip-Hop Duo Deen Squad Empower Hijabi Women with New Single 'Cover Girl,'" *Al Arabiya*, March 7, 2017, https://english .alarabiya.net/en/features/2017/03/08/Islamic-hip-hop-duo-Deen-Squad -empower-hijabi-women-with-new-single-Cover-Girl-.

20. 3ilm, "The Queen of the Land (Feat D-Clique)," YouTube, September 27, 2009, https://www.youtube.com/watch?v=3krv4f7VLRI.

21. *Urban Dictionary*, s.v. "broad," accessed February 2, 2020, http://www .urbandictionary.com/define.php?term=broad.

22. Glennisha Morgan, "Why Is Rapsody Still 'Hard to Choose'? [interview]," *Ebony*, September 17, 2014, http://www.ebony.com/entertainment-culture /why-is-rapsody-still-hard-to-choose-interview-403#axzz49q8KuKOP.

23. Max Goldberg, "9th Wonder and Co. Bring Laid-Back Soundscapes on 'Jamla Is the Squad,'" XXL, January 31, 2014, http://www.xxlmag.com /rap-music/reviews/2014/01/9th-wonder-jamla-is-the-squad-album -compilation-review/.

24. "Hip-Hop Mad and Still a Good Muslim," *Straits Times*, September 7, 2003.

25. Jake Tupman, "From Refugee to Rap Star: Soosan Firooz, Afghan Woman Rapper," *Muftah*, October 17, 2013. See also "From Refugee to Rap Star: Soosan Firooz, Afghan Woman Rapper," Women Development, December 23, 2013, http://womendevelopmentorg.blogspot.com/2013/12/.

26. Tupman, "From Refugee to Rap Star."

27. Tupman, "From Refugee to Rap Star."

28. Farid Shefayi interview for Star Educational Services, "Music with a Message—Musicians on a Mission: An Interview with Paradise and Diverse

from 143Band," Facebook, May 25, 2016, https://www.facebook.com /stareducationalsocietyafg/posts/music-with-a-message-musicians-on-a -missionan-interview-with-paradise-and-divers/1073855796019706/.

29. Max Page, "First Female Afghan Rapper Talks Music, Difficulties, Life After Taliban." *Popdust*, June 4, 2014, http://popdust.com/2014/06/04/afghan -female-rapper-paradise-photos143-band-diverse-videos-taliban-music/#slide1.

FIVE

—ᵐ—

ENEMY OF THE STATE

ON JANUARY 20, 2013, AT Obama's second inauguration celebration, the audience watched in shock as American Sunni Muslim rapper Lupe Fiasco was dragged offstage by a number of burly security guards. The Chicago-born Grammy Award winner and headliner at the party was supposed to celebrate his fellow Chicagoan's reelection but instead had used the stage to criticize the president for his policies. During his performance, he announced that he did not vote for Obama and spent half an hour delivering his antiwar track "Words I Never Said," chastising Obama, among other things, for not responding when Gaza was bombed:

> Limbaugh is a racist
> Glenn Beck is a racist
> Gaza Strip was getting bombed
> Obama didn't say shit
> That's why I ain't vote for him, next one either.

Since then, British Muslim hip-hopper Kareem Dennis, a.k.a. Lowkey, has sampled Lupe's lyrics from that track for his own song "Obama Nation (Part 2)." Just weeks before Lupe's appearance, former first lady Michelle Obama was criticized for inviting Common, an artist linked to the NOI, to a poetry event at the White House due to his critical lyrics challenging the government.

This was not the first time Lupe Fiasco, whose real name is Wasalu Muhammad Jaco, had denounced his country's leader. The previous summer, Lupe had criticized Obama for commissioning drone attacks in foreign lands. In 2006, in a CBS News interview, he accused the United States and Obama of being "the biggest terrorists" and pointed out the United States government as the root cause of terrorism: "My fight against terrorism, to me, the biggest terrorist is Obama in the United States of America. I'm trying to fight the terrorism that's actually causing the other forms of terrorism. You know, the root cause of terrorism is the stuff the U.S. government allows to happen. The foreign policies that we have in place in different countries that inspire people to become terrorists."[1] Lupe's love-hate relationship with the government is best captured in his 2009 mixtape, *Enemy of the State: A Love Story*.

The potency of hip-hop as a vehicle for social and political activism often puts it at odds with the establishment. Governments the world over serve as the most important gatekeepers of hip-hop. Understandably, the range of state responses very much depends on the nature of each state's leadership. The hip-hop community was shocked in 2018 to hear that China, the most populous country in the world, had just banned hip-hop culture on mainstream media at the height of its popularity and despite the success of shows like *Rap of China*. China's State Administration of Press, Publication, Radio, Film and Television (SAPPRFT) was explicit in stating that its television program would not feature hip-hop culture, subculture, or dispirited culture. This statement was made shortly after China removed renowned rappers GAI, PG One, VaVa, and Triple H from various television programs, singing competitions, and streaming sites, resulting in the wrath of China's hip-hop fans, who took to social media to vent their frustrations. *Time* magazine reported how netizens on Weibo, China's version of Twitter, ranted, "SARPPFT is so trashy! They didn't want to give Chinese hip-pop singers any chance of survival! We can go back to ancient times." Another lamented, "How can a government with high culture have such childish logic?"[2] The announcement of the ban came just five years after Daddy Chang gave an optimistic view on the hip-hop scene in China in 2013:

> My work is received by the Chinese hip-hop community as mostly political rap and one that has the [audacity] to touch on sensitive topics here [be] cause I criticize the communist government all the time and touch on topics that many don't touch over here cause they know they [are] going [to] get censored anyways or invited by officials to drink tea with them and warn us to shut up kindly. But as I grew more popular here, they censor less and less of my work cause they know that the more they censor, the more people will criticize and prove themselves right. So freedom of speech here grows freer and freer everyday not only from our community of hip-hop but on shows, radios, and blogs of other artists and writers. People here in China fought and improved freedom of speech thru internet and blogs which is heavily tied to how we operate hip-hop in China nowadays as well. It's the way indie

artists work today and we provide a platform for more artists to do that as well. A lot of hip-hop kids here assume they haven't invited me to drink tea is probably [be]cause of my Republic of China (Taiwan) passport, no mainland; mainland is PRC; citizen as well as me [being a] Canadian citizen. Means I'm not really a Mainlander citizen so they can't arrest me cause I am basically a foreigner Chinese, haha. So yeah, the guy that raps politics to some, raps truth to some, and a lunatic to some. But definatly [sic] one of those that contribute much to Chinese Hip Hop for sure.[3]

Affirming that his brand of no-holds-barred political rap is becoming more accepted, albeit grudgingly, Chang attributes the advent of the digital age as critical in opening the space for him and his comrades to be able to practice their craft. His liminal Chinese identity and his foreign passports make it difficult for the state to clamp down on him. However, with the recent ban, it remains to be seen to what extent rappers like Daddy Chang can still operate and to what degree they can reach a widespread Chinese audience. What is certain is that the Internet remains a domain where states have very little control, and, as Chang mentioned, the hip-hop scene in China is mainly fostered through cyberspace. In this vein, this chapter compares state management of hip-hop across a wide spectrum of political climates—from liberal to authoritarian and even despotic political regimes.

MUSLIM HIP-HOP OF THE "FREE WORLD"

The backlash against Muslims in the post–September 11 United States, and in many other Western liberal states, has had a tremendous effect on Muslim-hip-hop. State laws and policies meant to curb terrorism have had a negative impact on Muslim communities, including but not limited to violence against Muslims and those who are perceived as Muslim, police profiling, immigration controls, travel bans, and economic hardship. Muslim hip-hop that depicts these social realities and criticizes the establishment generally flourishes. This is mainly due to the fact that in liberal Western regimes, Muslim hip-hop is part of a larger landscape that thrives on the freedom of artistic and political expressions. Censoring measures are hardly ever utilized successfully by the state. Such attempts are countered by protracted public debates on civil liberties, supported by Muslims and non-Muslims, with the debates typically increasing the publicity of the alleged offensive medium. Be that as it may, the creative license for hip-hop artists to project their Islamic identity or Muslim cause has to be negotiated within the commercial sphere, albeit with varying degrees of success.

Riz MC's journey to hip-hop is an extraordinary one. An Oxford-educated, London-born rapper of Pakistani origin named Rizwan Ahmed, he polished his MC skills while studying at Oxford and initiated the Hit & Run club night scene during his time there. In 2006, his song "Post 9/11 Blues" caught the social media world by storm. In his introduction to the music video, Riz MC lamented that the track "wasn't played by any TV or radio stations, for being 'too controversial' despite huge internet support – the song then received global media attention, and was forced back onto the airwaves . . . what do you think?"[4] As the lyrics portray:

What can I do? I got the post 9/11 blues
On the telly nothin but the post 9/11 news
War, Iraq, suicide bombs
Stop hogging the limelight
And make some room for my songs!!
Anyway its all re-runs
We need a new war, Bush go get Iran, I heard them talking "bout your mum!"
Change the channel, watch some telly for kids, but what's this?
"Hi kids welcome to fun-fun-fundamentalist"
In the breaks, Nike's advertising bomb-proof kicks
They're even showing Bin Laden's cave on Cribs!
So I picked up a respectable magazine
It told me about the new post 9/11 categories—
Israeli fighters are soldiers, Irish are paramilitary
And darkie ones are terrorists—how simple can it be?
But not me . . . my friends go: "Riz is still one of us"
But if I haven't shaved, they won't sit with me on the bus!
. . . Post 9/11 I been getting paid
Playing terrorists on telly, getting songs made
"But will it get airplay geeza?"
Well, if BBC don't want it I'll send it to Al-Jazeera

The track was initially deemed too politically sensitive for public distribution. Speaking out against the negative portrayals of Muslims that are "hogging the limelight," demanding "some room for my songs," and challenging the "new post 9/11 categories" while at the same time making a career out of "playing terrorists on telly"—all were direct criticisms of the press and media generally. Riz MC's comment on the song and the media's response to it is as follows: "It is about how the contours of our society have been distorted since 9/11, and how that affects every area of our lives . . . it's not a rant from an angry young Muslim, it's funny, and the music is quite poppy and radio-friendly. It's a shame that a satirical song like this is seen as a threat."[5] Yet the fact that the song "was forced back onto the airwaves" due to its global recognition shows the futility of censorship and the potency of the Internet's commercial value in determining the circulation of Muslim hip-hop tracks in the West. News outlets and radio stations that are always vying for novel content took note of Riz MC's poetic threat, "Well, if BBC don't want it I'll send it to Al-Jazeera." Today, Riz MC is a much-decorated artist in the mainstream hip-hop scene, even winning the MTV Video Music Award for Best Video with a Social Message in 2016 (renamed Best Fight Against the System in 2017) for his work "Immigrants (We Get the Job Done)."

Riz MC's influence as an artist goes beyond hip-hop. Although he started out making films rooted in the 9/11 experience, he later earned a name for himself as a successful Hollywood actor, gaining roles in mega productions such as *Rogue One: A Star Wars Story* and *Nightcrawler*. In 2006, Riz was detained and investigated under terrorism laws at a United Kingdom airport on his way home from the Berlin Film Festival, where he had presented his film *Road to Guantanamo*. An official at the airport, concerned about his political films, asked him point blank, "Did you become an actor mainly to do films like this, to publicize the struggles of Muslims?"[6] Undeterred, Riz went on to participate in other productions featuring the struggles of the September 11 generation. Some of these include *Britz* (2007), *Four Lions* (2010), and *The Reluctant Fundamentalist* (2013). Despite his brushes with the establishment, Riz subsequently received multiple awards and nominations in the United Kingdom and the United States for the comedy *Four Lions*, where he played a jihadi who is critical of Western imperialism.

The link between hip-hoppers and the film industry did not take long to form after the birth of the musical genre. In the United States, there has been a barrage of hip-hop-themed movies since the 1980s. Besides films based on biographies of hip-hop superstars such as Eminem (*8 Mile*), 50 Cent (*Get Rich or Die Tryin'*), and Notorious BIG (*Notorious*), other movies have attracted big-name actors like Wesley Snipes (*New Jack City*, 1991), Chris Rock (*CB4*, 1993), Taye Diggs (*Brown Sugar*, 2002), and Terrence Howard and Taraji P. Henson (both starred in *Hustle & Flow*, 2005). Queen Latifah and Muslim hip-hop icon Mos Def are common features in this genre. Since 9/11, hip-hop-themed films, whether commercial movies or critical documentaries, have become increasingly popular and are allowing Muslim voices to be heard worldwide. The level of popularity and success nonetheless differs, and films produced outside the West usually face greater challenges and often require Western patronage to get any kind of distribution.

While Riz MC's success can be attributed to his broad-based appeal, other Muslim hip-hop artists of varying niche areas also thrive in the West, albeit by engaging in slightly different strategies. Mainstream hip-hop turned *nasheed* superstar Maher Zain shot to fame by creating a platform on Facebook and uploading his music on YouTube. Within eighteen months of having an online presence, Maher became the first Muslim musician to have two million fans on Facebook. His track "Insha Allah" (God willing) has been viewed 90 million times and his "Number One for Me" 115 million times on YouTube. The Swedish singer of Lebanese origin sees the Internet and "online word of mouth" as ways to circumvent his marginalization from both the mainstream hip-hop platforms and the mainstream local radio shows. Owing to their Islamic content, Maher's songs are regarded as problematic for mainstream hip-hop charts. He attributes this to the hesitance of music labels and producers to play his songs on mainstream channels like the MTV.

Maher Zain's Internet success prompted him to take on an ambitious tour in 2010 and 2011, performing sold-out concerts in Asia, the Middle East, Europe, and North America. He recorded songs in local vernaculars, which added to his initial Internet success. The song "Insha Allah," for example, is now available in English, French, Arabic, Turkish, Malay, and Indonesian versions. He recorded the song "Allahi Allah Kiya Karo" (continuously repeating the word *Allah*) in Urdu, featuring Pakistan-born Canadian singer Irfan Makki. His reach extends even to Southeast Asia despite not rolling out a single promotional campaign in the region. He has about seventy-three thousand followers on his Maher Zain Indonesia Fans Club Facebook page while the Malaysian chapter has a staggering three hundred thousand followers. Even tiny Singapore accounted for about nine thousand fans. Likewise, Maher collaborated with Southeast Asian hip-hoppers to record his songs in the region's lingua franca, Malay. In Indonesia, he collaborated with Andi Fadly Arifuddin, iconic local singer and leading vocalist of the rock group Padi, to record "Insha Allah" and "For the Rest of My Life" in the local language, bahasa Indonesia. Beyond the affinities brought about by spoken languages, much of the Muslim world also hears in his songs the language of political change they have been yearning for.

Down under, the Muslim hip-hop landscape in Australia has been very much influenced by the migrant nature of the majority of Muslims, their ethnic and cultural diversities, and life in the working-class suburbs that is marginalizing in and of itself. It has been documented that many young Muslims have resorted to minimizing their Muslim identities on job applications to increase their likelihood of securing employment. Many cited examples of changing their names to "non-Muslim-sounding" ones and their addresses to locations with lower concentrations of Muslim residents. As in the United States, hip-hop in Australia is increasingly utilized as a form of social glue that rapidly becomes assimilated into mainstream society. In addition to the Melbourne-based grass-roots performing arts group ARAB, mentioned in chapter 2, the Australian government also recognizes the potential of appropriating hip-hop in order to reach young people. In carrying out outreach programs with different Muslim social groups in New South Wales and Victoria, the Australian Department of Immigration and Citizenship's Race Discrimination Unit showcases hip-hop music as an icebreaker to bridge the gaps between local Muslim youth.

Besides being a tool for connection and assimilation, Muslim hip-hop is also gaining a foothold in shaping national conversations. The Australian group the Brothahood has a cosmopolitan makeup, with members from Leba-nese, Egyptian, Turkish, and Burmese backgrounds. To a certain extent, the direction of their music parallels that of Australian hip-hop in general, inso-far as it calls for a strengthening of the country's multicultural identity. The Australian Human Rights Commission also recognizes the group's commit-ment to social activism. Since then, the Brothahood has taken their activism to capital cities in the Muslim world, such as Abu Dhabi, Jakarta, and Kuala Lumpur. Even so, since the release of their Islamic-based pilot album, *Lyrics of Mass Construction*, the group has adopted a different strategy. In their 2012 release, *MIXTAPE 2.0*, the group toned down their Islamic lyrics in an attempt to rid themselves of the "Muslim stigma" in mainstream society while fram-ing their activism within a more universal context. Despite these changes, they still rap about life as young Muslims in post–September 11 Australia, the Palestinian predicament, the Arab Spring, and the misrepresentation of Muslims in the media. This strategy has had the added benefit of allowing the group to be noticed for their musicality as well as their message. Their current release features legendary American hip-hop acts such as the Outlawz and Bone Thugs-n-Harmony, itself a ringing endorsement of their musical skills.

Aside from national and global reach, one Australian artist has uniquely presented himself from the lens of neighborhood nationalism. Matuse, a Mus-lim rapper of Lebanese and Syrian descent, has become popular in the Sydney hip-hop scene in the past few years. Matuse has been actively performing in Sydney and giving back to the community—among other things, by holding hip-hop workshops at the Bankstown Art Centre. He is one of the cosmopoli-tan members of Sydney vs Everybody, a hip-hop movement launched at the beginning of 2015. The movement is akin to a form of urban citizenship through "neighborhood nationalism" and "our area" discourses where the sense of place trumps other ideological and physical variations or differences of creed. Les Back (1996) has successfully employed this concept in exploring youth strategies for confronting issues of race and ethnicity within a particular locality. The Sydney vs Everybody movement focuses on the development and promotion of local hip-hop artists and is a response to the 2014 track "Detroit vs. Everybody," featuring Eminem, Royce da 5'9", Big Sean, Danny Brown, Dej Loaf, and Trick Trick. The track was inspired by the clothing line Tommey Walker designed to "rebuild Detroit's image through the restored pride of Detroiters universally."[7] The brand and its ideals of taking pride in one's locality have been embraced by the American hip-hop community, with celebrities such as Rick Ross, Young Jeezy, Drake, and Nas lending their weight to the movement.

Damien Arthur (2006) posits that "tensions within the glocal culture" are also seen with the representation of place in Australian hip-hop in cities like Adelaide, Melbourne, and Sydney. For example, he cited a comment made by Lo Quay, an editor of an Australian hip-hop magazine, about the competition and allegiance to particular local hip-hop fashions and brands, saying: "(The consumption of local Hip Hop brands is) a statement about, you know, representing local Hip-hop, and maybe Melbourne Hip-hop, depending on the shirt. Or to the point where sometimes, because there's different local clothing companies in different cities, like Sydney's got a couple, Melbourne's got a couple, so you find the Sydney people normally levitate towards the Sydney, Melbourne towards the Melbourne, and it's kinda like a friendly clothing rivalry I think as well" (Arthur 2006, 151). In his verses in the Sydney vs Everybody rendition, Matuse rapped about being singled out by a section of white Australia for his ethnic background rather than his lyrical skills. This is despite him proclaiming his allegiance to his country of residence with numerous mentions of "Australia," "Down Under," "Sydney," and the "Southwest" in his verses:

> Young & Arabian Mesopotamian alien first generation Australian
> Claiming the land that I initially came up in
> Mention my name to the lames in the game I'm in
> Watch the reaction from all of the factions
> All of the racists and bigots won't dig it
> But they will admit it's too vivid with passion
> Live it and spit it
> Ain't speaking of bridges
> Whenever I'm listing the biggest of Sydney's attractions
> Yeah
> We from Down Under, B
> Where the down and under be

Underdog till they down & under me
Sydney the city I'm repping regardless
Heavily hardened we stepping well guarded
The media's lies
& the devils bombarded
Speak for the hearts of my brothers that's martyred
The police is racist they charge us regardless
Regardless regarded
The hardest of artist freestyling around these garages
Southwest is what I represent
Where it's more than evident
They willing to arrest its residence of Lebanese decent
With no evidence
Our prime minister's sinister
Wickeder than an indigenous pillager
Figure the reason they quicker to stop me
Boss Lady will warn them
From Sydney to Harlem
I'm starving to barge in
And rep for my akhis
It's us against everybody

While cyberspace provides avenues for participation and expression, it is also rife with harsh personal attacks due to the anonymity it allows. As if on cue, immediately following the release of the track, Matuse was singled out for online abuse. One commentator on YouTube wrote, "I would've been happy if it ended before Matuse started. Track fell off HARD from then on," while another comment puts it bluntly, "I was enjoying it until the Muslim reared his head."[8] This latter criticism of Matuse, hating him for his religious beliefs, led to a strong pushback from the hip-hop community in support of their fellow artist. Sounds of the Zulu Nation anchor Johnny Bell, also known as DJ Host MK-1, articulated his disappointment of the episode and expressed his unequivocal support for Matuse in a lengthy Facebook post.[9] Despite these challenges, Matuse has also experienced much commercial success. He now travels between Sydney and New York for performances and other musical collaborations.

Such examples highlight how Muslim hip-hop can truly thrive in Western liberal states regardless of their various religious and political slants. These Muslim hip-hop artists negotiate issues of commercial viability by appealing to global or specific niches and, at the same time, enjoy protection against state sanctions despite their oppositional nature by reason of the West's encouragement of the rights of freedom of speech and expression. The same cannot be said for Muslim hip-hop artists in other parts of the world.

"ARABIAN" KNIGHTS

The global and cosmopolitan outlook brought about by the human rights messages of Muslim hip-hop has led to mixed reactions from the various gatekeepers of Muslim youth culture in different countries. Shannahan and Hussain (2011), for example, examined the state machinery at work in curtailing the Tunisian rap scene. In 2009, Amnesty International released a report stating that the Tunisian "authorities continue to use their 'security and counter-terrorism' concerns to justify arrests and other repression of Islamists, and political dissent in general—including the rights to freedom of expression, association and assembly—and arrests and harassment of alleged Islamist youth are common" (2009, 6). In Turkey, *bandrols*—a form of endorsement sticker affixed on media products—are stringently disseminated by the Ministry of Culture. A hip-hop group's application for a sticker might be turned down due to their political content. Banned from making any sort of impact in the mainstream commercial market, groups find their way to the underground scene. Here, they put up their anthems on websites or distribute them as cassettes and demo CDs (Solomon 2005, 5–6). While speaking up for their rights through music, hip-hop artists need to creatively negotiate an environment where excessive violence to quell protests is not uncommon and restrictions are imposed on the Internet and the media.

One of these precarious environments relates to the geographic separation of Muslim hip-hoppers. Jackie Reem Salloum's *Slingshot Hip Hop* (2008), showcasing Palestinian rap acts, has been screened in many general and Palestinian film festivals in cities like Toronto and Singapore. The documentary features Lyd residents DAM, Abeer Zinati (dubbed "the first lady of Palestinian rhythm and blues"[10]), and Mahmoud Shalabi (formerly of the Palestinian hip-hop crew MWR); Gaza Strip–based group the Palestinian Rapperz; and the West Bank–based group Arapeyat, a duo of female MCs, Safa and Nahwa. Salloum shared: "There is a very real geographic separation within the Palestinian hip-hop movement.... These groups are all restricted physically by the Israeli government, and the film shows how they use their music to channel their frustrations and connect with their peers." Hence, the Internet becomes the main platform for exchanges between Palestinian hip-hop outfits and the wider hip-hop *ummah*. While in Lebanon screening her documentary to large groups of Palestinian youth in the three refugee camps in Bedawi, Bourj el-Barajneh, and

Chatila, Salloum explains the plight of the hip-hoppers in her film: "They can't travel to see each other, so they trade beats and vocal tracks over the Internet. Right now, all the groups are reaching out to other Arab rappers throughout the world: the U.S.-based crews The Philistines and The NOMADS, the Iraqi hip-hop crew from Canada, Euphrates; and they are also working on collaborations with several African and Latin-America-based hip-hop crews."[11]

Cyberspace is also the platform for hip-hop acts in refugee camps to reach out to the world. In an innovative account of groups who live under severe restrictions, Yaseen of I-Voice informed the Middle East and North Africa (MENA) media watch group, Menassat, in 2008 that he and his sidekick, TNT, are working with both Dam and Ramallah Underground from the West Bank from the confines of the Lebanese refugee camp in Bourj el-Barajneh. He dreams of performing together with his Palestinian comrades, although he realizes this would be more possible in the West than in Lebanon or Palestine.

Many scholars and media observers have also pointed out that hip-hop and rap music were the soundtrack to the Arab Spring as the protest movements chanted to the poetics of young, influential rappers. For middle-class youth, the name Hamada Ben Amor, a.k.a. El General, has become synonymous with the revolutions. In an interview with *Time* magazine, he declared that he was inspired by the revolutionary lyrics of American hip-hop icon Tupac Shakur and that he was rapping "for the good of the people."[12] *Time* magazine credited a track by then twenty-one-year-old El General as "the rap anthem of the Mideast revolution," a movement that began in the rapper's backyard during the Jasmine Revolution in Tunisia. His song "Rais Lebled" (President of the country) was released on Facebook a week before the self-immolation of a fruit vendor that triggered a domino effect, with protests spreading from Tunisia to Egypt:

> Mr. President, your people are dying
> People are eating rubbish
> Look at what is happening
> Miseries everywhere Mr. President
> I talk with no fear
> Although I know I will only get troubles
> I see injustice everywhere.

The song quickly went viral. The fast-spiraling revolution induced him to pen another song, "Tunisia Our Country," that led to his arrest by the secret police. Huge public furor ensued, with incessant demands from protestors against his incarceration by the government, which lasted for three days. The Tunisian government banned his works from airing on the radio and forbade him from releasing new albums or staging any performances. Before being released from police custody, he was coerced into signing a declaration not to produce any more political tracks. Nonetheless, tens of thousands of protestors in the streets were already chanting verses from the track in unison, demanding that the president step down.

El General's revolutionary anthem echoed in the songs of other rappers. Following El General's arrest, another Tunisian rapper, Lak3y, released a nine-minute song, "Touche Pas a Ma Tunisie" (Don't touch my Tunisia). By the end of the next month, during the Egyptian revolution, "Rais Lebled" had replaced the regular Qur'anic recitation, national anthem folk poetries, and the like and was being sung in Tahrir Square in Cairo (Ibrahim 2016). Groups like the Cairo-based hip-hop trio Arabian Knightz immersed themselves in the Tahrir Square protests and posted their track "Rebel" online,[13] hoping to mobilize more people. El General, who had started the hip-hop revolution, continued to receive numerous invitations to join his hip-hop comrades and fellow Arab protestors. Indigenous hip-hop groups like the Arabian Knightz were releasing their own tracks to lend their voices, but it was El General's song that had quickly captured the imaginations of angry young Arabs in Yemen, Bahrain, Libya, and Syria. Although unable to accept any of these invitations, he wrote a new song, "Vive Tunisie!" not only to honor the fallen heroes of the Jasmine Revolution but also as a tribute to the freedom movements in Egypt, Algeria, Libya, and Morocco.

As conflicts grew throughout the Arab world, other rappers followed a similar model to call for action. Days after violence erupted in Syria, an anonymous rapper put out a track entitled "Biyan Raqam Wahid" (Communique no.1) that called for mass revolt against the government of Bashar Assad. Similarly, Libyan hip-hoppers Ibn Thabit and MC Swat criticized Gaddafi for his excesses. In 2011, then twenty-three-year-old Youssef Ramadan Said, also known as MC Swat, released "Hadhee Thowra" (This is revolution), in which he beseeched Libyans to take to the streets and rebel against the dictator. He has since been arrested a few times for his confrontational style and for criticizing the post-Gaddafi regimes, and he is trying to seek political asylum in Europe.

Hip-hop in the Arab Spring was used in two ways. At one level, it was a tool of mass mobilization, spreading positive messages about the protests through rap. The tracks symbolized the anger of the people and harnessed the collective emotion of the populace, condensing it into rhythmic verses. Scholars of moral protests have rightly singled out emotions as central in the social solidarity of moral protests (Jasper 1997; Kamaludeen 2017). However, as Julius Bailey emphasizes in *Philosophy and Hip-Hop* (2014), contrary to popular belief in the savageness of Muslims, Arabs and rap and hip-hop culture as a whole denounce violence. This point cannot be emphasized enough in the current climate of Islamophobia and the war on terror, where Arab and Muslim violence is overpublicized and overpoliticized. Against this backdrop, young Muslim hip-hoppers measure their responses, scathing and directly critical of the failings of the ruling regimes but at the same time not justifying bloodshed as a solution. The second level at which hip-hop operates is toward the global audience to solicit attention, support, and ultimately aid for the cause of the protesters. Through hip-hop culture, rappers often make the case that the Muslim fight for liberty against authoritarian regimes is similar to the African American struggle for civil rights and equality.

The year 2011 was a major turning point, not just in the relationship between young Muslims and hip-hop but in the history of hip-hop culture in the Middle East and Northern Africa. Balti, a former member of Wled Bled, was Tunisia's most famous rapper in the 1990s and early 2000s when rap was relatively unknown and police crackdowns had driven his contemporaries into exile—including Ferid El Extranjero for, among other works, his song "3bed Fi Terkina" (In an open-air prison). After his arrest by the Interior Ministry, Balti turned to commercial rap for a chance to make a living out of his music. Soon he was earning substantial income from ticket sales, of which a large portion went to the Tunisian government, who saw him as a lucrative revenue source. Despite maintaining that he was merely working on his art and was not beholden to the state, his popularity plummeted in the aftermath of the fall of Ben Ali, Tunisia's embattled president of twenty-three years. The landscape for Tunisian hip-hop, as with similar regimes, had shifted in favor of revolutionary tunes, with the country's rappers eager to establish their revolutionary credentials. Rap journalist El Mekki was quoted in *SPIN* magazine: "Now everyone is looking at rappers as the new elite of the country.... When everyone was silent, they spoke up. When everyone was at home, they went to the streets shouting and fighting against the police. So today, the old generation is feeling guilty and giving rap much more respect" (Peisner 2011b).

In the mid-2000s, closely following the rise of these new "elites" and the fact that it was no longer easy for oppressive regimes to co-opt hip-hop, another revolution occurred: social media. Underground rap and other similar social movements already existed, but without an ideal medium for revolution. As David Peisner (2011a) observed, amid the mostly Arabic and French graffiti sprawled on the barrier surrounding a makeshift monument to the Tunisian revolution, one slogan in English stood out: "THANK YOU FACEBOOK."

Social media posts had become the proxy for liberal journalism in these oppressive regimes, and they were accepted as legitimate references for journalists
and broadcasted by mainstream media outlets such as CNN, the BBC, and
especially Al Jazeera. The "CNN effect," which had a profound influence on foreign policies in the late Cold War period, had found its successor in Facebook.

The relationship between hip-hop and authoritarian countries entered a
new era due to the increasing strife in the region over the last decade. The
chaos in Syria, for example, has ironically benefitted Syrian hip-hop by catapult-
ing it into the global scene. Intense surveillance from the state has increasingly
driven hip-hop acts like Damascus-based LaTlateh out of the country, forcing
the group to widen their audience and travel the Middle East to perform. Abu
Koulthoum, a third of the group LaTlateh, which also includes Al Sayyed Dar-
wish and Watar, professed defiantly: "The most important thing right now is
to create a space for free expression—a freedom of expression that was stifled
to the point that two or three years ago we could not even imagine that a revolution would even happen. . . . Whatever happens—whether the regime falls
or not—we need to create this space and enlarge it."[14] Middle Eastern hip-
hoppers often have to operate outside their own localities and with overseas
sponsorship. His groupmate Watar, although acknowledging support from the
United States and its allies, lamented the insufficiency of the funding and the
difficulties of making music before the uprisings: "Our problems were pretty
simple. There was simply no support. We did our first concert by paying for
it ourselves. . . . We did other concerts with money from the US embassy and
French cultural centre—but it was only really symbolic funding. Of course
there are always problems with cultural activities in Syria. The regime was
afraid of cultural expression."[15] These "foreign interests," whether journalistic,
academic, or economic, undoubtedly fueled anxiety on the part of the regime,
particularly due to the strategy of what scholars and observers are calling "hip-
hop diplomacy," which is regularly deployed by Western powers in Muslim
countries. Utilizing music in US foreign policy is not new. During the Cold
War, the United States engaged in "jazz diplomacy," which involved renowned
artists such as Louis Armstrong and Duke Ellington performing overseas.

Hence, the homological imagination, the sense that young Muslim kids are
imagining themselves as sharing a similar destiny with their African American
sisters and brothers, is not entirely conceptualized by the former. It is nourished
and concretized by those at the center of hip-hop through collaborations and
visits to Muslim lands in the name of solidarity. The United States Embassy
has been actively engaging in hip-hop diplomacy since 2005, at times working hand in hand with its other September 11 policy initiative in the Muslim

world, which is sponsoring Sufism. Fait Muedini's *Sponsoring Sufism: How Governments Promote "Mystical Islam" in Their Domestic and Foreign Policies* (2015) meticulously maps out how countries are now aligning themselves with mystical Islam as they perceive Sufism to be apolitical and hence not a threat to their continued dominance. These alliances also confer on the patron regimes a sense of credibility for being Muslim friendly. In the same vein, Hisham Aidi's *Rebel Music* (2014) delves into how, after September 11, governments and their apparatuses started to chart the ways Sufism could be appropriated in Asia, Africa, and the West. For instance, the RAND Corporation's *Civil Democratic Islam: Partners, Resources, and Strategies* (2003, 63) encourages Western governments to support folk Islam through embracing those who practice Sufism while simultaneously provoking "disagreements between traditionalists and fundamentalists." Also in 2004, the Nixon Center held a conference to discuss how Sufism could be used as a tool of US foreign policy. Likewise, the American Center for Strategic Intelligence Research produced a monograph proposing Sufism as "an exploitable fissure in the bulwark of Islam" (Lambert 2005, 168). Music, of course, also plays a very significant part. These multipronged initiatives are best encapsulated by the comment by former secretary of state Hillary Clinton, who candidly talked about hip-hop diplomacy as a form of soft power: "I can't point to a change in Syrian foreign policy because Chen Lo and the Liberation Family showed up [laughter]. But I think we have to use every tool at our disposal. We move a lot of different pieces on the chess board every day."[16]

These initiatives involve inviting influential native groups to make pilgrimages to the United States to showcase their talent in front of key players in the hip-hop industry and encouraging American artists to perform in the Muslim world. In 2013, Tariq Snare, an American drummer and author of *Children Can Play Hip-Hop Drums* who converted to Islam, was sent to the Middle East as part of the ongoing initiative. Tariq cuts a popular figure and straddles the mainstream and Muslim hip-hop scenes, having collaborated with Queen Latifah, Native Deen, Sami Yusuf, and legends like Stevie Wonder. Tariq, noticing the rise of hip-hop from Tunisia to Egypt to Saudi Arabia, lauded the reach of the popular genre, "Hip hop has so much to do with changing and letting people who have no voice [speak]; some people can't even read and write but they can rap."[17] In talking to journalists, he noted links between Muslim youth in the region and African American youth in the Bronx, emphasizing hip-hop's twin abilities to give voice to the voiceless and to express the aspirations of the underclass.

Attempts at hip-hop diplomacy are not limited to the United States government. In 2010, the Australian government presented its Hip-Hop Is Harmony in Diversity Tour, which included Omar Musa and the Brothahood. The hip-hoppers toured Surabaya, Yogyakarta, and Jakarta in Indonesia, performing with local acts Kua Etnika, Jogja Hip-hop, Saykoji, and JFlow. The tour in Southeast Asia was funded by the Australia International Cultural Council, which is Australia's main cultural diplomacy organ within the Australian Department of Foreign Affairs and Trade. This effort at hip-hop diplomacy is explicitly advertised on the Australian Embassy Indonesia website.[18]

Unsurprisingly, these attempts at hip-hop diplomacy are not always successful. Kendra Salois (2014), in her work on the US government's efforts in Morocco, captures the tensions surrounding this diplomacy. There are many reasons why these collaborations can become difficult. Language is one, as some Arab rappers are not conversant in English. A second difficulty lies in the different styles adopted by the hip-hoppers both in terms of performance and lyrical content. Another challenge that is not always obvious is the potential for fierce criticism faced by those who participate in the program. Chen Lo from the Lo Frequency writes in his blog: "Though we acknowledge the US's *attempted* use of hip-hop, and other forms of art and culture, as a tool to serve the interests of the US, that didn't impact the music we performed on tour *or the sincerity of our movement.* Our intent was and still is to share our music and experiences with the world and to connect with real people in ways we can all relate to" (Salois 2014, 245). Chen Lo's sentiment reflects the agency among most, if not all, hip-hop practitioners to be authentic to their craft. This is a challenge for hip-hoppers who have been drafted by the state or are perceived to be associated with the state. Youssef Ben Ismail, in his interview with some members of Zomra, a collective of Tunisian hip-hoppers, recorded the group's frustration at being reduced to a symbol of political representation at the expense of their artistic creation. According to Zomra member Castro: "You know that not long ago I was a campaigner in UGET? I am very political! Political rap, the idea of critical rap, it's important. We do it in Zomra too. But it's the artist's responsibility to resist being confined to a symbol. The moment an artist becomes the bearer of a single message, of a single idea, he becomes a puppet."[19]

More specific to this book, there has been a proliferation of hip-hop-based films and documentaries released over the last decade or so that portray the social realities of the September 11 generation from a Muslim perspective. Arabic hip-hop has been well-represented in Joshua Asen's *I Love Hip-Hop in Morocco* (2007), Ahmad Abdalla's *Microphone* (2010), and Nicholas Mangialardi's *Egyptian Underground* (2012). They do not just depict young Arabs mimicking black culture but also, for instance, mixing sounds borrowed from the West with music from classical Arabic singers. This is one strategy Muslim hip-hoppers have devised to introduce hip-hop culture into their native countries. This approach enables groups to test the market on the receptivity of their new sounds, to create a niche for themselves and their unique brand, and to attempt to convert listeners of classical indigenous music to their form of music.

Because governments are aware of the potency and popularity of hip-hop culture among urban minority youth, a trend has arisen among conservative societies to liberalize the music landscape to attract foreign talent and respond to the increasing desire of youth for more access to sounds heard on the Internet. Today, hip-hop music has even found its way to conservative Saudi Arabia. Saudi hip-hop group Dark2Men was one of eight finalists from the Middle East in an MTV Arabia show, launched in 2007. The group has discussed the intense pressure they faced from family, the workplace, and the state in creating and performing their music. Owing to the stringent socioreligious laws in their native country, which prohibit the free association of males and females who are unrelated and even forbid music studies in school, Dark2Men had never performed in public going into the regional competition. This was in stark contrast to the other rappers in the competition from Lebanon, Egypt, and the UAE who were relatively seasoned performers. Undeterred, the group, who met virtually through a rap website, was committed to making history in the conservative kingdom. Tamer Farhan of the three-man outfit fondly recounts the support they received from the September 11 generation, "Young guys come up to us and say: 'We thought that pursuing a dream in Saudi Arabia was impossible. You guys made it in hip-hop with everyone against you. That gives us hope that even here, anything is possible.'"[20]

Qusai Khidr, also known as Don Legend, a pioneering Saudi rapper, defends himself and other hip-hoppers in the documentary *Lyrics Revolt*, stating: "We're not politicians. We're not businessmen. We're not soldiers. We are hip-hop artists."[21] Qusai hosted MTV Arabia's popular show *Hip-Hop Na* (My hip-hop) with Farid "Fredwreck" Nassar. Fredwreck, a Palestinian American music producer, is noted in the Arab hip-hop scene for having collaborated with American superstars 50 Cent and Snoop Dogg. The overwhelmingly favorable response to the show caught the eye of foreign investors enticed by the staggering youth market. It is no surprise, then, that in 2011, the first Saudi hip-hop radio show, *Laish Hip-Hop* (Why hip-hop), became a huge success not only in the Arab region but also internationally. Its Jeddah-born host, Hassan Ahmad Dennaoui, a.k.a. Big Hass, who counts Middle Eastern rappers like Narcicyst, Shadia Mansour, Omar Offendum, and Lowkey among his inspirations, has catapulted to fame and has been invited to emcee across the globe.

Muslim hip-hop in this region, therefore, leverages very different strategies to thrive amid the profound state management in their countries—from utilizing the Internet to navigate geographical separations preventing them from uniting on a common stage to harnessing the power of social media in the relentless project of speaking truth to power, which in some cases has led to its demise. Other strategies employed by Muslim hip-hoppers facing strict state control include leveraging foreign cultural diplomacy projects to finance their craft and simply riding the wave of liberalization, however limited, for commercial purposes. Despite the common perception of the ultraconservative nature of their societies, these hip-hoppers have managed to gain widespread recognition in their countries. And, amid these indigenous concerns, they still strive to remain authentic to the genre.

HIP-HOP IN THE MUSLIM ARCHIPELAGO

Although many Muslims reside in the Middle East, Indonesia has the largest Muslim population in the world, with Muslims making up 40 percent of the population in the Southeast Asian region. In Malaysia, 61 percent of the population is Muslim, and in Indonesia, it is 87 percent. Both are secular states, although Malaysia adopts Islam as its official religion and Indonesia's first principle in its state ideology of Pancasila is the "Belief in One God." Of the three countries discussed in this section, Singapore is the only one with a minority Muslim population, at about 15 percent. However, Singapore's cultural and religious flow with Malaysia and its proximity to Indonesia necessitate the state to act carefully in matters pertaining to religion and its Muslim population (Kamaludeen, Pereira, and Turner 2010). Looking at Muslim hip-hop in this region entails not only a provincialization of Muslims from the Middle East but also that of hip-hop from its African American roots. The "soft authoritarian" model of state management in Indonesia, Malaysia, and Singapore, which is the focus of this section, is vastly different from the models of liberal democracy in the West and the autocratic regimes of the Arab world. In this region, these states have generally adopted democratic frameworks of government, achieved considerable economic and social development, and had nation-building success of varying degrees. Although they eschew granting absolute freedom, these countries are less likely to use state machinery, such as the secret police, to clamp down on dissent. As such, the state management of hip-hop, as with many other matters, must intricately straddle the various stakeholders in society through a plethora of means, such as the sporadic use of legal tools, the procurement of other cultural (often religious) gatekeepers, and the promotion of co-opted, sanitized, and/or commercial versions of hip-hop.

Much of the peripheralization of hip-hop from the airwaves in Muslim-majority countries can be attributed to the concerns of indigenous moral entrepreneurs regarding its compatibility with Islamic tenets. The conversations in this regard are dynamic and at times tense and involve various strata of society. In this region, hip-hop has even been addressed by national leaders. Singapore, for example, has been historically suspicious of its youth cultures. The rapport between the state and its young Muslims hit low levels between the 1970s and 1990s, when rock culture was at its peak. The stereotypes attached to these *Mat* rockers (*Mat* being a Malay derivative of the common Muslim name Muhammad, much like Mo in the UK) have often caused these youth great unease. They were often seen as uneducated, drug abusers, and rebels against the religious *da'wah* movement. Compounding their predicament, in the 1970s the government rolled out policies specifically intended to stem "hippie" culture among Singaporean youth. Long hair, for example, was illegal for men. Despite some amount of public outcry, the state maintained that this was a necessary measure to maintain social cohesion in Singaporean society. Eager to snub the influence of "decadent" Western values, Rajaratnam, a former Singaporean minister, was famously noted to have proclaimed in 1972, "If our citizens are asked to sacrifice a few inches of dead cells [long hair] to keep Singapore safe from the scrounge of hippism, I would not believe for a moment that democracy is dead in Singapore. It is not founded on hair."[22] The approaches of moral entrepreneurs such as the state and Islamic religious organizations evolved on almost parallel trajectories. Despite the general reluctance to demonize rock and pop in the 1980s, the reemergence of the perils of Western cultural influences and a reassertion of "Asian (Confucian) values" (Kong and Yeoh 2003) in state discourse form the context for the decision to ban slam dancing in 1992. Slam dancing, which was closely associated with the music of the other (defined as the West), was considered immoral.

Despite the region's difficult relationship with rock culture, rock music has seen a reversal in fortunes of late. In Malaysia, the conservative Islamic Party PAS recently featured rockers such as Amy Search, Ali XPDC, and Sham Kamikaze at their events amid their newly embraced mantra of *hiburan Islam* (Islamic entertainment), fronted by its youth activists. Known for shunning pop music and engaging in regular protests of concerts showcasing Western artists such as Michael Learns to Rock, Avril Lavigne, rapper Pitbull, and hip-hop artist Rihanna, the party has taken a new stance to appropriate music as a form of *da'wah*, as long as it is performed by good Muslims who do not portray a sinful lifestyle or present immoral messages in their lyrics and stage shows (Mueller 2014).

In Indonesia, rock music has been rejuvenated by virtue of the spectacular endorsement of none other than the head of state, Jokowi Widodo, a well-known metalhead. The president has been a regular fixture at rock concerts since his youth in the 1990s and has no qualms professing his affinity for Metallica, Megadeth, and Napalm Death. In 2013, Widodo's known passion for heavy metal got him into some trouble. He was given a bass guitar signed by Metallica's Robert Trujillo while serving as the governor of Indonesia's capital city of Jakarta. The Ibanez guitar became the center of controversy when it was seized by anticorruption officers, who alleged the guitar was a bribe. In seizing the instrument, Indonesia's Corruption Eradication Commission (KPK) declared that their reasoning was due to the handwritten message on the guitar, which reads, "Giving back . . . Keep playing that cool, funky bass"; as the authorities argued, "In Indonesian, [those] words could have a meaning of asking for something in return."[23] However, it is undeniable that Widodo's patronage of rock culture endeared him to throngs of young voters in the country. If Obama is known as the first hip-hop president (Alim and Smitherman 2012), Widodo is referred to as the first heavy metal president by his supporters.[24] In 2017, the prime minister of Denmark presented the Indonesian president with a set of Metallica's records during a visit to the Bogor Palace and then sent a tweet celebrating the event. Widodo, smiling contentedly, promptly acknowledged his Danish counterpart for having understood his favorite music.[25]

Muslim Southeast Asia's recent embrace of Western popular music has been marked by a flurry of academic works documenting this turn of events (Lockard 1998; Weintraub 2011; Daniels 2013; Schmidt 2017). These significant trends aside, unadulterated Western music, which is not amalgamated with local tastes and fused into indigenous sensitivities such as *dangdut* and *nasheed*, faced a difficult start in Southeast Asia. This is the main thrust of the monographs and compilations on popular culture and Islam in Southeast Asia. Despite the scholarly field's eagerness to document the diverse strains of music that have made inroads into the Muslim populace, it is strange that hip-hop, the dominant popular culture today, still remains elusive and has been given only minor attention thus far.

As with rock music, hip-hop endured a sketchy relationship with the power holders in the region. Hip-hop music in Indonesia faced a high-profile dismissal in the mid-1990s. The former Indonesian president Badaruddin Jusuf Habibie, then in his capacity as minister of research and technology, famously voiced his discontent over suggestions to organize a national rap festival, proclaiming: "The younger generation shouldn't want to be enslaved by an aspect of foreign culture which isn't even liked in its own country. It's not even appropriate over there, much less in Indonesia, it's not suitable. . . . I don't agree with it because it's of no use whatsoever, especially for the young generation" (Massardi 1995, 106).[26] Habibie went on to criticize hip-hop music as lacking in art. After watching a rap performance at a television station on New Year's Eve, he gave a damning verdict of the genre and advised his citizens that not all culture from developed countries should be held in high esteem. To the contrary, the lyrics of rap music can be outright dirty, ugly, tasteless, and hence an overall negative force. A strategy taken by hip-hop outfits like JHF and Jahanam (Destruction) to counter the state censure of their craft is to position themselves as custodians of their ethnic culture and heritage by adopting a hybridized or glocalized version of hip-hop. Both groups rap in their own Javanese dialect and focus on literary folk tales in their lyrics, fusing hip-hop beats with traditional indigenous instruments.

In Malaysia, the multiaward-winning 2010 reality show *Showdown*, which showcased the best hip-hop break-dancers, krumpers, and poppers in the country vying for the top prize, was turned into a feature film six years later with the same name. To even begin to understand the struggles of hip-hoppers in finding a niche in the conservative local music industry and to grasp the significance of the release of *Showdown*, it is important to understand the context in which the movie emerged. The movie was released more than two decades after hip-hop arrived in the country with the breakout of Malay all-male groups, including 4U2C and KRU, and all-female groups Res 2 and Feminin. To be marketable at that time, these groups had to infuse their music with pop sounds. They gained widespread acceptance for their blend of music and were even featured in Malaysia's 1993 Temasya Aidilfitri show celebrating the end of Ramadan that aired on national television. Armed with moves from 1990s sensation Vanilla Ice, the groups took to the stage announcing rap as the choice of the new generation and then ended their gig with a proclamation of their love for the nation.

Censorship is likely for hip-hop acts that do not comply with the norms of what is considered acceptable entertainment. Within weeks of the release of Malaysia's first "genuine" hip-hop album in 1995 by hip-hop collective Naughtius Maximus, nine tracks from the album were abruptly banned by Radio Televisyen Malaysia for being "too Westernized."[27] Even with their massive commercial success, KRU was also banned in 1995 for their demeanor, fashion sense, and social commentaries. In 1997, they had difficulties securing the permits for their KRUmania tour, in part owing to the authorities' objection to the term *mania*, as the state was concerned that it would have an adverse impact on young people. Unfortunately, the financial crisis of 1997 was the end of many of these burgeoning acts.

Much has changed since 9/11. The new millennium has seen hip-hop make a comeback in Malaysia with renewed vigor. In 2010, three of Malaysia's biggest rappers, SonaOne, Joe Flizzow, and Altimet, collaborated on a track called

"Who Do It Better." In the song, Altimet rhymes in Malay about being schooled by hip-hop's earliest stars while pointing to his Eric B & Rakim T-shirt. Four years later, Joe Flizzow and SonaOne collaborated on a track called "Apa Khabar" (How are you) that discusses how far hip-hop has come in Malaysia. The track went on to win two national music awards. That same year, SonaOne, who is part of a group of Malaysian hip-hop producers called G.O.D. Music (Gentlemen on Dinosaurs), was awarded the best song for "No More"—the first time an English song had managed to clinch the title in the Malaysian *Anugerah Industri Muzik*'s entire twenty-one year history.[28]

Digital media at the turn of the millennium proved to be influential for hip-hop culture in the Muslim Archipelago. In a study on youth in Indonesia conducted through the lens of youth innovation and the effects of new media, Juliastuti (2006) argued that since the year 2000, Indonesia has experienced a proliferation of youth publications that have shifted from the normal discussion of the political issues of the day to a "celebration of communities and self-existence." The youth-produced new media, often in the form of photocopied publications disseminated within the youth networks of Indonesian cities, is used as a platform for transmitting ideas. The publications range from poetry to short stories, films, visual arts, rave parties, and even writings that critique the influence of capitalism in the music industry. It was reported in 2004 that 223 alternative media, run by people who were born in the 1980s, existed in Indonesia (Juliastuti 2006, 142). Although some of these publications are short-lived, the range illustrates the consumption of global trends in everyday life. Coupled with a rising number of personal blogs, new media has given young people a newfound sense of freedom to fulfill their desires for self-expression and a medium to publicize their private space. These expressions are further fueled by the explosion of information brought about by the proliferation of social media.

As seen in the case of Indonesia, the collision of authoritarianism and hip-hop culture does not necessarily lead to outright censure by the state. This relationship is increasingly characterized by uncertainty, ambiguity, and the realization of the implausibility of a total clampdown on hip-hop in the digital age. The following comment from Yaacob Ibrahim, Singapore's former minister-in-charge of Muslim affairs, provides insight into this evolving relationship between illiberal regimes and hip-hop in some countries in Southeast Asia:

> For instance, some of us may wonder about the effect that hip-hop culture has on our youth. How should we view this? Is it good or bad? Is it a passing phase that some young people go through or is it a symptom of alienation? Is it a negative influence or can it be harnessed to bring across positive messages

to our youth? As we explore, we realize it is just not possible to have black or white perspectives on this issue and indeed, on many issues that affect young people. Perhaps, a more useful approach to understanding youth phenomena is to start by finding out how young people themselves view the world, while holding in check our own assumptions and premature judgments. Understanding the thoughts and aspirations of our young people is the first step towards integrating the youth into the community. This Conference is therefore a useful platform that will help us understand the various perspectives and worldviews of our youth. It is only by understanding our youth that we can start finding better ways to engage young people and help them bring out the best in themselves. (Kamaludeen 2016b, 83)

The comment by the former minister shows an obvious shift in the way the state is managing youth consumption of Western-influenced music.

The government's change in its approach to young people may be partially attributable to the state's concern with hip-hop, violence, and, particularly, terrorism. In 2007, the Singapore government estimated that there were six thousand webpages sponsoring radicalism, with a significant number featuring "rap music and MTV-style editing" in order to appeal to the younger demography. Chat rooms and other platforms for social networking clearly attract the media-savvy generation. Video images of persecuted Muslims globally, such as those involved in the Israeli-Palestinian conflict, call upon Muslims' opposition to Western encroachment. The websites even feature hip-hop and rap musicians who push for jihadism (Mohamed 2008). As *self-radicalization* becomes the buzzword in Singapore's terrorism industry, the Internal Security Department of Singapore adopts a more youthful, engaging method in reaching out to young Muslims in local institutes of higher learning. Hairulanuar Bohari, a twenty-one-year-old student from the Institute of Technical Education, was among a group of youth who promoted the role of musicians in stamping out extremist ideologies. In a youth workshop, one of the ideas raised by participants was for cafes and music studios to be incorporated within mosques in order to entice young people (Zakir 2008).

In a strategy not unique to the region, the Singapore government's recognition of hip-hop's popularity and power has resulted in its co-option of the music. Along with national trends to liberalize Singapore's music landscape to serve as a magnet for foreign talent and respond to the increasing consumption of these genres in the digital age, the state and Muslim organizations have immersed themselves in a celebration of hip-hop culture. By extension, local Muslim organizations, including mosques, have slowly become more embracing of aspects of hip-hop culture. The presence of hip-hop performers alongside *nasheed* groups is a commonplace at Malay/Muslim community events. One of the Islamic Religious Council of Singapore (MUIS) annual events, Ramadan Youth Challenge, called upon local R&B singer Imran Ajmain, along with other performing artists. Several mosques, with MUIS's sponsorship, have also organized a Malay songwriting competition in honor of the Prophet's life, allowing the participants to infuse diverse elements, including hip-hop and R&B.[29] Malay/Muslim organizations like the 4PM group also organized a "hip-hop battle" to attract young Muslims to their various activities.

Although the relationships of the Singapore government and religious authorities with Muslim youth and rock music have been relatively straightforward and well-documented (Fu and Liew 2009; Kong 2006), the dynamics of state, youth, and hip-hop in the post–September 11 era are more complex. Hip-hop has been periodically appropriated by the Singapore state to spread national messages and "propagandistic slogans" (Tan 2009, 115). This is evident in several music videos, including one made in 2007 by the Media Development Authority featuring high-level Chinese bureaucrats rapping and another released in 2003 featuring local comedic icon Phua Chu Kang disseminating information about measures needed to fight the outbreak of the SARS disease. This state-engineered rap was argued to be the state's "hegemonic player (broadcast media), valiantly co-creating with and co-opting the grassroots through appropriating rap for its presumed accessibility to larger demographics and disseminating this (eventually over the Internet) via a music video (narrow-cast media)" (Tan 2009, 126).

Even Singapore's opposition group, the Singapore Democratic Party (SDP), has cashed in on the popularity of hip-hop culture over the past few years, with several videos released on YouTube, entitled "Roo Boys Hip-Hop from Queenstown Prison," documenting the release of two of its Muslim youth activists from prison; they were waited on by a group of supporters that included the former SDP chairman Jufrie Mahmood. The activists had been detained for wearing T-shirts picturing a kangaroo in a judge's gown during the defamation hearing between Minister Mentor Lee Kuan Yew and the Singapore Democrats.[30] With one of the released activists shouting *"Merdeka!"* (freedom), a banner with the words "Hip-Hop Hooray" was hoisted in the background, with the rest of the group breaking into a song. While the rap anthem "Hip-Hop Hooray" was made famous by the American group Naughty by Nature in 1993, reaching number one on the *Billboard* charts, the version belted out by the small crowd was an unrecognizable melancholic one.

Singapore Muslim hip-hop and critical hip-hop are primarily produced by Singapore Malay Muslim youth for Singapore Malay Muslim youth. Mainly as a result of out-of-bounds, or OB markers laid down by the state, which ensures that critical issues surrounding interethnic dynamics and state-society relations are not broached on national radio and television channels, mainstream hip-hop in Singapore tends to be uniquely insular. The most successful outfit, Ahli Fiqir (Thinking group), devotes their songs to deriding the Malay Muslim community for stereotypical traits such as the community's perceived laziness and propensity for a life of crime. This narrative is best encapsulated in their popular track "Samseng," which means "gangster" in the Chinese dialect of Hokkien. In the song, the group chastises those who slip into deviant lifestyles and consequentially contribute to the stigmatizing of the entire community.

The other form of hip-hop that states in this region have allowed to flourish is that of popular, or commercial, hip-hop. In Malaysia and Indonesia, the Muslim market is large enough to even support the *nasheed*-hip-hop fusion discussed in chapter 2. The voices of Muslim scholars in these countries are influential enough to induce Muslim hip-hop artists in Malaysia and Indonesia to seek collaborations with established *nasheed* groups in a bid to flaunt the genre's compatibility with Islam. Given Singapore's minority Muslim population, however, these developments are uncommon, leaving commercial hip-hop among Singapore Muslims to address the more popular themes of love and life, if not the self-reflexive form like that performed by Ahli Fiqir.

Even so, limited economic opportunities in Singapore have created a talent drain of Singapore youth to neighboring Malaysia. Sleeq, formed in 2005, is arguably one of Singapore's most successful hip-hop acts, winning Singapore's Most Popular Artist award at the regional awards show, Anugerah Planet Muzik, together with Taufik Batisah and Hady Mirza in 2007 and 2008. The duo, composed of cousins Ahmad "Syarif" Syarifullah and Alif Abdullah, broke into the Malaysian market some years ago, performing in Malaysia's Merdeka Day Hip-Hop Festival and winning some preliminary acknowledgments, like the Maxis Malaysia's Artist of the Month. Syarif, who also won Singapore's Malay TV channel's Most Popular Male Personality award, remarked, "In Malaysia, people really look at their actors and singers as idols. . . . In Singapore, you don't really get the same response. Because we're such a small country, you can bump into anyone anytime, anywhere."[31] In 2010, their song "Untuk Dia" also topped Brunei's Pelangi FM Charts for four consecutive weeks. They made the permanent move to Malaysia in 2013 under the advice of Singapore's acting icon Aaron Aziz. Thirty-nine-year-old Aaron, who earned Malaysia's Most Popular Artist award in both 2011 and 2013, moved to Kuala Lumpur in 2004. Sleeq, formerly managed by Imran Ajmain's Beats Society, signed with Aaron Aziz Productions, Aaron's management-cum-production company, in 2011.

For these artists, their "ouster" was not due to the state's overt policies against the hip-hop genre but rather the dismal socioeconomic conditions in the musical and sporting arenas where Malay youth tend to flourish. In 2012, Sleeq, in collaboration with Aaron, released a track called "Salam Semua" (Peace to all) where they talked about the pain of having to live in self-imposed exile to ply their craft.

For Singaporean hip-hop artists, issues of national representation tend to come to the fore because of the populist nature of their hip-hop, which ignores universal concerns such as human rights. The trend of Singaporean artists crossing the causeway to the land of their Malay brothers and sisters in Malaysia in search of better economic opportunities has attracted controversy. At home, they are criticized for forgetting their roots and thinking they are too good for their own country, themes that are also expressed in the "Salam Semua" track. In the host countries, some Malaysian artists also registered their anger at Singaporeans' success in their entertainment industry. After Aaron's national award, a Malaysian artist wrote on his blog and on Twitter, "I'll be more proud if a Malaysian had won!!! Thank you fellow Malaysians for encouraging foreign artistes to tarnish our art!"[32] This othering of Singaporeans has led to an enhanced striving by Singaporean entertainers not just in terms of effort but also in public exhibitions of loyalty to their newfound home. As a case in point, Aaron's public proclamation that he preferred Malaysian prime minister Najib to his Singaporean counterpart predictably became an issue of intense debate, especially in the island city-state.[33]

An interesting point of comparison between Muslim hip-hop in this region as opposed to other parts of the world concerns the appropriation of Islam or Islamic terminologies. Whereas the term *Allah* has been freely adopted by the NOI and Five Percenter Muslims in the West in innovative ways, it proves particularly contentious in an Islamic space like Southeast Asia, especially when it is used by non-Muslims. In August 2016, Malaysian Chinese rapper Namewee was arrested after about twenty nongovernmental organizations reported him for insulting Islam in his track "Oh My God!" The video included backdrops of places of worship in Malaysia with interjections of "Allah" punctuating its lyrics. In his defense, Namewee contends that his intention was to promote religious harmony.

Recently, Malaysians have had a troubling history of stopping non-Muslims from appropriating the Arabic word *Allah* to refer to God. In 2014, Malaysia's highest court decided against the Catholic Church in their appeal to overturn a ban on the use of the word *Allah* in their publications. The verdict was the culmination of a seven-year wrangle that started when the Ministry of Home

Affairs threatened to rescind the permit for the Catholic Church's *Herald* newspaper for its use of the word *Allah* in its Malay editions. While the Christian hierarchy contended that the word predates Islam, having existed in Bibles and other religious documents, the authorities were concerned that it would lead to apostasy among Malay Muslims and cause public disorder amid religious tensions in the country. Several cases of attacks against the churches were reported over the years, as some Malays found the church's prolonged court battles to be outright provocations against Islam. In a diverse country where Malay Muslims make up more than half of the population, and Christians who are predominantly from Chinese, Indian, and indigenous communities number around 10 percent of the population, the tendency to appropriate racial and religious politics for the incumbent regime is high. Interestingly, the ruling came in the aftermath of the 2013 Malaysian general elections, where the ruling party, Barisan Nasional, lost the popular vote for the first time, by more than 3 percent, to the opposition party, Pakatan Rakyat.

The ban took the Muslim world by surprise. Within the region, Indonesian cleric Yahya Chohil, from the country's most represented religious organization, Nahdlatul Ulama, expressed his bewilderment at the claim that the word *Allah* is exclusive to Muslims, saying that he could not find a similar idea in any Islamic debates in the past. Wan Saiful Wan Jan, the executive director of the Institute for Democracy and Economic Affairs, a research foundation based in Malaysia's capital city, stated succinctly: "This Palestinian guy came up to me and said: The world is laughing at you. I'm from an Arab country and everyone uses the word, every day."[34]

Despite Indonesian tolerance regarding the use of the word *Allah* when speaking of the Malaysian experience, the country has not been spared from controversy when it comes to appropriating Islam to fit with popular culture. In May 2015, Ade Armando, a lecturer at the University of Indonesia, triggered a public outcry and was reported to the local police when various national media sources reported the headline, "Allah Pleased if the Quran Is Read in the Style of Hip-Hop."[35] The news reports carried Armando's comment on his Facebook and Twitter accounts: "Allah is not an Arab. For sure Allah will be pleased if His verses are read in the style of Minang, Ambon, Chinese, hip-hop, blues."[36] His comment attracted death threats and a barrage of attacks from many quarters amid claims of apostasy. The criticisms were made on two fronts. The first condemnation was ontological and revolved around the reduction of Allah to an Arab person. How can God be compared to man? And, if the two cannot be likened, then how is man able to grasp the likes and dislikes of God except those that He has revealed in the divine scripture and through his messengers?

The second criticism is less philosophical and more pertinent in the context of this book.

Many voiced their displeasure with Armando's proposal to appreciate the Islamic sacred text through mediums like hip-hop. Anne Rasmussen contends that infusions of Qur'anic recitation in musical form are sacred performances that draw heavily from the Middle East and rely on the Arab aesthetics and the "imagination of Arab authenticity" (2010, 169). Thus, following Rasmussen, the amalgamation of the Qur'an even with sounds indigenous to the Malay community was controversial. Most hip-hop artists, even those who see the craft as a powerful tool for *da'wah,* shun the incorporation of Qur'anic verses, in its original Arabic form, into their lyrics. Hence, it is no surprise that the comment by Armando drew such a furor as it can be perceived as gradations of authentic dilution away from Arab aesthetics and closer to Malay forms and even to Western cultural practices.

Given the management of hip-hop by states, often with the support of various religious and cultural gatekeepers, "underground" hip-hop has become an undeniable part of the landscape. A vibrant "underground" hip-hop culture exists in Singapore, flourishing in large part due to the strong state control of the free-to-air television and radio stations and the demarcation of race, religion, and politics as OB markers. As a result, Singaporean hip-hoppers like Akeem Jahat (Bad Akeem) have been gaining a following through posting tracks and mixtapes on YouTube; Bad Akeem's 2014 mixtape garnered about thirty-two thousand views in less than a year. The mixtape, entitled *SeluDOPE,* a play on the Malay word *seludup,* meaning "smuggle," contains provocative tracks such as "L.K.Y." and three versions of "Berita Hairan" (Strange news), the latter a criticism of the "strange" reporting of the Malay national newspaper, *Berita Harian* (Daily news). In addition, the tracks are punctuated with occasional profanity, such as "motherfucker," and laden with references to drinking vodka, in addition to sexually explicit lyrics, encapsulated in the title of the track "Sundalrella," the word *sundal* meaning "slut" in Malay. These lyrically explosive tracks are set against references of prostrating to God and running to the mosque if one is afraid of confronting the rapper. Hence, it is little wonder that Akeem does not make the mainstream radio stations. The same can be said about other popular acts, such as talented hip-hopper/producer Rauzan Rahman, whose hit songs "Kasih Mengapa" (Why love) and "Hingga Ke Akhir" ('Til the end) were nominated for the 2007 Best Singapore Malay Song and the 2011 Most Popular Song in Singapore at the Planet Muzik awards. However, Rauzan's 2010 collaboration with the Crazy88 on the song "GILA" (Crazy), which has a uniquely local flavor, did not have the same mainstream acclaim, despite rapping in English and having more social media success, because of its use of expletives such as "fuck" and "bitch."

Some Southeast Asian Muslim rappers started off with an underground presence and later achieved mainstream commercial success. Before becoming Malaysia's latest hip-hop sensation, Mikael Adam Bin Mohd Rafee Michel Lozach, a.k.a. SonaOne, worked on songs like "Taik Lalat" (Mole) and "I Don't Care" where he disses local celebrities for their looks and smugness while mouthing expletives.

The themes broached by these "underground" or virtual hip-hoppers are also more controversial given Singapore's highly sanitized mainstream music landscape. Hip-hoppers like Miiko, in a track called "Mana Melayu Kita" (Where are our Malays), starts the song by rapping "Mana Melayu Kita, Mana Budaya Kita, Sri Tri Buana, Ini Tanah Kita Punya" (Where are our Malays, Where is our culture, Sri Tri Buana, This land is ours), with the Singapore flag in the background throughout the music video. The track makes an explicit mention of Malays as the indigenous population of Singapore that is enshrined in Article 152 of the constitution. The track by Miiko is critical because, although the special position of the Malays and their indigeneity are recognized in the constitution, official state narratives have always painted Singapore as a migrant or settler community that only consisted of a mere 150 people upon the arrival of Stamford Raffles in January 1819. Instead of mentioning Raffles, who has been established as the modern-day founder of Singapore, Miiko evokes the image of Sri Tri Buana, which in Sanskrit means "Lord of the Three Worlds," the legendary figure who founded Singapore at around 1299. Sri Tri Buana supposedly ruled the Srivijaya Empire, which was based in Palembang, Sumatra.

Mattar (2003) contends that the Internet allows Muslim youth consuming hip-hop culture to traverse national and ethnic boundaries by suspending their local identity and adopting a globalized black identity. He demonstrates in his article how Singaporean hip-hoppers appropriate Ebonics, a form of black street English, in their conversations online. This adoption of global solidarities is usually formed over the appraisal of the aesthetic qualities of musical commodities or how and where these music can be consumed. However, although a global consumption of hip-hop is present among Muslim youth, hip-hop production in the public sphere is mainly localized. These conversations are almost always carried out with a dose of Singlish, a colloquial form of Singapore English that infuses local dialects like Malay, Tamil, and Hokkien. Interestingly, the hip-hoppers have also juxtaposed the rivalry between the East Coast and the West Coast in American hip-hop to the Singaporean topography, which is strange given that Singapore is a tiny island where one can drive from one end to the other in pretty much an hour. These rivalries at times express themselves in racial tones, with the majority Chinese and the Malays at opposite ends of the spectrum. Even though Anthony Kwame Harrison (2009) notes that in the United States, there are signs that hip-hop is becoming more racially democratic and egalitarian, in countries where discussions on race and religion are heavily regulated, the underlying tensions can play themselves out in the underground and virtual scenes.

Many hip-hop acts that contest the neat and dominant narrative of the state are not represented in the mainstream media. In addition, Muslim hip-hop groups, especially those located in the West, were utilizing the Internet to spread their music even before September 11. Soldiers of Allah, from the United States, was one of the first groups to announce its arrival to the global hip-hop *ummah*. The group believes the concept of copyright does not exist in Islam facilitating the dissemination of their music on free file-sharing websites. Furthermore, it is imperative for researchers to take new media very seriously since using merely national mass media as a source of data does not paint a complete picture of hip-hop culture in many countries. This importance of examining online sources is especially pertinent in places like Singapore where there are undeniable authoritarian aspects, which include draconian laws, control of political participation, and measures limiting civil and political rights and freedom of the press (Mauzy and Milne 2002, Kamaludeen and Turner 2014). In addition, the *Berita Harian*, the Malay national paper, traditionally grooms employees for positions of high political office. The close relationship between the state and Malay/Muslim journalists can be traced back to the pioneering Malay Muslim members of parliament and even the first president of Singapore, Yusof Ishak (Kamaludeen and Aljunied 2009).

This chapter has shown the relationships between hip-hop and the state in varying contexts. I offered some frameworks to analyze the state management of hip-hop, especially beyond the Western context. It is worth studying how hip-hop practitioners interact with the state because, to a large extent, hip-hop groups who produce socially conscious music are at the forefront of building a *society of publics*. In *The Power Elite* (1956), C. Wright Mills describes a process of change through which a society of publics gives way to a mass society. A society of publics is one in which there is a two-way flow of communication between governing elite and citizenry and the opinions of citizens are based on their own direct experiences of social reality. In addition, opinion is not passive but is realized in social actions. Mass society has the opposite characteristics: one-way communication, elite-guided understanding, and passive opinion. This is where examining the cybersphere when studying social groups who function within the landscape of authoritarian or soft authoritarian political regimes can be more liberating. The mainstream media in countries where the press is stifled becomes problematic, especially for groups who operate at the peripheries of society, as coverage of events is inevitably skewed in favor of the power holders.

NOTES

1. Marcus Riley, "Lupe Fiasco Calls Obama a 'Terrorist': Popular Rapper Criticizes Fellow Chicagoan," *NBC Chicago*, June 8, 2011, https://www.nbcchicago .com/news/local/lupe-fiasco-calls-obama-a-terrorist/1903309/.

2. Casey Quackenbush and Aria Chen, "'Tasteless, Vulgar and Obscene': China Just Banned Hip-Hop Culture and Tattoos from Television," *Time*, January 22, 2018, https://time.com/5112061/china-hip-hop-ban-tattoos-television/.

3. Wang Daiyu, "Islam in China Interview with Daddy Chang," *Islam in China Project*, May 10, 2015, http://islaminchina.info/islam-in-china-interview -with-daddy-chang/.

4. Riz Ahmed, "Riz MC—Post 9/11 Blue," YouTube, May 19, 2006, https:// www.youtube.com/watch?v=AKTsJpfCoIQ.

5. Alice O'Keeffe, "Rapper Asks BBC to Play 9/11 Song," *Guardian*, April 9, 2006, http://www.theguardian.com/media/2006/apr/09/radio.arts.

6. Vikram Dodd, "Guantánamo Actors Questioned under Terror Act after Film Festival," *Guardian*, February 21, 2006, https://www.theguardian.com/uk /2006/feb/21/film.terrorism.

7. "Our Story," Detroit vs. Everybody, https://vseverybody.com/pages/our -story.

8. Sydney vs. Everybody (Hustle Hard Television Exclusive), YouTube, January 1, 2015, https://www.youtube.com/watch?v=i-nZXKa7-Jk.

9. "Open Letter to Sydney Hip-Hop Scene, RE: Sydney Vs Everybody, Written by DJ MK-1," Facebook, accessed December 12, 2015, https://www.Facebook.com /john.khilla/posts/10153067147349319.

10. Jackson Allers, "Slingshot Hip Hop Comes to Lebanon," *Electronic Intifada*, August 14, 2008, https://electronicintifada.net/content/slingshot-hip-hop-comes -lebanon/7671.

11. Allers, "Slingshot Hip Hop."

12. Vivienne Walt, "El Général and the Rap Anthem of the Mideast Revolution," *Time*, February 15, 2011, http://content.time.com/time/world /article/0,8599,2049456,00.html.

13. Hass Re-Volt, "Interview: Rebel through Hip Hop: Talkin' about a Revolution," *Mashallah News*, February 7, 2011, https://www.mashallahnews .com/rebel-through-hiphop/.

14. Samer Mohajer and Fay Rajpar, "Syria Conflict Finds a Voice in Hip-Hop," *BBC News*, August 3, 2012, http://www.bbc.com/news/world-middle-east-19017267.

15. Mohajer and Rajpar, "Syria Conflict Finds a Voice."

16. Tracy Smith, "US Diplomacy: Hitting the Right Notes," CBS News, July 4, 2010, https://www.cbsnews.com/news/us-diplomacy-hitting-the-right-notes/.

17. Rand Dalgamouni, "US Drummer Brings Hip Hop to Jordan," *Jordan Times*, February 13, 2013, http://vista.sahafi.jo/art.php?id=7384ad37863104654d8 38931312cb78993734f9d.

18. "Australian Hip Hop Artists Demonstrate Harmony in Diversity on Indonesian Tour," Australian Embassy Indonesia, October 13, 2010, http://indonesia.embassy.gov.au/jakt/MR10_083.html.

19. Youssef Ben Ismail, "Tunisia's Hip Hop Artists Are More than Symbols and Troublemakers," *Huffington Post*, December 6, 2017, https://www.huffpost .com/entry/zomra-a-tunisian-hiphop-c_b_8525332.

20. Faiza Saleh Ambah, "'An Earthquake That Shifted the World Around Us'; Beyond a Disapproving Kingdom, Untested Saudi Rappers Find Transformation and Victory, of Sorts, at Hip-Hop Contest in Dubai," *Washington Post*, March 7, 2008.

21. Allison L McManus, "Lyrics Revolt," *Jadaliyya*, October 7, 2013, https:// www.jadaliyya.com/Details/29598/Lyrics-Revolt.

22. Sinnathamby Rajaratnam, "Singapore and Long Hair: The Lifestyle Which Matted Locks Conceal," *Straits Times* (special edition), May 1972.

23. Sean Michaels, "Metallica Guitar at Centre of Indonesian Corruption Row," *Guardian*, May 29, 2013, https://www.theguardian.com/music/2013/may /29/metallica-guitar-indonesian-governor.

24. The BBC reported Randy Blythe, the singer of rock band Lamb of God, as saying on his Instagram, "Incredibly, ladies & gentlemen, the new President of Indonesia is a metal head AND a lamb of god fan. No, this is not a joke, yes the photos are real, yes he digs Napalm Death, Metallica, Megadeth, & lamb of god amongst others - holy crap! THE WORLD'S FIRST HEAVY METAL PRESIDENT!". "Indonesia: Metal Fans Cheer Joko Widodo Poll Win," *BBC*, July 25, 2014, https://www.bbc.com/news/blogs-news-from-elsewhere-28482456.

25. "Danish PM Surprises Jokowi with Metallica Box Set," *Jakarta Post*, November 28, 2017, https://www.thejakartapost.com/news/2017/11/28/danish -pm-surprises-jokowi-with-metallica-box-set.html.

26. Generasi muda jangan mau diperbudak unsur budaya asing yang di negaranya sendiri tak disukai . . . di sana saja tidak patut, apalagi di Indonesia, tidak cocok. . . . Saya tidak setuju karena tidak ada manfaatnya sama sekali, terutama bagi generasi muda.

27. "This (Incomplete) History of Malaysian Hip Hop," *Documentist Ride*, April 9, 2010, https://documentist.wordpress.com/2010/04/09/this-incomplete -history-of-malaysian-hip-hop/.

28. Lexi Davey, "I Wanna Be a Producer: Sona One," *Juice*, June 13, 2011, http://juiceonline.com/i-wanna-be-a-producer-sona-one/.

29. "[News] Singapore: Write a Song, Learn the Prophet Muhammad's Values," Forums.vr-zone, March 19, 2008, http://forums.vr-zone.com/chit-chatting/251117-news-singapore-write-song-learn-the-prophet-muhammads-values.html.

30. "Roo Boys (Isrizal) Hip-Hop from Queenstown Prison," hochoonhiong, streamed live on December 19, 2008, YouTube video, 00:3:05, https://www.youtube.com/watch?v=MAH17Sqw5nA. ; "Roo Boys (Shafiie) Hip Hop from Queenstown Prison," hochoonhiong, streamed live on December 18, 2008, YouTube video, 00:3:42, https://www.youtube.com/watch?v=JpYzS8Puveo; Singapore Democratic Party, "A Young Patriot Goes To Jail," December 11, 2008, https://yoursdp.org/news/a_young_patriot_goes_to_jail.

31. Juliana June Rasul, "Sleeq Move," *The New Paper*, August 28, 2013, https://www.asiaone.com/entertainment/sleeq-move.

32. "Sour-Grapes KL Actor Attacks Aaron Aziz for Winning Most Popular Artist Award," STOMP—Singapore Seen, April 10, 2012, https://blog2-hiburan.blogspot.com/2012/04/aaron-aziz-google-blog-search_11.html?m=0.

33. Clara Chooi, "Singapore Actor Says Prefers Najib to Hsien Loong," *Malaysian Insider*, October 14, 2011, http://lib.perdana.org.my/PLF/News_Online/2011/0005/TheMalaysianInsider%5B14Oct2011%5DSingapore%20actor%20says%20prefers%20Najib%20to%20Hsien%20Loong.pdf.

34. Thomas Fuller, "The Right to Say 'God' Divides a Diverse Nation," *New York Times*, November 4, 2014, https://www.nytimes.com/2014/11/04/world/asia/in-malaysia-allah-is-reserved-for-muslims-only.html.

35. Bilal Ramadhan, "Ade Armando: Allah Senang Jika Ayat Ayat Alquran Dibaca dengan Gaya Hip-Hop," *Republika*, May 20, 2015, https://www.republika.co.id/berita/nasional/umum/15/05/20/non3s4-ade-armando-allah-senang-jika-ayat-alquran-dibaca-dengan-gaya-hiphop.

36. Ade Armando, Facebook, May 2015, https://www.facebook.com/ade.armando.372/posts/10152907140402817?_rdc=1&_rdr.

SIX

— ɷ —

KEEPING IT REAL . . . KEEPING IT COOL

HIP-HOP CULTURE HAS BECOME SO fashionable that it is easy to think of it as a mere gimmick, a prefix and marketing ploy devoid of any substantive content. The term has been stretched so thin and is now used to describe anything and everything such that it is impossible for us to arrive at its essence. From this perspective, the age-old hip-hop axiom of "keeping it real" becomes paradoxical—how do we keep it real when the real does not exist or cannot be ascertained anymore? Through examining hip-hop culture from the lenses of piety, ethnicity, gender, rights, and state control, this book has both confirmed and departed from this idea. Muslim hip-hop is characterized by the complex dialectical ways that hip-hop culture evolves as young Muslims try to replicate and at the same time distance themselves from it.

Even though hip-hop is a globalized art form, it is undeniable that a center-periphery relationship still exists as African American identity remains the dominant currency of exchange in the hip-hop *ummah*. There is a certain degree of a fetishization of blackness that goes beyond the debates on hip-hop authenticity or the many aspiring Muslim hip-hoppers who look up to their more established compatriots from the United States, with their cutting-edge sounds or rhymes. Artists such as Mos Def and, to a lesser degree, Lupe Fiasco are idolized by many young Muslim conscious rappers. The fact that African American hip-hop groups from the NOI and the Five Percenters, such as Public Enemy, Wu Tang Clan, and Eric B & Rakim, to Sunni groups like the Soldiers of Allah and Native Deen, have seemingly limitless support among Muslim hip-hoppers is also a testament to this.

African American Muslims still hold much sway in Muslim migrant communities and among indigenous converts to Islam. The most influential,

Malcolm X, is hip-hop culture's beloved civil rights icon, and he is generally seen as the standard-bearer in the fight for equality. A homological imagination of African American hip-hop occurs as global Muslim hip-hop practitioners and consumers seek to appropriate its structural resonances. In the process, hip-hop and the African American experience confer upon young Muslim hip-hoppers "a cultural vocabulary and historical experience with which to bond and from which to draw elements for local repertoires of resistance" (Aidi 2004, 119). However, in the middle of the mass consumption of hip-hop among global Muslim youth, the lexicon of the NOI and Five Percenters' "Islamic" hip-hop has not only lost its original meaning but has been deconstructed to take on new meanings.

Hip-hop activism among globalized Muslim youth can be conceptualized as what Baudrillard has called "reality by proxy." I contend that the essence of global Muslim hip-hop lies in its simulation of a transient simulacrum of reality rather than an interaction with a known or "real" reality (Baudrillard 1988, 4–5). Going beyond the first- and second-level simulations of counterfeiting and production respectively, a revisionist approach to the understanding of Islamic orthodoxy indicates that the NOI and Five Percenter theology (and brand of hip-hop) have already appropriated Islamic iconography at the hyperreal level. Orthodoxy here does not refer to one particular brand of Islam, be it Sunni or Shiite, Salafi or Sufi, but rather, following Talal Asad (1993), is characterized by matrices of power whereby the orthodox version of the day in a particular community or nation has the power to discipline deviant ones. A "double hyper-realization" (Kamaludeen 2012) then occurs as mainstream Muslim hip-hoppers seek to reclaim the orthodoxy of their religion while maintaining the NOI and Five Percenters' hip-hop parlance as part of their homological imagination. In fact, in the context of the mass consumption of hip-hop culture among Muslim youth globally, the Islamic hip-hop lexicon of the poetic jihadis has shed the meanings originally embedded in the NOI and Five Percenter messages. Hip-hop jargons and black iconographies have been "violated" to take on a "realer than real" feel. Hence, the global Muslim youth hip-hop culture demonstrates a "generation by models of a real without origin or reality" and "is no longer a question of imitation, nor duplication, nor even parody. It is a question of substituting the signs of the real for the real, that is to say of an operation of deterring every real process via its operational double" (Baudrillard 1994, 1–2).

This double hyper-realization is achieved via two key processes that can be understood through an appreciation of the disciplining of language and the disciplining of the body. The process of disciplining the body is evident in how contemporary young Muslims Islamize the performativity of the NOI and Five Percenter hip-hop culture. The notion of bodily discipline is a strong feature of Islamic hip-hop. Its practitioners strive to conform to a body regimen that is in line with the tenets of Islamic principles. The other process of disciplining language aims at mainstreaming hip-hop jargons to give them more conventional and "authentic" connotations. These interpretations are made to either satisfy Sunni Muslim requirements or represent a more universal front to unravel global and inclusive interpretations. Muslim hip-hop of NOI and Five Percenter beginnings, a movement that is subversive within the domain of Islamic theology, has been co-opted into a more consumerist and palatable medium to voice Muslim youth discontent. Turning theological symbols on their heads, Muslim hip-hop culture can be seen as a social movement aiming not only to promote multicultural living but also to project a "real" Islam into hip-hop through the infusion of elements of *nasheed* and Islamic devotional music. Hence, having begun as a challenge to the supremacy of the white over the black man, hip-hop is repositioned as a global movement for Muslim youth of the September 11 generation. Lyrics within hip-hop music not only document struggles with the non-Muslim other but are part of the sartorial strategies of resistance within the religion itself. It is ironic that the quest for religious authenticity and justice further adds to the hyperreal nature of the endeavor. The entry of Muslim hip-hop jargon into the hip-hop landscape can thus be seen as what Baudrillard (1998) has termed "a carnival of signs."

To speak of hip-hop as hyperreal might seem blasphemous given how ubiquitous the notion of "keeping it real" is in the hip-hop world. Michael Jeffries's *Thug Life: Race, Gender, and the Meaning of Hip-Hop* (2011) unpacks the multiple dimensions of "keeping it real" through the prisms of culture and race. "Keeping it real" means a way of life to some, something you commit to. Others equate it to staying the way you are and being true to yourself no matter what. There are also those who see "keeping it real" as a mere hip-hop slang devoid of much meaning. Relevant as it is to have a firm grasp of what people mean when they say something and what they decode upon hearing particular jargons, this discussion on hyperreality is pertinent given the demography we are talking about. The September 11 generation has also been referred to as millennials, defined by many scholars as those born between 1980 and 2000, the eve of the twin tower attacks. This group is now not only a distinct generation but also an analytic in religious studies due to their sheer critical mass. To put this into perspective, in the United States, there are about eighty million people who can be classified as millennials. In the Arab world, this same generation makes up approximately one-third of the population at more than one hundred million people. The main shift in this generation's religious life is that due to a myriad of factors, the family has ceased to be the source and sustaining abode of religion. It is now the individual.

This move from congregational-based to individualized spirituality is characterized by significant amounts of religious tinkering in no small way facilitated by living in a digital age. The concept of bricolage has been widely used to describe religious tinkering of this sort: the act of putting together components that do not seem agreeable with one another—for instance, Islam and hip-hop. The prominence of digital culture, which underpins the ethos of the bricoleur, is what fuels millennial religiosity (Han and Kamaludeen 2016). Hence, the distinct marker of millennial religiosity is mixing and matching. Some custodians of institutionalized religion may view this as a loss of religiosity; however, this is not the case. Instead, bricolage is a process of religious diffusion, the deconstruction and reconstruction of different aspects of religion that exist either as parts or whole entities in other forms. The result of such a process has been the ability of young Muslims to rationalize their choice of fusing Islam with hip-hop culture, a medium that resonates deeply with them.

To others, the popularity of hip-hop culture can be seen as a facet of what Ritzer (2004) has termed "grobalization." Hip-hop's popularity among young Muslims suggests the cultural colonizing virtues of the Americanization of everything in life, including Islam. This has led some to advocate an essentialist and reductionist Americanization thesis in explaining the lived experiences of Muslim youth. The adoption of "black" culture among young Muslims, devoid of any direct mentorship, has thus been attributed to the amount of media exposure to "black" music. However, the consumption and production of hip-hop among Muslim youth contain various presuppositions that should not be taken for granted. Youth participation in hip-hop culture is structured to varying degrees by both national and transnational factors. Language also structures an individual's perspectives of the world and functions as the vehicle whereby these worldviews are communicated. In the case of the consumption of hip-hop culture, it can be argued that there is an attempt to replicate the struggles of not only the African American experience specifically but the hip-hop *ummah* as a whole (Alim 2006a, 2006b).

Besides Muslim hip-hop practitioners of African American origin, this book has featured a significant number of migrant and/or diasporic Muslim hip-hoppers. The latter group enriches our perspectives of Muslim hip-hop in many ways as it prevents any form of reductionist deduction regarding their practice of hip-hop. Diasporic young Muslims are subjected to their host countries' official doctrines of multiculturalism, which influence young Muslims' attitudes toward migrant status. In addition, their socioeconomic status is also often intimately linked to the locality where they reside. Migrant hip-hop is curtailed both at the level of how it can be performed as a global genre with its peculiar linguistic styling and at the level of local sensitivities in terms of institutional constraints and the management of multiculturalism in the country.

Australia and France demonstrate the unique manifestations of migrant hip-hop among Muslim youth. Australia's Western Sydney, the area where a significant number of Muslim migrants live, has long been stigmatized as unrefined and is distinguished by its high level of social problems. Accents originating from the particular locality, which are labeled *woggie* or *westie*, accumulate less cultural capital. *Wog*, in the Australian context, is a slur that refers to those of a non-Anglo-Celtic European background. Traditionally, it was used as a derogatory term for southern and eastern Europeans, including Greeks and Italians, but it is increasingly associated with people from Asian or West Asian backgrounds, like the Lebanese and the Turkish. Even so, the term *wog* has been turned on its head and appropriated by the abused as a form of empowerment. Three Lebanese youth from Sydney formed the hip-hop group W.O.G (World of Grimm), and they garnered considerable attention when they uploaded two of their songs, "3rd Eye Conspiracy" and "Righteous Creatures," on muslimrap.net. Somewhat similar in content to the Brotha-hood's song "The Silent Truth," "3rd Eye Conspiracy" narrates the difficulties of living as part of the September 11 generation, in the midst of the global war on terrorism. The track "Righteous Creatures" contains more overt Islamic lyrics, such as *La ilaha illAllah* (There is no God but Allah), and evokes symbols like the Qur'an and Mecca. A *nasheed* blog features W.O.G and Maher Zain as the two *nasheed* acts hailing from Lebanese migrant backgrounds.[1] Young Muslims in Western Sydney are also known to utilize an amalgamated form of language to challenge the power relationships that are embedded in a predominantly white Christian nation. "Lebspeak" has emerged among second-generation Lebanese youth to counter conventional decorum by in-gesting hip-hop jargons into their everyday speech. Then we turn to France. The influence of Arab and Muslim culture has been the subject of much study in French hip-hop (Moch 2017). The strong secular nationalism in France is resisted in its vibrant hip-hop scene. Through the borrowing of Muslim terms in their rap, such as *inch'Allah* (God willing) and *jéllabah* (long robe with full sleeves), artists like MC Solaar present the Northern African Islamic culture as not only harmonious with French culture but also enriching it.

The infusion of the Arabic language is, understandably, a key aspect of the hyperrealization of hip-hop. Sara Grewal (2013) contends that, at one level, through the use of Ebonics as the master language of hip-hop and the

peripheralizing of white mainstream English, the hip-hop nation has particu-
larized the life experiences of the black community as esoteric and inaccessible
to the white majority. This lingua franca of the hip-hop community makes it
difficult for an other to penetrate the scene and challenge or add to the prevailing discourses of black life. In turn, the fusion of Arabic words into the Ebonics
of hip-hop serves a dual function. In the contemporary climate characterized
by Islamophobia and xenophobia, the use of Arabic by Lupe Fiasco and Mos
Def at once rejects multiple forms of hegemonies. It counters the white cultural
supremacy embedded in standard English by using Ebonics and at the same
time "foreignizes" the adopted language of the hip-hop nation by declining to
translate Islamic terms such as *Bismillah ar-rahman ar-raheem* (In the name
of God the Most Gracious, the Most Merciful) and *Assalamu alaykum* (Peace
unto you) from Arabic. At the same time, their localized usage of the Arabic
language in terms of pronunciations and meanings violates the Arab cultural
hegemony in favor of a subcultural understanding of Islam.

So potent is this form of appropriation that it has also found its way into
mainstream Western hip-hop. Hip-hop superstar Kanye West, in his song
"Power," with Jay-Z and Swizz Beatz, raps:

> Now everything I'm rhyming on cause a Ramadan
> Been a don, praying for the families lost in the storm
> Bring our troops back from Iraq, keep our troops out of Iran
> So the next couple bars, I'mma drop 'em in Islam
> They say as-salamu alaykum say wa alaikum assalam

Kanye's use of Islamic terminologies like Ramadan, signaling the Muslim holy
fasting month, and *salam*, which is the Muslim greeting of peace, is not merely
a declaration of his solidarity with his Muslim comrade, Swizz Beatz, who declared in an interview that "I have no bosses, only Allah, The Most High is my
boss.... That's it."[2] Kanye's cypher demonstrates something more significant—
the normalcy of Islam within hip-hop culture as well as its growing and enduring role in the United States' cultural landscape.

The same can be said of the 2018 hit "Family Feud," a collaboration of Jay-Z
and Beyoncé, hip-hop's "first couple," in which Jay-Z raises his hands in supplication, Muslim style, and utters *Humdu Allah* (Praises due to Allah). Four
years before this, Jay-Z received colossal Internet attention when he attended
an NBA game in Brooklyn, sitting courtside with his wife, Beyoncé, wearing a
Five Percenter medallion. This was a year after he released the song "Heaven,"
in which he spits the Five Percenter cyphers: "Arm, leg, leg, arm, head—this
is God body / Knowledge, wisdom, freedom, understanding, we just want our

equality," beseeching his fans to "Question religion, question it all / Question existence until them questions are solved." His sporting of Five Percenter regalia raised many questions for the general public as well as within the group itself. Some asked why he was wearing a symbol of black supremacy from a radical group and wondered whether he was advocating reverse discrimination. Others opined that a reawakening of the diminished Five Percent movement was occurring within popular culture. A small proportion of commentators thought the act was disrespectful to the group, with those within the movement itself questioning Jay-Z's right to wear the symbol if he had not fully embraced the lifestyle of the Nation of Gods and Earth. A representative of the Five Percenters, Saladin Allah, stated: "Jay Z is not an active member—no one has vouched for him. . . . It was always understood that you don't wear the regalia if you don't totally subscribe to the life."[3] Since Jay-Z has never addressed these questions head on, speculation continues. Notwithstanding, it is known that hip-hop artists often use popular culture to commodify images of a rebellious group and merchandize them to look cool.

The intricate relationships between Muslims and non-Muslims can be illustrated by hip-hop's interreligious couples. One of the most high-profile couples is Swizz Beatz, who is Muslim, and his wife, Alicia Keys, who prefers to be known more as a spiritual person rather than be associated with a particular religion. In her words:

> I would call it spirituality because I think religion gets very sticky. I think it's beautiful to have a belief in something and that's where religion comes in. It's perfect in the sense of believing in something bigger and greater and having faith and hope. But for me it's definitely spirituality in the sense of having integrity and certain morals I stand by. I pray a lot. I think prayers are like affirmations, things that you speak out loud and therefore they can come to you. I believe a lot in the power of words. That's why I love them so much.[4]

In early 2017, Alicia Keys came under intense criticism when she posted a tweet with an image of a sexualized woman donning an *abaya* and a *niqab* in which she called for the acceptance of a woman's choice of dress. Keys swiftly took down the post after receiving a barrage of criticisms from both Muslims and non-Muslims. Keys found herself caught between two camps at opposite ends of the spectrum. One side argues that women who adorn the *abaya* and the *niqab* are necessarily oppressed and are being forced to do so. Even if women choose to wear them voluntarily, this group denies the agency of these women and assumes they have somehow internalized the patriarchal gaze. Hence, these critics were enraged by Keys's post, which they believed "glamorized the niqab" and "romanticized oppression."[5] The other camp was equally offended by Keys's post, claiming that Keys had disrespected and sexualized articles of clothing that are supposed to be upheld as symbols of modesty. That Keys elected to accentuate and expose the female form these clothes were designed to hide was met with contempt.

Disciplining language and disciplining the body are often intertwined to such a degree that many hip-hoppers believe fashion and hip-hop music cannot be separated. Much of the hip-hop persona is about how one dresses, which is the primary reason so many hip-hop artists have created successful clothing lines. Inadvertently, Muslim hip-hoppers are reinterpreting the dress code for their own industry. Beyond the gender divide, choice of clothing is a primary source of concern for male Muslim rappers, too, as they seek to express their connectivity to the audience.

Some Muslim artists choose to dress in a neutral way, stripped of their "Islamic" or "hip-hop" identifiers. This deliberate strategy of not associating themselves with either Islam or hip-hop makes them more palatable to audiences on both sides of the divide. According to Maher Zain: "We [Muslims] are not a boring people, you know. We don't just sit and pray. . . . The way I dress, inshallah, is a way of showing that people can be good Muslims no matter how they look" (quoted in Janmohamed 2016, 104). His comment reflects the stance of some diasporic Muslim artists in the West who have struggled to bridge the gulf among their Arabic, Islamic, national, and subcultural identities. He talks about his challenges of identity formation in his track "Insha Allah" in an abstract way:

> Every time You feel like you cannot go on
> You feel so lost and that you're so alone
> All you see is night and darkness all around
> You feel so helpless you can't see which way to go
> Don't despair and never lose hope
> 'Cause Allah is always by your side.

Other artists take a different route by presenting specific cultural identifiers. Members of the Indonesian outfit JHF regularly incorporate cultural batik designs into their dress code both on and off the stage. The renowned batik design, which has been exported globally and is extremely popular among Muslims in Southeast Asia, traces its roots to Java, Indonesia. Yogyakarta, in central Java, the group's hometown, is known among locals as the center of Javanese culture. Donning the batik as part of the traditional costume on their promotional posters or matching it together with the customary hip-hop gear of baseball caps, baggy pants, and sneakers during their gigs, JHF present themselves as being part of the masses even as they are delivering what many conservatives in their community consider a controversial art form. In 2014, in line with a host of American hip-hop artists who have launched their own clothing lines, such as Jay-Z (Rocawear), Pharrell (Billionaire Boys Club), Puff Daddy (Sean John), and Kanye West (Yeezy), JHF announced that they were developing their own batik apparel line called Bom Batik. The leader of the group, Kill the DJ, declared, "We want this because this is identity."[6]

Indonesia's Lady Gan's and Jeri Taufik's 2018 track, "Burn It Up," is another example. In the music video, Lady Gan, who recently embraced the hijabi lifestyle, wore the label of daukyfashion, Indonesia's renowned hijab fashion house. Also sporting a gold chain with a huge pendant reading "Happy" and alternating her hoodie with traditional but fashionable Muslimah garb, she rapped about her experience of being a Muslim female rapper:

Jangan ungkit yang sudah berlalu,	Do not dig up the past,
Ku tak hidup lagi jaman itu	I do not live in that time anymore
Gak peduli ocehan mereka	Do not care about their babbling
Kini kau lihat semua sudah berbeda	Now you see everything is different
Sekarang udah enggak bandel	Now I am not stubborn
Alhamdulillah gue enggak nyesel	Alhamdulillah I do not regret
Bukan buatan, ini asli, original	Not artificial, this is original, original
They'll call me rap superstar	They'll call me rap superstar
Bukan banci panggung, bukan porn star	Not a stage sissy, not a porn star

This collaboration also marked a new beginning of hijabi Muslim rappers working with fellow native artists who take on a contrary presentation of hip-hop performance. Jeri Taufik's previous music video, "Mantra," released just a few months before "Burn It Up," features a scantily clad tattooed woman in her bikini and lingerie, along with booze, drugs, and the use of expletives— everything that is provocative in conservative Indonesia, a Habibiean nightmare. This self-confidence among the Indonesian hip-hop community to flaunt their own cultural and religious identities in their music, especially from its women artists, did not come early. The initial forms of hip-hop in Indonesia in the 1990s were more akin to mimicking the streets of the United States in terms of outlook.

Basketball, and especially the allure of the NBA in Southeast Asia, has played a significant role in introducing hip-hop culture to young Southeast

Asian Muslims prior to September 11. For some time, hip-hop and the NBA undoubtably have been two of the United States' most successful cultural exports. Elena Romero's book *Free Stylin': How Hip Hop Changed the Fashion Industry* (2012) devoted an entire chapter to the symbiotic relationship between basketball and hip-hop culture.

Many NBA players identify with hip-hop culture off the court, and during NBA games, popular tracks are blasted at high volume to entertain the crowd and cheerleaders incorporate hip-hop dance into their routines during timeouts, all while rappers sit courtside bantering with the athletes. In 2018, during a Clippers–Nuggets game, Drake's smash hit "God's Plan," which peaked at number one in various music charts, blared in the background as the players went through their paces. Within a few weeks of Drake dropping his track, Deen Squad released a spin-off version, called "Allah's Plan," that garnered about three million views on YouTube in just one month.

Iwa K, famous for his patronage of basketball, is regarded as one of the pioneers of Indonesian hip-hop. Iwa K sold 100,000 copies of his first album in 1992 and 260,000 copies of his second album, *Topeng* (Mask), in 1993. Iwa K frequently dresses in oversized jerseys, and his music videos, such as "Bebas" (Free), often take place on the basketball court. Doubling up as a commentator for basketball games, he created a track called "Nombok Dong" as a tribute to the sport. The song's chanting of "Bola Basket, Bola Basket!" became a mantra for the expanding number of hip-hop basketball fans in the region. Sports and music are potent ingredients in the new generation's creation of a cool identity.

One of the most significant ways that Muslim hip-hop culture has reinvented its bodily regimen is through the adoption of the "Muslim cool" identity. In the *New Muslim Cool* documentary,[7] rapper Hamza Pérez puts it this way:

> It's a new generation, man ... that wants traditional Islam by using technology and the culture of society. We created our own clothing, you know ... our own way of talking, you know ... our own music, you know ... saying our own slang. Instead of listening to garbage rap music I'm listening to some music that speaks about spiritual belief and social change, you know ... instead of wearing clothing that has Scarface on it I may have a shirt with a positive message on it. I'm Islamifying my clothing, taking the culture and making it more spiritually identifiable for us. Being in this society but not compromising our identity.

The Muslim cool movement subverts the hegemonic understanding of "cool" in hip-hop culture that has been unfortunately attached to gun culture, drugs, sexual promiscuity, and a generally hedonistic lifestyle. Lupe Fiasco, in his track "The Cool" (2006), challenges the wisdom of engaging in such vices within the hip-hop community:

> This life goes passing you by
> It might go fast if you lie
> You born, you live, then you die
> If life goes passing you by
> Don't cry
> If you're breaking the rules
> Making your moves
> Paying your dues
> Chasing the cool

Lupe's lucid takedown of the hip-hop community in "The Cool," where he talks about bling, liquor, rocks, and bullets, was symptomatic of conscious hip-hop's ability to speak truth to power and keep it real.

To counter this reduction of hip-hop to mere mimicry and a hyperreality devoid of an essence, Muslim hip-hoppers bring back the importance of the "streets" and being grounded to their community as a way of keeping it real. The Brothahood speaks about the group's extensive engagement with their community to encourage people to remain rooted, conducting workshops for students of all age groups and organizing events for the local Muslim community. Many Muslim hip-hoppers the world over, from DAM to Omar Offendum and the Brothahood, pride themselves on engaging with all layers of society. The streets thus do not merely reflect the downtrodden who sleep on the sidewalk but include those who cruise down the road in their posh automobiles—the haves and the have-nots. In the words of El General: "I started rapping not for money but just to get my voice across. . . . I wanted to focus particularly on politics and wanted to defend Islam through my music."[8]

This is the most significant objective of global Muslim hip-hop, and young Muslims are fighting back from the projects in Brooklyn to the streets of Berlin and the lanes of Jericho. Hip-hop continues to be one of the most common expressions of youth culture, extending beyond its traditional description as the "Black folks' CNN" (according to a rapper from Public Enemy quoted in Gilyard 2008, 98). Playing on the same analogy, Palestinian rappers DAM affirmed hip-hop's influence in the Muslim world, stating, "Every village now has hip hop. . . . Hip-hop is our CNN" (Wright 2011, 127). Such expressions attest to the role of hip-hop music in representing a strand of social reality and also serve as a response to conventional media's distorted portrayals of these groups. References to hip-hop music as an alternative source of information can be understood as a rejection of mainstream media's misrepresentations of groups that exist at the margins of society. For many hip-hop activists, particularly in authoritarian states, hip-hop music is a means of presenting the sentiments of the oppressed majority.

One would be remiss to see hip-hop activism and the poetic jihadis' struggle for justice as merely aimed at confrontations between Muslims and non-Muslims and/or citizens and the state. The vibrancy within the hip-hop *ummah*, itself characterized by a rereading of the religion, cannot be taken for granted. A significant part of Muslim hip-hop has been about claiming agency to interpret Islam, especially with regard to issues of gender and the limits of participation in hip-hop and if hip-hop is even compatible with Islam in the first place. The nascence of the poetic jihadis among the Muslim hip-hop *ummah* appears to have bridged the gap between the genres of *nasheed* and hip-hop, with the notion of jihad as central to their endeavors. This has led to interesting concepts such as the coining of the term *G-had*, inspired by Fun-Da-Mental's album *All Is War (The Benefits of G-had)*. Inadvertently, a double hyperrealization occurs as the producers of mainstream Muslim hip-hop seek to maintain the Five Percenter lexicon of G while also subverting elements of it.

Through all these, I have demonstrated the ingenious and disingenuous ways young hip-hoppers and moral entrepreneurs have appropriated hip-hop's musical content and the culture that surrounds it. Specifically, in conversation with Islam, hip-hop culture has morphed over the decades as it has been subjected to sociopolitical conditions, state intervention, digital technology, and events that shape the psyche of a generation. Hip-hop culture as practiced by the Muslim hip-hop *ummah* exists in dialectical relationships with government institutions, political parties, media, religious groups, and young people themselves, who attempt not only to claim and assume moral guardianship but to redraw existing moral boundaries. These practices do not exist as dualisms (such as a conflict between structure and agency) but rather accentuate the consequences of young people living within a structure. Youth attain their dispositions, consciously or unconsciously, from a structural framework. The challenge remains to reconcile themselves with seemingly colliding social norms. Furthermore, as I have shown in the previous chapters, realizing the incongruence with American hip-hop culture, there are many conscious attempts by Muslim hip-hoppers to provincialize hip-hop from its black roots. This can be conceptualized, although not all the time, via the homological imagination. These transformations force young people to reread what it means to be Muslim and what it means to do hip-hop.

The hip-hop scene is therefore an ideal laboratory to study the contentious nature of the September 11 generation. From the lenses of religion and Muslim hip-hop specifically, an artist is considered representative and authoritative if he is seen as a "real" Muslim, and the withdrawal of this validation often manifests itself in the form of stigmatization. This is set against what Mahmood Mamdani alleges as the tendency in mass media and even academic circles to describe "good" Muslims as "modern, secular, and Westernized, but bad Muslims as doctrinal, anti-modern, and virulent" (2004, 24).

Carrying the Muslim label and being expected to be the mouthpiece of Islam is a heavy responsibility, one that artists, both men and women, would at times rather do without. Miss Undastood wanted to carry the flag for Muslim women early in her career but has since retracted her stance, and her male counterparts have been known to express similar sentiments. Lupe Fiasco, who innovatively made a remix of Kanye West's "Jesus Walks," entitled "Muhammad Walks," declared on MTV's *Rap Fix* that although Islam informs everything he does, "I don't like putting my religion out there, I don't like wearing it like that, because I don't want people to look at me as the poster child for Islam. I'm not. I don't want them to look at my flaws and be like, 'Oh, that's the flaws of Islam.'"[9] Similar to Miss Undastood, who declared, "I am done being a poster girl for Islam,"[10] these artists want others to see them for their "real" selves and not as "an ideal" who represents either a version of Islam— be it NOI, Five Percenter, Sunni, or Shiite—or the entire Muslim *ummah*. Other hip-hoppers have found the constant labeling of Muslims into categories to be extreme. According to Native Deen: "As American Muslims, we feel like our voices have been drowned out by the extremists on both sides. . . . As musicians, we know the power of music and hope to reach out to our fellow Americans through this song."[11] Native Deen responded powerfully by releasing a music video entitled "My Faith My Voice," which takes its name from a campaign showcasing the diverse voices in the Muslim community.

To speak of the global Muslim *ummah* necessitates provincializing on multiple fronts—the most intuitive being that of geography—but it also requires an astute understanding of the various cultural and religious repertoires. Chakrabarty suggests that an important element in the process of provincializing is to reopen the discussion on one European word, *imagination*. It might seem somewhat of a paradox to want to breathe heterogeneity into the word *imagination* since one would think the essence of the word is already heterogeneous in nature, but it can no longer be taken for granted as a forgone conclusion. In his article "The Time of History and Times of Gods," Chakrabarty (1997) illuminates the problems faced by secular subjects like history and sociology in handling imaginations in which gods, spirits, or the supernatural have agency in the world and how secularism translates itself into the writing of history. Chakrabarty also points to the limitations of language as an intermediary. "Events," according to him, may not be completely accessible by language, and language and representations always form a "thin film" between us and the world. This explains the difficulties of Muslim rappers in appropriating jargons and other symbolisms from hip-hop culture and their struggles with authenticity.

In *Islam and the Blackamerican*, Sherman Jackson puts forth that for Islam to continue to invoke real meaning in the lives of its adherents, it needs to be able to straddle two seemingly conflicting spheres. It needs to be able to discuss head on the social conditions and structures bearing down on society. At the same time, it should not lose its God centeredness and emphasis on personal piety and success in the afterlife, although these may not have any direct relevance to the first sphere. What this means is that today's young Muslims do not have to "choose between piety and protest, activism and spirituality, or secular interest and eschatological success" (2005, 172). Jackson's modest argument aimed at African American Muslims could certainly be extended to include the globalized Muslim youth of the September 11 generation. This, in its essence, is the project of socially conscious Muslim hip-hop I have tried to demonstrate.

Following Tricia Rose's *Hip-Hop Wars* (2008), this book has attempted to show the nuanced way hip-hop has been embraced by the younger generation. I have demonstrated how the other—in this case, globalized Muslim youth—in seeing themselves as the "new blacks," are responding critically to the warring between two camps: those who are critical of the vices within hip-hop and want to dump it into the rubbish bin of history versus those who are defending hip-hop with rose-tinted glasses, excusing it for all its misogyny and pleasuring of the self. Granted, though, these are not the only two ways the September 11 generation is responding to this conflict. Among those who have embraced hip-hop culture, there are variations in terms of attempts at reconciling it with Islam, both in form and degree.

Perhaps, in engaging with subaltern theories, we can further conceptualize how we might provincialize normative understandings of hip-hop culture and re-world the earth by attempting to tell alternative developments of hip-hop and giving reason a different place by analyzing its interactions with the global hip-hop generation. When do we call a tradition "real"—that is, not invented? Having "demystified" a particular ideology as invented, what then does one put in its place? The "real"? Although not without its problems, this particular framework of "invented traditions"—to a large extent, Muslim hip-hop artists are in the business of inventing and rereading traditions—is showing us that the picture of a changeless or static past is usually a construction of early-modern European historical and sociological thinking. It has seldom been the Muslim *ummah*'s way of describing itself until recently, when it has internalized the dominant gaze of the West. As I have shown extensively in this book, young Muslims resist the simplistic categorizing that has characterized much of the post-9/11 rhetoric that caricatures them into neat dichotomies. Hip-hop provides the platform for this.

NOTES

1. "Profile W.O.G (Rap Muslim)," All about Nasheed (blog), June 27, 2012, http://allaboutnasheed.blogspot.ae/2012/06/profile-wog-rap-muslim.html; "Maher Zein's Biography," All about Nasheed (blog), August 3, 2011, http:// allaboutnasheed.blogspot.com/2011/08/maher-zeins-biography.html.

2. "Swizz Beatz: 'I Have No Bosses. Only Allah, the Most High Is My Boss. That's It.' [Preview 2013]," Booska-P.com, streamed live on July 16, 2013, YouTube video, 00:01:45, https://www.youtube.com/watch?v=JUSt3m5UhVs.

3. Gary Buiso, "Jay Z's Bling from 'Whites Are Devils' Group," *New York Post*, April 6, 2014, https://nypost.com/2014/04/06/jay-zs-medallion-bears-logo -of-five-percent-radical-group/.

4. Mary W. and Darina S., "Singer Alicia Keys," *Teen Ink*, https://www.teenink .com/nonfiction/interviews/article/5341/Singer-Alicia-Keys/.

5. Leyal Khalife, "Alicia Keys Posted a Photo of a Woman in Niqab . . . and People Aren't Happy," *Step Feed*, March 29, 2017, https://stepfeed.com/alicia -keys-posted-a-photo-of-a-woman-in-niqab-and-people-aren-t-happy-1087.

6. Sabtu, "Jogja Hip Hop Foundation siapkan album dan buku," Antaranews. com, February 8, 2014, http://www.antaranews.com/berita/418033/jogja-hip -hop-foundation-siapkan-album-dan-buku.

7. Jennifer Maytorena Taylor, *New Muslim Cool* (Specific Pictures, 2009), documentary.

8. David Peisner, "Inside Tunisia's Hip-Hop Revolution," *SPIN*, August 24, 2011, https://www.spin.com/2011/08/inside-tunisias-hip-hop-revolution/.

9. "Lupe Fiasco and Sway: Talk about Islam," Walker Brooks, streamed live on September 26, 2009, YouTube video, 00:04:28, https://www.youtube.com /watch?time_continue=12&v=gnt4GlQGirs.

10. "Muslim. Woman. Hip Hop. Artist." *Islamic Monthly*, January 13, 2015, https://www.theislamicmonthly.com/muslim-woman-hip-hop-artist/.

11. "Hip Hop Confronts Islamophobia," *Fame Magazine*, September 29, 2010, https://www.famemagazine.co.uk/hip-hop-confronts-islamophobia/.

REFERENCES

Abdul Khabeer, Su'ad. 2007. "Rep That Islam: The Rhyme and Reason of American Islamic Hip-Hop." *Muslim World* 97 (1): 125–41.

———. 2016. *Muslim Cool: Race, Religion, and Hip-Hop in the United States.* New York: New York University Press.

Abu-Jamal, Mumia. 2006. "'A Rap Thing,' 'On Rapping Rap,' and 'Hip-Hop or Homeland Security.'" In *The Vinyl Ain't Final: Hip-Hop and the Globalization of Black Popular Culture*, edited by Dipannita Basu and Sidney J. Lemelle, 23–26. London: Pluto.

Abu-Lughod, Lila. 2013. *Do Muslim Women Need Saving?* Cambridge, MA: Harvard University Press.

Ackfeldt, Anders. 2012. "'Imma March' toward Ka'ba': Islam in Swedish Hip-Hop." *Contemporary Islam* 6 (3): 283–96.

Ahmad, Salman. 2010. *Rock and Roll Jihad: A Muslim Rock Star's Revolution.* New York: Free Press.

Aidi, Hisham. 2004. "Verily, There Is Only One Hip-Hop Umma: Islam, Cultural Protest, and Urban Marginality." *Socialism and Democracy* 18 (2): 107–26.

———. 2014. *Rebel Music: Race, Empire, and the New Muslim Youth Culture.* New York: Pantheon.

Alameddine, Rabih. 2008. *The Hakawati.* New York: Knopf.

Alexander, Claire E. 2000. *The Asian Gang: Ethnicity, Identity, Masculinity.* Oxford: Berg.

Alim, H. Samy. 2005. "A New Research Agenda: Exploring the Transglobal Hip Hop Umma." In *Muslim Networks from Hajj to Hip Hop*, edited by Miriam Cooke and Bruce B. Lawrence, 264–74. Chapel Hill: University of North Carolina Press.

———. 2006a. "Re-Inventing Islam with Unique Modern Tones: Muslim Hip-Hop Artists as Verbal Mujahidin." *Souls* 8 (4): 45–58.

———. 2006b. *Roc the Mic Right: The Language of Hip-Hop Culture.* New York: Routledge.

Alim, H. Samy, and Geneva Smitherman. 2012. *Articulate While Black: Barack Obama, Language, and Race in the U.S.* New York: Oxford University Press.

Allen, Harry. 1991. "Righteous Indignation: Rappers Talk about the Strength of Hip-Hop and Islam." *Source* 48: 48–53.

Amnesty International. 2009. *Tunisia: Continuing Abuses in the Name of Security.* London: Amnesty International Publications.

Anderson, Elijah. 1999. *Code of the Street: Decency, Violence, and the Moral Life of the Inner City.* New York: W. W. Norton.

An-Na'im, Abdullah. 1990. *Towards an Islamic Reformation: Civil Liberties, Human Rights, and International Law.* Syracuse, NY: Syracuse University Press.

Anselmi, William. 2011. "Long Played Revolutions: Utopic Narratives, *Canzoni d'autore.*" In *Popular Music and Human Rights: World Music,* edited by Ian Peddie, 7–16. Farnham, UK: Ashgate.

Arthur, Damien. 2006. "Authenticity and Consumption in the Australian Hip Hop Culture." *Qualitative Market Research: An International Journal* 9 (2): 140–56.

Asad, Talal. 1993. *Genealogies of Religion: Discipline and Reasons of Power in Christianity and Islam.* Baltimore: The Johns Hopkins University Press.

Asante, Molefi K. 2008. *It's Bigger than Hip-Hop: The Rise of the Post-Hip-Hop Generation.* New York: St. Martin's.

Back, Les. 1996. *New Ethnicities and Urban Culture: Racisms and Multiculture in Young Lives.* London: Routledge.

Bailey, Julius. 2014. *Philosophy and Hip-Hop: Ruminations on Postmodern Cultural Form.* New York: Palgrave Macmillan.

Barendregt, Bart. 2006. "Cyber-*nasyid*: Transnational Soundscapes in Muslim Southeast Asia." In *Medi@sia: Global Media/tion In and Out of Context,* edited by Todd Holden and Timothy Scrase, 170–87. London: Routledge.

———. 2011. "Pop, Politics, and Piety: Nasyid Boy Band Music in Muslim Southeast Asia." In *Islam and Popular Culture in Indonesia and Malaysia,* edited by Andrew N. Weintraub, 235–56. London: Routledge.

Baudrillard, Jean. 1988. *The Ecstasy of Communication.* Edited by Sylvere Lotringer. Translated by Bernard and Caroline Schutz. Brooklyn, NY: Autonomedia.

———. 1994. *Simulacra and Simulation.* Translated by Sheila Faria Glaser. Ann Arbor: University of Michigan Press.

———. 1998. *The Consumer Society: Myths and Structures.* Translated by Chris Turner. London: Sage Publications.

Beckford, James A., Daniele Joly, and Farhad Khosrokhavar. 2005. *Muslims in Prison: Challenge and Change in Britain and France.* Basingstoke, UK: Palgrave Macmillan.

Benard, Cheryl. 2003. *Civil Democratic Islam: Partners, Resources, and Strategies.* Santa Monica: RAND Corporation.

Bennett, Andy. 2000. *Popular Music and Youth Culture: Music, Identity and Place.* London: Macmillan.

Bielefeldt, Heiner. 2000. "'Western' versus 'Islamic' Human Rights Conceptions?: A Critique of Cultural Essentialism in the Discussion on Human Rights." *Political Theory* 28 (1): 90–121.

Bonnette, Lakeyta M. 2015. *Pulse of the People: Political Rap Music and Black Politics.* Philadelphia: University of Pennsylvania Press.

Boubekeur, Amel. 2005. "Cool and Competitive: Muslim Culture in the West," *ISIM Review* 16: 12–13.

Bourdieu, Pierre. 1984. *Distinction: A Social Critique of the Judgement of Taste.* London: Routledge.

———. 1988. *Homo Academicus.* Cambridge, UK: Polity.

———. 1990. *The Logic of Practice.* Cambridge, UK: Polity.

Boyd, Todd. 2002. *The New H.N.I.C: The Death of Civil Rights and the Reign of Hip-Hop.* New York: New York University Press.

Bunt, Gary R. 2009. *iMuslims: Rewiring the House of Islam.* Chapel Hill: University of North Carolina Press.

Butcher, Melissa. 2008. "FOB Boys, VCs and Habibs: Using Language to Navigate Difference and Belonging in Culturally Diverse Sydney." *Journal of Ethnic and Migration Studies* 34 (3): 371–87.

Butler, Paul. 2010. *Let's Get Free: A Hip-Hop Theory of Justice.* New York: New Press.

Cameron, D. 2003. "Feeling Like an Outsider, Habib? FOBs and Multis Know the Feeling." *Sydney Morning Herald*, May 31.

Chakrabarty, Dipesh. 1997. "The Time of History and the Times of Gods." In *The Politics of Culture in the Shadow of Capital*, edited by Lisa Lowe and David Lloyd, 35–60. Durham, NC: Duke University Press.

———. 2000. *Provincializing Europe: Postcolonial Thought and Historical Difference.* Princeton, NJ: Princeton University Press.

Cheney, Charise. 2005. *Brothers Gonna Work It Out: Sexual Politics in the Golden Age of Rap Nationalism.* New York: New York University Press.

Clay, Andreana. 2012. *The Hip-Hop Generation Fights Back: Youth, Activism and Post-Civil Rights Politics.* New York: New York University Press.

Clegg, Claude Andrew III. 1997. *An Original Man: The Life and Times of Elijah Muhammad.* New York: St. Martin's Griffin.

Common (with Adam Bradley). 2012. *One Day It'll All Make Sense.* New York: Atria Books.

Curtis, Edward E. IV. 2006. *Black Muslim Religion in the Nation of Islam, 1960–1975.* Chapel Hill: University of North Carolina Press.

Curtis, R. M. Mukhtar. 1994. "Urban Muslims: The Formation of the Dar ul-Islam Movement." In *Muslim Communities in North America*, edited by Yvonne Haddad and Jane Idleman Smith, 51–73. Albany: State University of New York.

Dalacoura, Katerina. 2007. *Islam, Liberalism and Human Rights*. London: I. B. Tauris.

Daniels, Timothy, ed. 2013. *Performance, Popular Culture, and Piety in Muslim Southeast Asia*. New York: Palgrave Macmillan.

Daulatzai, Sohail. 2012. *Black Star, Crescent Moon: The Muslim International and Black Freedom beyond America*. Minneapolis: University of Minnesota Press.

Dawson, Ashley. 2002. "'This Is the Digital Underclass': Asian Dub Foundation and Hip-Hop Cosmopolitanism." *Social Semiotics* 12 (1): 27–44.

Dixon, Matthew. 2002. "UK–Music and Human Rights." In *Music, Music Therapy and Trauma: International Perspectives*, edited by Julie Sutton, 119–32. London: Jessica Kingsley Publishers.

Drissel, David. 2009. "Hip-Hop Hybridity for a Glocalized World: African and Muslim Diasporic Discourses in French Rap Music." *Global Studies Journal* 2 (3): 121–42.

Dwyer, Kevin. 1991. *Arab Voices: The Human Rights Debate in the Middle East*. Berkeley: University of California Press.

Edmunds, June, and Bryan Turner. 2005. "Global Generations: Social Change in the Twentieth Century." *British Journal of Sociology* 56 (4): 559–77.

Emon, Anver M., Mark S. Ellis, and Benjamin Glahn, eds. 2012. *Islamic Law and International Human Rights Law*. Oxford: Oxford University Press.

Esposito, John. 2008. "W. D. Mohammed: A Witness for True Islam." *Washington Post*, September 10.

Fauset, Arthur Huff. 2001. *Black Gods of the Metropolis: Negro Religious Cults of the Urban North*. Philadelphia: University of Pennsylvania Press.

Fernandes, Sujatha. 2011. *Close to the Edge: In Search of the Global Hip-Hop Generation*. New York: Verso.

Fink, Steven. 2012. "For the Best of All Listeners: American Islamic Hip Hop as Reminder." *Journal of Religion & Society* 14: 1–23.

Fischlin, Daniel, and Ajay Heble. 2003. *Rebel Musics: Human Rights, Resistant Sounds, and the Politics of Music Making*. Montreal, Canada: Black Rose.

Flores, Juan. 2000. *From Bomba to Hip-Hop: Puerto Rican Culture and Latino Identity*. New York: Columbia University Press.

Floyd-Thomas, Juan. 2003. "A Jihad of Words: The Evolution of African American Islam and Contemporary Hip-Hop." In *Noise and Spirit: The Religious and Spiritual Sensibilities of Rap Music*, edited by Anthony Pinn, 49–70. New York: New York University Press.

Fu, Su Yin, and Liew Kai Khiun. 2009. "Deghettoizing Subcultures: The Multicultural Evolution of Mat Rock in Singapore." In *Race and Multiculturalism in Malaysia and Singapore*, edited by Daniel P. S. Goh, Matilda Gabrielpillai, Philip Holden, and Gaik Cheng Khoo, 157–72. London: Routledge.

Gardner, Rod, Yasemin Karakaolus, and Sigrid Luchtenberg. 2008. "Islamophobia in the Media: A Response from Multicultural Education." *Intercultural Education* 19 (2): 119–36.

Gazzah, Miriam. 2008. "Rhythms and Rhymes of Life: Music and Identification Processes of Dutch-Moroccan Youth." ISIM Dissertations. Amsterdam: Amsterdam University Press.

Gilroy, Paul. 1993. *The Black Atlantic: Modernity and Double Consciousness*. London: Verso.

Gilyard, Keith. 2008. *Composition and Cornel West: Notes toward a Deep Democracy*. Carbondale: Southern Illinois University Press.

Goodey, Jo. 2001. "The Criminalization of British Asian Youth: Research from Bradford and Sheffield." *Journal of Youth Studies* 4 (4): 429–50.

Grewal, Sara Hakeem. 2013. "Intra- and Interlingual Translation in Blackamerican Muslim Hip Hop." *African American Review* 46 (1): 37–54.

Grewal, Zareena. 2014. *Islam Is a Foreign Country: American Muslims and the Global Crisis of Authority*. New York: New York University Press.

Han, Sam, and Kamaludeen Mohamed Nasir. 2016. *Digital Culture and Religion in Asia*. London: Routledge.

Harrison, Anthony Kwame. 2009. *Hip-Hop Underground: The Integrity and Ethics of Racial Identification*. Philadelphia, PA: Temple University Press.

Hill, Joseph. 2016. "Baay Is the Spiritual Leader of the Rappers": Performing Islamic Reasoning in Senegalese Sufi Hip-Hop." *Contemporary Islam* 10 (2): 267–87.

Huntington, Samuel P. 1996. *The Clash of Civilizations and the Remaking of World Order*. New York: Simon & Schuster.

Hutnyk, John. 2011. "Pantomime Paranoia in London, or, 'Lookout, He's behind You!'" In *Popular Music and Human Rights: British and American Music*, edited by Ian Peddie, 51–66. Farnham, UK: Ashgate.

Ibrahim, Awad. 2016. "Critical Hip-Hop Ill-Literacies: Re-mixing Culture, Language and the Politics of Boundaries in Education." *Journal of the American Association for the Advancement of Curriculum Studies* 11 (1): 1–14.

Irama, Rhoma, translated by Andrew Weintraub. 2011. "Music as a Medium for Communication, Unity, Education, and Dakwah." In *Islam and Popular Culture in Indonesia and Malaysia*, edited by Andrew Weintraub, 185–92. London: Routledge.

Isoke, Zenzele. 2015. "'Why Am I Black?' Gendering Hip-Hop, and Translocal Solidarities in Dubai." In *Intercultural Communication with Arabs*, edited by Rana Raddawi, 309–26. Singapore: Springer.

Jackson, Sherman A. 2005. *Islam and the Blackamerican: Looking Towards the Third Resurrection*. New York: Oxford University Press.

Jacobson, Jessica. 1998. *Islam in Transition: Religion and Identity among British Pakistani Youth*. London: Routledge.

Janmohamed, Shelina. 2016. *Generation M: Young Muslims Changing the World*. London: I. B. Tauris.

Jasper, James. 1997. *The Art of Moral Protest: Culture, Biography and Creativity in Social Movements*. Chicago: University of Chicago Press.

Jeffries, Michael P. 2011. *Thug Life: Race, Gender, and the Meaning of Hip Hop.* Chicago: University of Chicago Press.

Joppke, Christian. 2009. *Veil: Mirror of Identity.* Cambridge: Polity.

Juliastuti, Nuraini, translated by Camelia Lestari. 2006. "Whatever I Want: Media and Youth in Indonesia Before and After 1998." *Inter-Asia Cultural Studies* 7 (1): 139–43.

Kamaludeen Mohamed Nasir. 2007. "Rethinking the 'Malay Problem' in Singapore: Image, Rhetoric and Social Realities." *Journal of Muslim Minority Affairs* 27 (2): 309–18.

———. 2012. "The Homological Imagination: Hip-Hop Culture and Muslim Youth." In *Handbook of Hyper-Real Religions,* edited by Adam Possamai, 321–38. Leiden: Brill.

———. 2015. "The September 11 Generation, Hip-Hop and Human Rights." *Journal of Sociology* 51 (4): 1039–51.

———. 2016a. "Antipodal Tattooing: Muslim Youth in Chinese Gangs." *Deviant Behavior* 37 (8): 952–61.

———. 2016b. *Globalized Muslim Youth in the Asia Pacific: Popular Culture in Singapore and Sydney.* New York: Palgrave Macmillan.

———. 2017. "Boycotts as Moral Protests in Malaysia and Singapore." *International Sociology* 31 (4): 396–412.

———. 2018a. "Hip-Hop Islam: Commodification, Cooptation and Confrontation in Southeast Asia." *Journal of Religious and Political Practice* 4 (3): 374–89.

———. 2018b. "'Policing the Poor' and 'Poor Policing' in a Global City." *Journal of Poverty* 22 (3): 209–27.

Kamaludeen Mohamed Nasir and Syed Muhd Khairudin Aljunied. 2009. *Muslims as Minorities: History and Social Realities of Muslims in Singapore.* Bangi: National University of Malaysia Press.

Kamaludeen Mohamed Nasir, Alexius Pereira, and Bryan Turner. 2010. *Muslims in Singapore: Piety, Politics and Policies.* London: Routledge.

Kamaludeen Mohamed Nasir and Bryan S. Turner. 2014. *The Future of Singapore: Population, Society and the Nature of the State.* London: Routledge.

Keyes, Cheryl. 2002. *Rap Music and Street Consciousness.* Urbana: University of Illinois Press.

———. 2017. "'Ain't Nuthin' but a She Thang': Women in Hip Hop." In *Issues in African American Music: Power, Gender, Race, Representation,* edited by Mellonee V. Burnim and Portia K. Maultsby, 306–27. New York: Routledge.

Khan, Adviya. 2011. "Muslim Women in Hip-Hop: An Ethnographic Study of 'Poetic Pilgrimage.'" Master's diss. submitted to Cardiff University School of History, Archaeology, and Religion.

Kibria, Nazli. 2008. "The 'New Islam' and Bangladeshi Youth in Britain and the US." *Ethnic and Racial Studies* 31 (2): 243–66.

Kitwana, Bakari. 2002. *The Hip-Hop Generation: Young Blacks and the Crisis in African-American Culture*. New York: Basic Civitas.

———. 2005. *Why White Kids Love Hip-Hop: Wankstas, Wiggers, Wannabes, and the New Reality of Race in America*. New York: Basic Civitas.

Knight, Michael Muhammad. 2007. *The Five Percenters: Islam, Hip-Hop and the Gods of New York*. Oxford: Oneworld.

Kong, Lily. 2006. "Music and Moral Geographies: Constructions of 'Nation' and Identity in Singapore." *GeoJournal* 65 (1–2): 103–11.

Kong, Lily, and Brenda S. A. Yeoh. 2003. *The Politics of Landscapes in Singapore: Constructions of "Nation."* Syracuse, NY: Syracuse University Press.

Lambert, Stephan P. 2005. *The Sources of Islamic Revolutionary Conduct*. Washington, DC: Center for Strategic Intelligence Research.

Lee, Martha Frances. 1996. *The Nation of Islam: An American Millenarian Movement*. Syracuse, New York: Syracuse University Press.

Lemelle, Sidney J. 2006. "'Ni Wapi Tunakwenda': Hip-Hop Culture and the Children of Arusha." In *The Vinyl Ain't Final: Hip-Hop and the Globalization of Black Popular Culture*, edited by Dipannita Basu and Sidney J. Lemelle, 230–54. London: Pluto.

LeVine, Mark. 2008. *Heavy Metal Islam: Rock, Resistance, and the Struggle for the Soul of Islam*. New York: Three Rivers.

Lockard, Craig A. 1998. *Dance of Life: Popular Music and Politics in Southeast Asia*. Honolulu: University of Hawaii Press.

Low, B. E. 2011. *Slam School: Learning through Conflict in the Hip-Hop and Spoken Word Classroom*. Standford, CA: Stanford University Press.

Maira, Sunaina. 2008. "'We Ain't Missing': Palestinian Hip-Hop—A Transnational Youth Movement." *CR: The New Centennial Review* 8 (2): 161–92.

———. 2016. *The 9/11 Generation: Youth, Rights, and Solidarity in the War on Terror*. New York: New York University Press.

Mamdani, Mahmood. 2004. *Good Muslim, Bad Muslim: America, the Cold War, and the Roots of Terror*. New York: Pantheon.

Mandaville, Peter. 2009. "Hip-Hop, Nasheeds, and 'Cool' Sheikhs: Popular Culture and Muslim Youth in the United Kingdom." In *In-Between: Spaces Christian and Muslim Minorities in Transition in Europe and the Middle East*, edited by Christiane Timmerman, Johan Leman, Hannelore Roos, and Barbara Segaert, 149–68. Brussels, Belgium: Peter Lang.

Manganyi, Noel Chabani 1982. "Identity, Culture and Curriculum." In *Education, Race and Social Change in South Africa*, edited by John A. Marcum, 91–97. Berkeley: University of California Press.

Mannheim, Karl 1952. "The Problems of Generations." In *Essays on the Sociology of Knowledge*, edited by Paul Kecskemeti, 276–323. London: Routledge.

Marranci, Gabriele. 2009. *Faith, Ideology and Fear: Muslim Identities within and Beyond Prisons*. London: Continuum.

Masquelier, Adeline, and Benjamin F. Soares, eds. 2016. *Muslim Youth and the 9/11 Generation*. Albuquerque: University of New Mexico Press.

Massardi, Yudhistira A.N.M. 1995. "Si Bawel Kena Omel." *Gatra* 21:106–7.

Mattar, Yasser. 2003. "Virtual Communities and Hip-Hop Music Consumers in Singapore: Interplaying Global, Local and Subcultural Identities." *Leisure Studies* 22 (4): 283–300.

Mauzy, Diane K., and R. S. Milne. 2002. *Singapore Politics under the People's Action Party*. London: Routledge.

Maxwell, Ian. 2003. *Phat Beats, Dope Rhymes: Hip-Hop Down Under Comin' Upper*. Middletown, CT: Wesleyan University Press.

Mayer, Ann Elizabeth. 1995. *Islam and Human Rights: Tradition and Politics*. Boulder, CO: Westview.

McDonald, David. 2013. *My Voice Is My Weapon: Music, Nationalism, and the Poetics of Palestinian Resistance*. Durham, NC: Duke University Press.

McMurray, Anaya. 2008. "Hotep and Hip-Hop: Can Black Muslim Women Be Down with Hip-Hop?" *Meridians: Feminism, Race, Transnationalism* 8 (1): 74–92.

Mernissi, Fatima, translated by Mary Jo Lakeland. 1993. *The Forgotten Queens of Islam*. Minneapolis: University of Minnesota Press.

Miah, Shamim, and Virinder S. Kalra. 2008. "Muslim Hip-Hop: Politicisation of Kool Islam." *South Asian Cultural Studies Journal* 2 (1): 12–25.

Middleton, Richard. 1990. *Studying Popular Music*. Philadelphia: Open University Press.

Miller, Monica. 2013. *Religion and Hip-Hop*. New York: Routledge.

Mills, C. Wright. 1956. *The Power Elite*. New York: Oxford University Press.

Mills, C Wright. 1959. *The Sociological Imagination*. New York: Oxford University Press.

Miyakawa, Felicia M. 2005. *Five Percenter Rap: God Hop's Music, Message, and Black Muslim Mission*. Bloomington: Indiana University Press.

Moch, Michał. 2017. "Language, Migration and Globalization: French Hip-Hop versus Arabic Diaspora Hip-Hop." In *Moving Texts, Migrating People and Minority Languages*, edited by Michal Borodo, Juliane House, and Wojciech Wachowski, 41–51. Singapore: Springer.

Mohajer, Samer, and Fay Rajpar. 2012. "Syria Conflict Finds a Voice in Hip-Hop." BBC News, August 3. http://www.bbc.com/news/world-middle-east-19017267.

Mohamed, Ali. 2008. "War against Terror: Countering the Threat of Self-Radicalisation." *Straits Times*, February 7.

Mordue, Mark. 2014. "To a Hip-Hop Beat, Omar Musa Reveals the Beauty of the Streets." *Australian*, July 19.

Morgan, Marcyliena. 2009. *The Real Hiphop: Battling for Knowledge, Power, and Respect in the LA Underground*. Durham, NC: Duke University Press.

Muedini, Fait. 2015. *Sponsoring Sufism: How Governments Promote "Mystical Islam" in Their Domestic and Foreign Policies*. New York: Palgrave Macmillan.

Mueller, Dominik. 2014. *Islam, Politics and Youth in Malaysia: The Pop-Islamist Reinvention of PAS*. London: Routledge.

Mushaben, Joyce Marie. 2008. "Gender, HipHop and Pop-Islam: The Urban Identities of Muslim Youth in Germany." *Citizenship Studies* 12 (5): 507–26.

Nair, Ajay, and Murali Balaji, eds. 2008. *Desi Rap: Hip-Hop and South Asian America*. Lanham, MD: Lexington Books.

Nashashibi, Rami. 2011. "Islam in the 'Hood: Exploring the Rise of Ghetto Cosmopolitanism." Unpublished PhD thesis, University of Chicago.

Nijhon, Raeshem Chopra. 2008. "Making Brown Like Dat: South Asians and Hip-Hop." In *Desi Rap: Hip-Hop and South Asian America*, edited by Ajay Nair and Murali Balaji, 79–108. Lanham, MD: Lexington Books.

Ntarangwi, Mwenda. 2016. *The Street Is My Pulpit: Hip Hop and Christianity in Kenya*. Urbana: University of Illinois Press.

Nuruddin, Yusuf. 1994. "The Five Percenters: A Teenage Nation of Gods and Earths." In *Muslim Communities in North America*, edited by Yvonne Haddad and Jane Idleman Smith, 109–32. Albany: State University of New York Press.

———. 2006. "Ancient Black Astronauts and Extraterrestrial Jihads: Islamic Science Fiction as Urban Mythology." *Socialism and Democracy* 20 (3): 127–65.

Ong, Aihwa. 1999. *Flexible Citizenship: The Cultural Logics of Transnationality*. Durham, NC: Duke University Press.

Orlando, Valerie. 2003. "From Rap to Raï in the Mixing Bowl: Beur Hip-Hop Culture and Banlieue Cinema in Urban France." *Journal of Popular Culture* 36 (3): 395–415.

Peddie, Ian, ed. 2011. *Popular Music and Human Rights*. Farnham, UK: Ashgate.

Peisner, David. 2011a. "Inside Tunisia's Hip-Hop Revolution." *SPIN*, August 2011.

———. 2011b. "Youth in Revolt." *SPIN*, September 2011.

Pennington, Rosemary, and Hilary E. Kahn, eds. 2018. *On Islam: Muslims and the Media*. Bloomington: Indiana University Press.

Perkins, William Eric. 1992. "Nation of Islam Ideology in the Rap of Public Enemy." In *The Emergency of Black and the Emergence of Rap*, edited by Jon Michael Spencer, 41–50. Durham, NC: Duke University Press.

Perry, Imani. 2004. *Prophets of the Hood: Politics and Poetics in Hip Hop*. Durham, NC: Duke University Press.

Peterson, James Braxton. 2014. *The Hip-Hop Underground and African American Culture: Beneath the Surface*. New York: Palgrave Macmillan.

Petley, Julian, and Robin Richardson, eds. 2011. *Pointing the Finger: Islam and Muslims in the British Media*. London: Oneworld Publications.

Poole, Elizabeth, and John E. Richardson, eds. 2006. *Muslims and the News Media*. London: I. B. Tauris.

Rahim, Lily Zubaidah. 1998. *The Singapore Dilemma: The Political and Educational Marginality of the Malay Community.* Kuala Lumpur, Malaysia: Oxford University Press.

Rantakallio, Inka. 2013. "Muslimhiphop.com: Constructing Muslim Hip Hop Identities on the Internet." *CyberOrient* 7 (2): 8-41.

Rasmussen, Anne K. 2010. *Women, the Recited Qur'an, and Islamic Music in Indonesia.* Berkeley: University of California Press.

Rasul, Juliana June. 2006. "Mandarin Also Can, Mah! All-Malay Group Performs Chinese Songs with Aplomb at Channel U's Band Search." *Today*, May 29, p. 30.

Ritzer, Goerge. 2004. *The Globalization of Nothing.* Thousand Oaks: Pine Forge Press.

Rivera, Raquel Z. 2003. *New York Ricans from the Hip Hop Zone.* New York: Palgrave Macmillan, 2003.

Romero, Elena. 2012. *Free Stylin': How Hip Hop Changed the Fashion Industry.* Santa Barbara, CA: Praeger.

Roose, Joshua. 2016. "The Brothahood: 'Australia's Mine Too.'" In *Political Islam and Masculinity*, 51–85. New York: Palgrave Macmillan.

Rose, Tricia. 1994. *Black Noise: Rap Music and Black Culture in Contemporary America.* Middletown, CT: Wesleyan University Press.

———. 2008. *The Hip-Hop Wars: What We Talk about When We Talk about Hip-hop—and Why It Matters.* New York: Basic Civitas.

Sachedina, A. 2009. *Islam and the Challenge of Human Rights.* New York: Oxford University Press.

Said, Edward. 1997. *Covering Islam: How the Media and the Experts Determine How We See the Rest of the World.* New York: Random House.

Salois, Kendra. 2014. "The US Department of State's 'Hip-Hop Diplomacy' in Morocco." In *Music and Diplomacy from the Early Modern Era to the Present*, edited by Rebekah Ahrendt, Mark Ferraguto, and Damien Mahiet, 231–49. New York: Palgrave.

Sardar, Ziauddin. 2006. "Can British Islam Change?" *New Statesman*, July 3. https://www.newstatesman.com/node/195560.

———. 2013. "The Shadows of Muslim Men." *Critical Muslim* 8: 3–17.

Sarkissian, Margaret. 2005. "'Religion Never Had It So Good': Contemporary Nasyid and the Growth of Islamic Popular Music in Malaysia." *Yearbook for Traditional Music* 37:124–52.

Schloss, Joseph G. 2009. *Foundation: B-Boys, B-Girls, and Hip-Hop Culture in New York.* New York: Oxford University Press.

Schmidt, Leonie. 2017. *Islamic Modernities in Southeast Asia: Exploring Indonesian Popular and Visual Culture.* Washington, DC: Rowman & Littlefield.

Schur, Richard L. 2009. *Parodies of Ownership: Hip-Hop Aesthetics and Intellectual Property Law.* Ann Arbor: University of Michigan Press.

Senghaas, Dieter. 2002. *The Clash within Civilisations: Coming to Terms with Cultural Conflicts.* New York: Routledge.

Shannahan, Dervla Sara, and Qurra Hussain. 2011. "Rap on 'l'Avenue'; Islam, Aesthetics, Authenticity and Masculinities in the Tunisian Rap Scene." *Contemporary Islam* 5 (1): 37–58.

Sharma, Nitasha Tamar. 2010. *Hip Hop Desis: South Asian Americans, Blackness, and a Global Race Consciousness.* Durham, NC: Duke University Press.

Sharpley-Whiting, Tracy. 2007. *Pimps Up, Ho's Down: Hip-hop's Hold on Young Black Women.* New York: New York University Press.

Shaw, Danny. 2015. "Why the Surge in Muslim Prisoners?" *BBC News*, March 11.

Solomon, Thomas. 2005. "Living Underground Is Tough: Authenticity and Locality in the Hip-Hop Community in Istanbul, Turkey." *Popular Music* 24 (1): 1–20.

———. 2011. "Hardcore Muslims: Islamic Themes in Turkish Rap between Diaspora and Homeland." In *Muslim Rap, Halal Soaps and Revolutionary Theater: Artistic Developments in the Muslim World*, edited by Karin Van Nieuwkerk, 27–54. Austin: Texas University Press.

Soysal, Levent. 2004. "Rap, Hiphop, Kreuzberg: Scripts of/for Migrant Youth Culture in the WorldCity Berlin." *New German Critique* 92:62–81.

SpearIt. 2016. "Sonic Jihad: Muslim Hip-Hop in the Age of Mass Incarceration," *Islamic Monthly*, April 27. https://www.theislamicmonthly.com/sonic-jihad/

Stephenson, Peta. 2010. *Islam Dreaming: Indigenous Muslims in Australia.* Sydney: University of New South Wales Press.

Swedenberg, Ted. 2001. "Islamic Hip-Hop vs. Islamophobia." In *Global Noise: Rap and Hip-hop Outside America*, edited by Tony Mitchell, 57–85. Middletown, CT: Wesleyan University Press.

———. 2002. "Hip-Hop Music in the Transglobal Islamic Underground." In *Black Culture's Global Impact*, edited by H. Samy Alim, 16–18. Special issue of *Black Arts Quarterly* 6 (3). Stanford, CA: Stanford University, Committee on Black Performing Art.

Tan, Shzr Ee. 2009. "Singapore Takes the 'Bad' Rap: A State-Produced Music Video Goes 'Viral.'" *Ethnomusicology Forum* 18 (1): 107–30.

Tibi, Bassam. 1994. "Islamic Law/Shari'a, Human Rights, Universal Moral and International Law." *Human Rights Quarterly* 16: 277–99.

Turner, Richard Brent. 2003. *Islam in the African-American Experience.* Bloomington: Indiana University Press.

———. 2006. "Constructing Masculinity: Interactions between Islam and African-American Youth since C. Eric Lincoln, *The Black Muslims in America*." *Souls* 8 (4): 31–44.

Utley, Ebony A. 2012. *Rap and Religion: Understanding the Gangsta's God.* Santa Barbara, CA: Praeger.

Wallach, Jeremy, Harris M. Berger, and Paul D. Greene. 2011. *Heavy Metal Rules the Globe: Heavy Metal Music around the World.* Durham, NC: Duke University Press.

Waltz, Susan Eileen. 2004. "Universal Human Rights: The Contribution of Muslim States." *Human Rights Quarterly* 26 (4): 799–844.

Warren, Andrew, and Rob Evitt. 2012. "Indigenous Hip-Hop: Overcoming Marginality, Encountering Constraints." In *Creativity in Peripheral Places: Redefining the Creative Industries,* edited by Chris Gibson, 141–158. London: Routledge.

Weintraub, Andrew, ed. 2011. *Islam and Popular Culture in Indonesia and Malaysia.* London: Routledge.

West, Cornell. 2001. *Race Matters.* New York: Vintage.

Williams, Patrick J., and Kamaludeen Mohamed Nasir. 2017. "Youth Cultures in Southeast Asia: Exploring Hijabista and Hijabster Phenomena." *Crime, Media, Culture: An International Journal* 13 (2): 199–216.

Wilson, Jonathan (Bilal) A. J. 2012. "Muslim Youth Culture: A New Wave of Hip Hop Grunge." *Halal Journal.* World Halal Forum special edition, 32–38.

Wright, Robin. 2011. *Rock the Casbah: Rage and Rebellion Across the Islamic World.* New York: Simon & Schuster.

Zakir Hussain. 2008. "Muslim ITE Students Discuss Ways to Combat Radical Views." *Straits Times,* February 12. https://www.asiaone.com/News/Education/Story/A1Story20080212-49223.html.

Zanfagna, Christina. 2017. *Holy Hip Hop in the City of Angels.* Berkeley: University of California Press.

Zine, Jasmin. 2001. "Muslim Youth in Canadian Schools: Education and the Politics of Religious Identity." *Anthropology & Education Quarterly* 32 (4): 399–423.

———. 2006. "Unveiled Sentiments: Gendered Islamophobia and Experiences of Veiling among Muslim Girls in a Canadian Islamic School." *Equity & Excellence in Education* 39 (3): 239–52.

INDEX

Abdalla, Ahmad, 149
Abdullah, Alif, 158
Abraham, Saul, 58
"abstracted empiricism," 12
Abstract Vision/Humanity, 90–91
Abu-Jamal, Mumia, 75–76
Abu-Lughod, Lila, 108
academia's representation of Islam and
  Muslims, 22–23
accessories associated with hip-hop, 52–53,
  54–55, 109
Ackfeldt, Anders, 51
activism/activists, hip-hop: addressing
  misconceptions of Islam, 30, 93, 109;
  and #AskAMuslim movement, 109; in
  authoritarian states, 178; broad scope of,
  93, 103; and Brothahood, 140; and "cool"
  Islam, 49; and *da'wah* of hip-hoppers,
  51; diverse backgrounds of, 60; and
  #FreePalestine tweets, 57; and gender
  equality, 109, 127; and hip-hoppers'
  departures from music scene, 57; and
  identity formation, 30; imprisonment of,
  157; on the Internet, 33–34; and Islamic
  hip-hop, 45; and Islamic revivalism, 45; as
  mandate of Islam, 78; and Mona Haydar,
  109; music as vehicle for, 93–94, 104, 135;
  and provincialization, 26; as "reality by
  proxy," 168; as vehicle of assimilation,
  30; and views of oppressed majority, 178.

See also human rights; *specific activists,
  including* X, Malcolm
Adam, Safe, 71
ADF (Asian Dub Foundation), 112–13
Afghanistan, 126–28
African Americans: and Afrocentric themes
  in hip-hop, 104; and #BlackLivesMatter
  movement, 78–83; and black masculinity,
  61–62; civil rights movement/struggles
  of, 17, 23, 29, 62, 85–87; and Ebonics, 162;
  and Far Right, 63; and hip-hop *ummah*,
  167; inequality experienced by, 17; and
  Muslims' identification with black
  culture, 28–29, 62, 64–65, 147, 162–63,
  167–68, 170, 178; and origins of hip-hop,
  17, 27; and police brutality, 17, 79–80; and
  provincializing hip-hop from African
  American roots, 27–30, 178; and skin
  tones, 129; and street culture, 59–61, 62, 64
Afrohumanism, 42
Ahli Fiqir (Thinking group), 46, 52, 158
Ahmad, Salman, 11
Ahmadiyyahs, 23
Aidi, Hisham, 8, 148
Ajmain, Imran, 157
Akhenaton, 65
Al-Ali, Nour, 95
Alameddine, Rabih, 69
Alexander, Claire, 64
Al-Falah Mosque, 48–49